MW00490444

TRAINING STUDENTS FOR URBAN MINISTRY:

AN EXPERIENTIAL APPROACH

———————————

A Dissertation

Presented to

the Faculty of the School of Intercultural Studies

Department of Intercultural Studies

Biola University

———————————

by

John Edwin Fuder

Wipf and Stock Publishers
150 West Broadway • Eugene OR 97401

Wipf and Stock Publishers
150 West Broadway
Eugene, Oregon 97401

Training Students for Urban Ministry
An Experiential Approach
By Fuder, John Edwin
©2001 Fuder, John Edwin
ISBN: 1-57910-698-6
Publication date: July, 2001
Previously published by NPP, 2001.

ABSTRACT

TRAINING STUDENTS FOR URBAN MINISTRY:

AN EXPERIENTIAL APPROACH

John Edwin Fuder

This descriptive work recounts the practical field experiences of

Christian college students from a formal educational setting involved in

training for urban ministry among disenfranchised subcultures. The specific

populations being explored are segments of the homeless, gangs, and

prostitutes peripheral to downtown Los Angeles. The students are also

exposed to diverse outreach models targeting these distinct groupings such as

the church, para-church, rescue mission, and Christian community.

The impetus for and foundation of the overall investigation is an

adherence to a sound biblical theology of the city and the poor. The dynamic

of teacher as coach and mentor in service with the students is demonstrated

as the concepts of experiential learning are applied to the urban environment.

An array of out of the classroom interactions provide face-to-face contact with

alienated individuals on the street, under bridges and in the various mission

settings.

These observations and encounters contain invaluable hands-on

educational opportunities as they are debriefed, reflected upon, and applied to

further learning. The study concludes with a review of the project's strengths, weaknesses, and pertinent discoveries for those who would implement a similar endeavor in training students experientially for urban ministry.

TABLE OF CONTENTS

LIST OF TABLES

LIST OF FIGURES

DEDICATION

To my friend Green Eyes, my mentor Dr. J., and my loving wife Nel, without whom this study would never have been conceived, conceptualized, or completed.

CHAPTER 1

TEXT AND CONTEXT IN URBAN MINISTRY TRAINING

THE SETTING

Urban America is one of the most neglected mission fields in the world today. Startling headlines bombard us on a daily basis with tragic news of gang violence, prostitution, drug abuse, homelessness and numerous other pressing issues emanating from the streets of our cities. Two rival members of Chicago street gangs share their perspective of a world that the average American knows little about. They comment, "Our boys are at war. We've seen our friends wounded and some have died...We live in a battle zone. And often it's the one who shoots first who lives to tell about it...That's what it's like...in urban America." (McLean 1991:9).

Urban America reflects a dynamic that is unique to this generation, in which God is urbanizing and internationalizing His world (Bakke 1987). By the year 2,000, the world will be more urban than rural (Greenway & Monsma 1989). Three quarters of the population in North America are already living in urban areas (Conn 1987). Studies project this trend to increase to over 90% by the turn of the century (Linthicum 1991a).

Cities act as "magnets" to attract diverse and often very needy people (McClung 1991:10). How should Christians respond then to an increasingly urban population? Scripture clearly reveals God's compassion for the Ninevahs of old and the enlistment of Jonah as His reluctant messenger. We

1

must recognize and embrace the challenge of this new emerging world which is coming to the city. Training institutions must be at the forefront of the evangelical response. Specifically, Christian colleges and seminaries, which have the distinct calling and opportunity to train men and women for effective ministry.

Nearly twenty years ago, Craig Ellison, one of many in a growing contingent of evangelical "urbanologists," spoke of a general lethargy and lack of "cutting-edge," creative urban ministry training models on the part of Christian schools. He credited this dearth to both faculty and students alike as products of a relatively monolithic culture. He suggested, as part of the solution, "direct exposure to the conditions and people of the city , as well as the opportunity for interracial, interethnic and intercultural exchange" (1974:80).

Ellison referred to the tendencies of seminarians to remain "ghettoized," a reflection of a traditional and outdated curricula. He concluded, "If the gospel is to be perceived as relevant by the...urban world, seminaries must provide the systematic opportunity for their students to deal with people from different classes, races, and economic backgrounds. They must learn more than theology in an elitist institution" (1974:81).

Two decades later, the challenge remains. Michael Pabarcus (1992:6) suggests, "The task of equipping ministers for present and future cities is the major challenge Christian colleges and seminaries face in the 1990's." Roger Greenway (1989:1) concurs:

> It has been difficult to get evangelical theologians to take seriously the phenomenon of modern urbanization...With few exceptions, our seminaries have not prompted young men and women to think

2

biblically about the complex urban issues so as to communicate the Christian message effectively, from an urban as well as a biblical perspective.

Of deep concern to the author (thereafter referred to as "I") is the desperate need of training men and women to effectively minister among the urban poor. Donald McGavran (1980:281) pointed out the historic tendency of missions to favor "the classes" (middle and upper) over "the masses" (the poor). I suggest that evangelical institutions have fallen into the similar trap and have neglected the opportunity to challenge our students with the overwhelming needs of the oppressed. Viv Grigg (1992:10) reminds us that the poor are collectively the most responsive people group, as demonstrated by Jesus' teaching and personal example (Luke 4:18) and confirmed by sociological analysis in general. Howard Snyder (1976:48) has also aptly noted, "A healthy emphasis on the gospel to the poor may be the surest antidote to institutionalism and irrelevant structures."

The most viable training model is the incarnational approach, patterned after Jesus' example. Living among the poor enables the urban worker to experience the triumphs and struggles of the people and to model the gospel message. But the intensity of such identification with needy people often produces frustration and discouragement and may lead to eventual burn-out. The best incarnational models recognize this and include time for reflection and rejuvenation as was demonstrated by Jesus when He drew apart from the crowds.

For most Christian colleges the incarnational model is unattainable. Faced with competing curriculum demands, few experienced staff, and dwindling financial resources, ministry among the urban poor has taken a backseat to other concerns. Despite their inabilities and limitations however, creative approaches to urban ministry training are being implemented. These run the gamut from the informal "urban plunge" or "tourist run" expeditions to such non-formal urban training models as SCUPE (Seminary Consortium for Urban Pastoral Education) in Chicago, CUTS (Center for Urban Theological Studies) in Philadelphia, CUME (Center for Urban Ministerial Education) in Boston, and the Bresee Institute in Los Angeles (Blackwood, Reichardt, and Schreiner 1992:iv).

Each of these context-specific programs is the urban residency component of a formal Christian college or seminary. Westmont's Urban Studies Program in San Francisco could also be included here. But the vast majority of formal schools of Christian higher education offer limited urban emphases in their curricula. There continues to be a need among students in those institutions for practical exposure to disadvantaged urban people and more extensive field education to complement classroom instruction. It is that audience to which this study is addressed.

Learning experiences in communities of need give a realistic perspective of disenfranchised subcultures and stimulate compassion for the city and its people. Attention must be given to training men and women within this educational context in order to understand the dynamics of such diverse urban "people groups" as gangs, prostitutes and the homeless and to help students develop effective ministry skills. Students must be challenged by face-to-face interaction with hurting people rather than mere cognitive input alone.

RESEARCH QUESTION AND PRIMARY OBJECTIVES

Given the inability of many schools to implement a contextualized training approach to urban ministry, how can students in such formal educational settings gain a perspective on and a passion for urban ministry among the poor? This dissertation proposes that compassion for the poor and experience in urban ministry can be personally realized by Christian college students through structured, short-term immersion in the city. The components of experiential learning [Kolb (1984), Schon (1987), Raths (1987), Hutchings and Wutzdorff (1988), et al.] are adapted and applied within the context of diverse ministry models and disadvantaged subcultures to accomplish this purpose.

Classroom instruction provides ongoing theory about and reflection on the city and its people, as well as the theological foundation and biblical basis of ministry among the poor. The essence of the training process is *exposure* to urban need and diverse ministry *experiences* with disadvantaged people, both structured and spontaneous. These intense encounters frequently leave the students in a state of *emotional disarray* as they struggle to make sense out of their observations and interactions. *Debriefing*, both in and out of the classroom, enables them to *reflect* on and draw meaning from these experiences and to *apply* their discoveries to *further learning*.

These components can be diagrammed as follows:

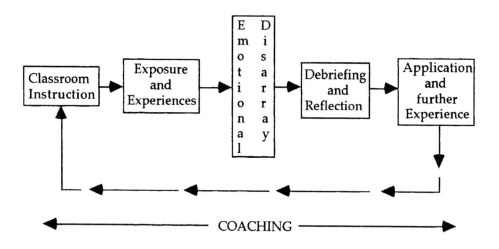

Fig. 1. The journey in experiential learning

I have chosen to portray this study by using the analogy of a journey in which teacher-coach and student alike travel together. Experiential learning, by its very nature, is process-oriented, fluid, and spontaneous. It unfolds before the learner much as one views the open road. The traveler is often unaware of what encounters may lie around the bend. The numerous stops enroute comprise the various observations and interactions leading to personal discovery. The periodic oasis allows for debriefing and reflection on the sights along the way. The journey is unique, however, in that the destination is the process itself, which leads to deeper understanding and application in the context of further experience.

The primary objectives of the study for the students are:

1. Intense exposure to the city and disadvantaged people.

2. Increased familiarity with urban ministry models.

3. Interaction with urban ministry leaders.

4. Hands-on urban ministry experiences.

5. Development of compassion for the poor.

6. Openness to future urban ministry involvement.

The study is admittedly an overview, a sweeping panorama of urban need and our brief exposure to the attempts of asserted evangelical institutions to intervene. Its goal is not necessarily to rate or critique those ministries as it is to view them through the students' eyes as a part of their learning process. The same is true of the subcultures themselves. The project is not designed to offer in-depth solutions to the myriad of issues faced by these individuals as it is to allow for initial access of the students into the same struggles. The classroom provides the context in which to further contemplate and discuss our discoveries and to formulate our approach in succeeding ministry endeavors.

SCOPE AND SIGNIFICANCE

This study utilizes several impoverished communities within metropolitan Los Angeles as the context for training students experientially in urban ministry. Specifically, the Pico-Union and Westlake districts, as well as skid row and a homeless encampment under a freeway overpass were used.

I mobilized a group of ten Biola University students, from a class of 22 enrolled in an Urban Research and Ministry course, to spend a 15-week semester with me in experiencing firsthand the needs of the city and becoming initially acquainted with selected urban ministries, both church and para-church.

This project applies the components of experiential learning within that intense environment in training these students from a formal Christian college and seminary context. It shows how they can participate in the urban setting so as to more effectively integrate faith and learning. It looks at this world of need through their eyes and reveals their struggles in coming face to face with gangs, prostitutes, drug addicts and street people. Numerous case studies of men and women in these subcultures emerge from the research as well as pertinent discoveries and conclusions in training students experientially for urban ministry.

These components of experiential learning are transferable to other cultural settings as well. Discoveries made as to the felt needs of people in these communities and the principles gleaned from immersing students in those contexts will be useful to others in similar training endeavors among equally needy settings across the land and throughout the world.

BACKGROUND AND LIMITATIONS

The foundation for my research was laid in twelve years of para-church urban ministry among the disadvantaged in San Jose, California. During that time I was exposed to numerous churches, ministries, and Christian leaders committed to the poor. My experiences included extensive involvement with inner-city youth, although limited contact with gang members. Through a rescue mission program I crossed paths daily with street people but had no occasion to develop a relationship with one personally. That opportunity took place during my studies, a year and a half prior to beginning the field work with the students.

While searching for an "informant" to fulfill the requirements of a class, I met a homeless man by the name of Green Eyes who was living on the street in the Westlake community. He was instrumental in putting me in touch with nearly everyone else whose stories unfold on the following pages. As I began to explore his networks I discovered an intriguing overlap of subcultures which were intricately intertwined and dependent upon each other. His significant relationships were with the homeless, prostitutes, and drug addicts. He also had contacts in the Orphans and Bonnie Brae Criminals (BBC) street gangs which roamed the community. Through Green Eyes I learned of the appalling environment of SRO hotels and became acquainted with landlords and social workers as well. He was my entree into their worlds and I followed his lead, bringing students along with me. Without Green Eyes, this study would never have materialized.

My interactions with Green Eyes gave a certain subjectivity to this study. He quickly surpassed the role of typical informant as he warmly welcomed me into his world. I was emotionally moved by those scarred individuals as I learned of their destructive lifestyles. My relationship with Green Eyes blurred the lines between the neutrality of the academic exercise and the instinctive desire to intervene in a compassionate manner as a Christian. I found that balance to be nearly impossible to maintain.

METHODOLOGY

Ethnographic Research

This study employs a qualitative research methodology, as it attempts
"to describe and develop a special kind of understanding for a particular social
situation...group, or interaction" (Locke, Spirduso, & Silverman 1987:84). It is
a journey in experiential learning that uses the ethnographic method to train
and expose the students to a whole culture, society, or community"
(Valentine 1978:134). Ethnographic research provides the opportunity to
observe specific behavior in a natural setting, gather pertinent data, and draw
conclusions and relevant strategies from it within the context or
environment (Wiersma 1991).

This research draws from a rich base of urban ethnographies done by
Whyte (1955), Ladner (1971), Stack (1974), Aschenbrenner (1975), Valentine
(1978), Keiser (1979), Williams (1981), Ezekiel (1984) and MacLeod (1987). Of
particular benefit has been the strong story-telling technique of Liebow (1967)
and his work with his key informant Talley. The gathering of succinct case
studies and oral histories by those ethnographers was emulated in my own
investigation through informal, open-ended interviews. Rosenthal's (1991)
data-gathering strategy of "hanging out with homeless people" proved to be
foundational to my interaction with those on the street as well.

Specifically, participant observation was the primary means of doing
the fieldwork and gathering the data. Spradley's (1980) model of the social
situation and its three primary elements of place, actor and activity was
considered not only in my own approach but in the students' as well. This
methodology allows "immersion in the setting" so as to "hear, see and begin

10

to experience reality as the participants do" (Marshall & Rossman 1989:79). It also helps one formulate sensible questions suitable to their world view and facilitates a better understanding of the meaning of what one is observing (Bernard 1988).

Ethnographic research is descriptive in nature. It "stresses the importance of context" (Marshall & Rossman 1989:46) and recounts the details of "what people actually say or do" (Locke, Spirduso, & Silverman 1987:84). I have purposely sought to preserve the flavor of the narrative in my research. My intent is to unfold the social situation and experiences of the actors in order to bring the reader directly into their world.

This then gives a sense of "being there" and captures "snapshots" of the people and events along the journey. It enables me to show how the students interact in a variety of settings and how their perceptions change in the experiential learning process. Ethnographic descriptions are at the heart of case studies and oral histories, which unlock the meaning of these diverse subcultures and provide "windows" through which we can see more clearly and gain a deeper understanding.

Experiential Learning

The project is grounded in the concepts of experiential learning, as noted in the works of Dewey (1938), Lewin (1951), Piaget (1971), Schon (1983) and Kolb (1984), et al. Numerous corollaries to experiential learning are seen in the literature as well. These include "applied studies" (Keeton & Tate 1978), "service learning" (Berte & O'Neil 1977), "field education" (Quinn & Sellars 1974), "engaged" or "problem-focused education" (Logan 1983), and

11

"integrated" (Hutchings & Wutzdorff 1988) or "holistic learning" (Joiner 1980).

Various definitions of experiential learning exist. The most basic is "learning through experience," "learning by doing," or simply, "How-to learning" (Brown 1980:47). Experiential learning reflects the process of "engaging students actively and directly rather than vicariously with the realities of a study subject" (Duley & Permaul 1984:18). It refers to "the learning that occurs when changes in judgment, feelings, knowledge, or skills result for a particular person from living through an event or events" (Chickering 1977:63).

Of particular interest to this study is the concurrent theme of "cross-cultural experiential learning" which specifically denotes growth from "direct contact with a culture other than one's own" (Neff 1981:2). Katherine Kendall explains, "One does not need to cross an ocean or a national border to find people whose ideas, values, attitudes, and behavior seem different and alien. The many cultures and subcultures within a community, city, or country offer a number of possibilities for experiential cultural learning" (Sikkema & Niyekawa-Howard 1977:iv-v).

One of the more significant models of experiential learning was developed by David Kolb (1976;1984), who drew heavily from John Dewey's (1938) "philosophy of educative experience." According to Dewey (1938:25), "all genuine education comes about through experience." Kolb recognized that experience and theory go hand in hand however, and his work has been hailed as "the missing link between theory and practice, between the abstract generalization and the concrete instance, between the affective and the cognitive domains" (Kolb 1984:ix).

In an article analyzing experiential learning theory, Murrell and Claxton (1987:6) summarize Kolb's model:

> Kolb described learning as a four-step process. Learners have immediate concrete experience, involving themselves fully in the experience and then reflecting on it from different perspectives. After these reflective observations, they engage in abstract conceptualization, from which they develop generalizations that help them integrate their observations into sound theories or principles. Finally, learners use these generalizations as guides to further action, or active experimentation, and experiment in new, more complex situations with what they have learned. Then they have another concrete experience and the cycle begins again, but this time the learner operates at a more complex level.

Several variants of Kolb's model have been postulated as well. Honey and Mumford (1983), operating from more of a managerial perspective, rephrase the four-stages as (a) having an experience, (b) reviewing the experience, (c) concluding from the experience, and (d) planning the next steps. Boot and Boxer (1980) suggest their version of the learning cycle, which they call "reflective learning," as personal experience, personal reflection, personal meaning, and personal action.

Concurrent with Kolb's (1976) initial discoveries was the research of Argyris and Schon (1974), who also investigated the relationship between knowing and doing. But in contrast to Kolb, whose model in essence sheds light on the "why" of experiential learning, Argyris and Schon sought to make explicit the "how" (Doherty, Mentkowski, & Conrad 1978:25). Hutchings and Wutzdorff (1988:7) summarize their contribution:

Argyis and Schon (1974)...developed the notion of a "theory of action," the set of assumptions, methods, and hypotheses that a professional acquires over time and through experience to tell him or her how to behave in a new situation. This theory of action is itself originally developed through the interaction between an "espoused theory" and a "theory-in-use." The espoused theory is the theory with which one enters the situation...once we must begin doing something with our espoused theory, a kind of imbalance is created. What we actually do, or what we see afterward that we could have done more effectively... [they] call the theory-in-use, which in turn modifies the original espoused theory, and so on.

Doherty et al. (1978:26-27) were struck with the congruency of both Kolb's and Argyris-Schon's experiential learning theories. Looking for a wider application of both models they overlaid the two to produce their own convergent theories. This they portrayed as "concrete experience subject to observation and reflection reveals theory-in-use modified to form a new espoused theory followed by testing espoused theories in new situations which lead to concrete experience."

Walter and Marks (1981:159-177) offer a detailed progression of the learning experience, broken down into the six phases of planning, introduction, activity, debriefing, summary, and evaluation. Of significance in their work is the inclusion of key events in each phase along with the roles and effects on the leaders and participants alike. One of the more crucial of these progressive phases of experiential learning is that of debriefing. James Raths (1987:25-27) supplies a helpful definition as well as an important clarification between debriefing and summarizing:

Debriefing is a process of helping students reflect on their learning experiences, attach personal meanings to them, and deepen their understandings...Debriefing is not the same as summarizing. Summarizing is often a task performed by others...But listening to a summary does not give a student the opportunity to make sense of

14

what has been taught or experienced, to operate on experience by organizing it...or to relate the experience to other events or ideas... The product of the debriefing process is an articulated sense of "meaning."

This aspect of reflection is then an integral part of experiential learning. Hutchings and Wutzdorff (1988:3) maintain, "self-reflection, or examination of oneself as a learner, is crucial to linking knowing and doing." Doherty et al. (1978:25) further state, "Only experience that is reflected upon seriously will yield its full measure of learning and the reflection must in turn aim at testing the newly refined understandings by further experience. Our duty as educators is both to provide the experiential opportunity and to make sure it can yield learning."

Donald Schon (1983;1987) took the model one step further by exploring the concept of "the reflective practitioner." This individual personifies one who is both knowing and reflecting in an active engagement with his or her surroundings. Schon (1983:68) clarifies, "When someone reflects-in-action, he becomes a researcher in the practice context...He does not separate thinking from doing...Because his experimenting is a kind of action, implementation is built into his inquiry."

Numerous strengths of experiential learning are evident in the literature. Walter and Marks (1981:151-154) point out that it is "above all an action approach to change" and that action "is tightly linked to commitment." They highlight several "forms of action" to include "exploration, experimentation, practice and performance." Commitment is seen as essential in that it "focuses the individual's will toward an action." Commitment is also significantly portrayed as the "transformer between being and action," but the converse is true as well that "action is fundamental to commitment building."

Walter and Marks (1981:3, 161, 282) note that experiential learning is "flexible in its uses" and both "process" and "present-oriented." Quinn and Sellars (1974:36) categorize it as "a dialogical approach to learning." Coleman (1977:57-60) mentions that "motivation is intrinsic" in learning experientially and that "self-assurance and a sense of accomplishment and mastery" are a direct result. He adds as well that experiential learning "appears to be less easily forgotten than learning through information assimilation."

Mary Ryan (1988:41) suggests, "Experiential learning is more active, concrete, and personal -and considerably less structured-than learning in the classroom...it represents a powerful and extended 'teachable moment,' when conditions for learning are ripe...." Hutchings and Wutzdorff (1988:76) comment, "A related characteristic is a focus on performance. To think of learning as performance is to think in terms of...applying what is learned. Performance is the integration of knowing and doing."

Non-traditional roles for student and teacher alike are central to experiential learning. Students function as "actor versus receiver" (Svinicki & Dixon 1987:144) and "subject" as opposed to "object" in the learning experience (Quinn & Sellars 1974:35). Murrell and Claxton (1987:13) mention that experiential learning refutes the "teaching as telling" approach to instruction.

Schon (1987) gives extensive, thought-provoking treatment to the crucial concept of teacher as "coach" in the learning process. He reveals (p.20), "...instructors function more as coaches than as teachers. In the early stages of the practicum, confusion and mystery reign. The gradual passage to convergence of meaning occurs by a distinctive dialogue of student and coach." This "distinctive dialogue" then takes the form of "telling and listening" (p.102) and "demonstrating and imitating" (p.107). He concludes (p.311), "The coach's legitimacy does not depend on his scholarly attainments or proficiency as a lecturer but on the artistry of his coaching practice."

Walter and Marks (1981:165) contribute several additional aspects to the nature of the coaching role such as"...encouraging and supporting, energizing, and even cheerleading." Ramsey (1974:52, 53) adds "guidance and direction," "interpretation," and "modeling" to the list as well. Hutchings and Wutzdorff (1988:65) also include "reading the environment" in which "faculty initially help students think about what they see and hear around them: to be good observers."

Howard Seeman (1988:29, 30) succinctly concludes:

> Experiential education instructors must be...value-clarifiers, facilitators...even counselors...They must be able to teach students how to discover relationships...how to see each experience from other perspectives...They must teach empathy...They have to learn to teach inductively...The instructor, not just the student, must take notes. He has to note the valuable aspects of students presented experiences in order to re-present them for further education. He must follow the class as well as lead it.

A corollary to experiential education is that of integrated learning. Hutchings and Wutzdorff (1988:5-19) identify the ingredients of "concreteness, involvement, dissonance, and reflection" as "strategies that allow students to bring knowing and doing into increasingly greater integration" (p.17). Noteworthy in the cycle is the third element of "dissonance," defined as the "mismatch between knowing and doing" or the

17

place where "cognition and affect collide" (p.15). It is also discussed as "throwing learners temporarily out of balance to move them toward deeper understanding" (p.14). The authors borrow a graphic phrase from Frick (1977:495-499) to shed further light on the cause of such disarray, namely, "new information crashing in on old ignorance."

Bill Joiner (1980:80) appeals for this "holistic" approach to education:

> Both the experiential and the formal mode have their strengths and their weaknesses. The weaknesses of each seem to become more predominant and problematic when either is applied in isolation from or in opposition to the other. I believe that integrating the strengths of both modes makes it possible to address the fundamental dilemmas faced by any educational enterprise more creatively and effectively. Our vision...needs to be expanded into a more holistic approach.

THEOLOGICAL FOUNDATION AND BIBLICAL BASIS

This carries us into the stream of Christian theological education. Conn and Rowan's (1984) extensive compilation of noted educators and missiologists reiterates concurrent themes of "contextualization" and "praxis education" in our missionary training. Wilson Chow (1982:51) echoed the premise of experiential learning in his comment, "There must be a functional integration between learning by precepts and learning by experience, between being and doing."

More recently, Greenway (1989:2) has said, "Theological education must provide the theological perspective, practical training, and strong motivation to make the Christian faith a transforming power in the cities throughout the world." Sidney Rooy (1992:236) adds, "Theological education for urban mission must equip Christians for making their faith a lived-out reality. This requires an education that is contextually aware and a theology of the city that moves beyond pietistic retreat."

In a noteworthy attempt toward a greater educational balance between our theology and practice, Roger Clark (1989:42) cited Holland's (1978) two-track analogy which was helpful in formulating my own thinking and approach in this study. The model includes cognitive input, ministry experience, dynamic reflection and spiritual formation, which undergirds both the theory and the practice.

Thomas Austin (1992:37) prods us toward relevant urban ministry training that spills out of the classroom and into the streets, "We must teach and model how to evangelize, disciple, counsel, motivate, preach to and pastor the urban dweller...All of these can be taught in the classroom, but they also need to be modeled and experienced in the city."

Stanley and Clinton (1992) focus on these ministry ingredients of teaching, modeling, discipling, counseling, and motivating within the context of mentoring. They expound upon the coaching dynamic to include imparting skills, confidence, linking with appropriate resources, observation, and evaluation (p. 82). They suggest the idea of a "sponsor" as one who opens up networks to another individual (p. 124). Green Eyes filled this role as he introduced me to his contacts on the street. Clinton and Clinton (1991) provide even more extensive detail on these functions, including apprenticeships and internships in informal training.

A holistic approach to ministry and ministry training, which embodies at its core an incarnational element, is well-represented in evangelical writings and has fueled my efforts and those of the students as well in this project. Perkins (1982) sounds the cry for holism and sensitivity to the "felt needs" of hurting people. Evans (1983) and Phillips (1985) address the priority of "identification" as foundational to loving and reaching people. Others who articulate the themes of incarnational, contextualized ministry include Grigg (1984; 1992), Greenway (1978; 1992), McClung (1991), and Lingenfelter and Mayers (1986).

Orlando Costas (1984:16) offers this penetrating remark, "The real issue is whether or not we as Christians are willing to be immersed in the concrete situations of the disenfranchised of our societies and witness to the lordship and saviorhood of Christ from within...Anything else is pure talk."

Isaac Canales (1989:36), in reference to ministry among Hispanic gang members, adds these comments, "The best strategy is...to be visible, available, sincere...committed to Christ...you must...hang out with them, go to bat for them, be insulted by them...and go to funerals with them. Nothing can take the place of being there...in other words, incarnational ministry."

Greenway's (Greenway & Monsma 1989:192) strong statement regarding a similar response towards the homeless framed my approach as well. He noted:

> "Feed My sheep," said Jesus. Sometimes pastors must find the sheep before they can feed them, just as Jesus did. I know where some torn and battered sheep are right now. They are scattered among the homeless on city streets, waiting for someone with a shepherd's heart to reach them ...Of all people, street people need pastors.

This incarnational, "pastoral" approach, fleshed out by Christenson (1988) in San Francisco and in particular detail by Van Houten (1988) in Chicago, gave direction to my own research on the streets of Los Angeles as I attempted to build relationships and make Christ relevant among the homeless, prostitutes, and gang members. Van Houten speaks of the priority of availability, day and night in some cases, to those in need. He emphasizes a commitment to consistently being with them over extended periods to demonstrate concern and earn the right to be heard. Included in this approach is the non-judgmental listening ear and the modeling of an alternative, Christ-like lifestyle. It involves a holistic advocacy with the disadvantaged that comprises not only their spiritual needs, but those of the physical, mental, emotional, and social as well.

[1]The Word of God specifically advocates our involvement with the poor and disadvantaged. Dubose (1984:65) cites over 300 references to the poor in the Bible, commenting that "nothing is clearer in Scripture than the fact that the God of the Bible is the Champion of the poor, the downtrodden, the exploited." Christ Himself proclaimed His calling "to preach the gospel to the poor" (Luke 4:18). Paul was exhorted "to remember the poor" (Gal. 2:10), and Jeremiah equates involvement with the poor as an expression of knowing God (Jer. 22:16).

The book of Proverbs has scores of references to the poor. Today's English Version translates Proverbs 14:31 to read, "...kindness shown to the poor is an act of worship." A few chapters farther along, in Proverbs 19:17, we catch a glimpse of God's "heavenly savings account." The verse informs us, "He who is gracious to a poor man lends to the Lord, and He will repay him for his good deed." Proverbs 21:12 simply states, "He who shuts his ear to the cry of the poor will also cry himself and not be answered."

Scripture continually emphasizes God's concern for "the widow, the orphan, the stranger, and the poor" (Zech. 7:10). Over 3,000 times in the Bible these four classes of people are specifically named. Although it is a very broad

---

[1]Unless otherwise indicated, Scripture references are to the New American Standard Bible.

categorization, each of these groups are represented in the community under study: "the widow" (single parents, street women), "the orphan" (street kids, gang members), "the stranger" (refugees, immigrants), and "the poor" (homeless).

Grant (1986:203) reminds us, "God's justice demands that those who are the most vulnerable, most susceptible, and most insecure be defended." Certainly these classes of people fit that criteria. The Psalms in particular give evidence of God's unique concern for their welfare. Psalm 9:9, "The Lord will be a stronghold for the oppressed." Psalm 140:12, "I know that the Lord will maintain the cause of the afflicted, and justice for the poor." Psalm 68:5 specifically portrays Him as "the protector of the widow," and Psalm 10:14 as "the helper of the orphan." Hosea 14:3 adds, "in Thee the orphan finds mercy."

God longs for His people to pattern their lives after His example. We are to feed the hungry, clothe the naked and shelter the homeless (Isa. 58:7; Ezek. 18:7). The very essence of our faith is to be categorized by a sensitivity to and advocacy on the behalf of orphans and widows (Isa. 1:17; Jas. 1:27). Reflecting on numerous biblical examples, Grant (1986:81) points out, "God's people have always shown the authenticity of their faith by caring for women and children in distress." There is no dichotomy in Scripture between our "being" and our "doing" as God's people. To walk with God in humility is to also walk with man in justice and compassion (Mic. 6:8).

22

An integral part of this study is the concurrent process of "learning" compassion (Matt. 9:13) as the students are immersed in communities of need. This is based solidly upon the powerful "seeing, feeling and acting" triad which was modeled by the Master in Matthew 14:14 and Mark 6:34. Appleby (1986:12-20) gives extensive treatment to this trio defining them as "eyes to see," "heart to feel," and "power to act," with the onus resting on the second crucial step. Henri Nouwan et al., in their challenging treatise on the subject, simply entitled *Compassion* (1982:4), provides an excellent definition of the same:

> The word "compassion" is derived from the Latin words "pati" and "cum," which together mean "to suffer with." Compassion asks us to go where it hurts, to enter into places of pain, to share in brokenness, fear, confusion, and anguish. Compassion challenges us to cry out with those in misery, to mourn with those who are lonely, to weep with those in tears. Compassion requires us to be weak with the weak, vulnerable with the vulnerable, and powerless with the powerless. Compassion means full immersion in the condition of being human.

This theme of "suffering together with" is expressed throughout Scripture, focusing on those "sinned against," the objects of compassion. It is the essence of God taking action on behalf of oppressed Israel in Exodus 3:7-10 and Christ's becoming flesh and making His home in our midst (John 1:14). It is a key concept in our Lord's Sermon on the Mount in which we are told, "Be merciful just as your Father is merciful" (Luke 6:36). Luke further reveals compassion as being central to the selfless response to human need on the part of the Good Samaritan (10:37) and the accepting, forgiving response of the Father upon the long-awaited return of his prodigal son (15:20).

Matthew 9:36 reiterates the pattern of how Christ "seeing" the multitudes, "felt" compassion and intervened in a personal and holistic manner. This particular expression of His burden for the "harassed and helpless" masses took place as He "was going about all the cities (verse 35)." It should also be noted that these "distressed and downcast" multitudes were ripe for the harvest and lacked only for workers to gather them into the kingdom (verses 37, 38).

It is this same urban arena into which the Bible commands our presence and involvement as God's "apostles to the city" (Greenway 1978). The prophet Jeremiah sounds the alarm for God's people to "return to these your cities" (Jer. 31:21). The Word of God as a whole clearly unfolds a divine concern for the metropolis, portrayed in such instances as Micah 6:9, "The voice of the Lord cries to the city," and Jonah 4:1, "...should I not have compassion on Ninevah, the great city...."

"The Bible is actually an urban book!" (Linthicum 1991a:21). It "begins in a garden and ends in a city" (Tonna 1982:121). Scripture contains 1400 references to the city, and there are at least 25 examples of what can be called urban ministry in the historical books alone (Greenway 1978). Jeremiah himself makes 137 references to cities (DuBose 1978).

Scripture pictures a tension and crucial battle being waged between good and evil in the city. This treatise is developed by Linthicum (1991a) and is plainly seen in the desperate straits of numerous urban dwellers. Psalm 55:9 says, "I have seen violence and strife in the city," and Lamentations 1:1, 2 reads, "How lonely sits the city...she has none to comfort her." Job 24:12 graphically states, "From the city men groan, and the souls of the wounded cry out."

As believers we are continually exhorted to be a leavening influence in this context of need. Jeremiah once more acts as spokesperson, beckoning us to "seek the welfare of the city" (29:7). The term "welfare" is actually the Hebrew word "shalom" and literally means "just-peace." It was addressed as part of a mandate to make the city one's home (verses 4-6) and embodies the challenge of embracing a broken environment and compassionately entering into the struggle for justice and reconciliation.

THEORETICAL REVIEW

Homelessness

Homelessness in America has been one of the most pressing social problems of recent decades and continues to be an ongoing dilemma today. Various definitions of homelessness have been proposed in an attempt to capture the diversity of those caught within its grasp. It can simply refer to a person's lack of a stable residence, including a place to sleep and receive mail. A broader sociological definition would consider the quality of social interaction as well as social and material supports (Ropers 1986). Michael Harrington (1984:101) pointed out, "A home is not simply a roof over one's head. It is the center of a web of human relationships. When the web is shredded, as a result of social and economic trends, a person is homeless even if he or she has an anonymous room somewhere."

For the purpose of this study, the following definition of the homeless, suggested by the United States General Accounting Office (1985:5) will be used: "Those persons who lack resources and community ties necessary to provide

25

for their own adequate shelter." These people are found in shelters, SROs, on the streets, in abandoned buildings, under bridges, in cars, and in the bushes.

Reflecting the urgency of the situation, 1987 was declared "The International Year of the Homeless" (United Nations General Assembly 1985). Three years prior to that the United States Department of Housing and Urban Development (HUD), issued a substantial report. Their research concluded that there were 250,000 - 350,000 homeless people in America. The Urban Institute, doing a follow-up study 3 years later however, estimated a homeless population between 500,000 - 600,000 (Burt & Cohen 1989). Former homeless advocate Mitch Snyder, claimed that these figures were drastically low and projected their numbers to be as high as 2 to 3 million (Redburn & Buss 1986).

Los Angeles County has the dubious distinction of containing the largest homeless population in the nation. The Los Angeles Times (June 30, 1993) quotes a recent study by Shelter Partnership Inc., estimating that "more than 77,000 people were believed to be living on the streets in mid-1992," an increase of at least 13% from the previous year. The downtown skid row is "home" to over half of this population (Koegel et al. 1990).

The underlying causes of such an extensive social dilemma are the subject of a diversity of opinions. Ropers (1988) identifies a number of the perceived roots of homelessness, such as deindustrialization, the low income housing crisis, recession and record low unemployment, cutbacks in social welfare programs, increased family instability and domestic violence, and deinstitutionalization of the mentally ill.

Compounding the situation is the reported intensity of need in studies done among homeless individuals. As many as one third of the homeless population are said to suffer from mental illness (Tessler & Dennis 1989), and the United States Conference of Mayors (1990) reported that over a third were substance abusers. Koegel, Burnam, and Farr (1988) reported that 28% of their sample of homeless individuals in Los Angeles were suffering from chronic major illness. An earlier study by Koegel and Burnam (1988) found as many as 64% of their inner-city homeless sample in Los Angeles reflecting a dependency on alcohol.

HUD estimates (1984), arguably low, put the number of homeless people across the country who are living in shelters at 69,000. There are more than a dozen rescue mission type shelters alone in the skid row district of Los Angeles providing over 2,000 beds a night (Rowe & Wolch 1990). This still leaves the vast majority of the homeless both here in Los Angeles and across the nation living on the streets or in subsistence level SROs. Many simply lack access to or avoid missions and shelters altogether (Redburn & Buss 1986). In fact, several studies have noted large numbers of people living on the streets even when shelter space is available (Baxter & Hopper 1982).

The last two decades have seen the rise of "the new urban homeless" (Rossi 1989; Stefl 1987; Hopper & Hamberg 1986). The contemporary homeless no longer resemble the derelict and hobo stereotypes of a past generation. They now include the elderly, the disabled, and Vietnam veterans (Ropers 1986). They are also no longer exclusively male. Homeless women began to appear on the streets in the 1970's and now include children and entire families (Hopper & Hamberg 1986). Women are still a minority among the homeless, but do constitute about 20% of the population (Ropers 1986). Many homeless women and adolescent females report that they left their homes after repeated incidents of abuse, rape, incest, and desertion (Stoner 1983).

Bahr and Garrett (1976) cited homeless women as characterized by a history of wrong choices, personal failures, drunkenness, shoplifting, abusing their children and neglecting their obligations. Many are forced to panhandle, deal drugs or become prostitutes and trade sexual favors for food, shelter and other necessities (Stoner 1983). Rowe and Wolch (1990), in their study among homeless women on skid row in Los Angeles, report the tendency of women to enter into a lover or spouse relationship, motivated in part by their need for protection and emotional support. Many homeless women reflect frustrated desires for conventional monogamous relationships and intense conflicts following coercive sexual encounters (Stoner 1983).

Richard Ropers has done extensive empirical research among the homeless in Los Angeles (1986, 1988). His findings reveal a disproportionately nonwhite population, over 50%, including 32% Black and 10% Hispanic. 78% are male, with a median age of 37. He further notes that 75% have lived in Los Angeles for two years or more. His research (1988:67, 68) includes an insightful analysis of those living in SRO hotels, whom he describes as "the sheltered homeless." These individuals comprise a distinct subpopulation of the larger homeless community, although manifesting similar conditions of "economic and social displacement and psychological isolation."

Despite being on "the top" of the stratification system, many SRO residents are just one step away from being on the streets. Some gravitate back and forth between the two. Recent research reveals as many 15,000 SRO residents in downtown Los Angeles, with two-thirds of those in skid row (Ropers 1988). As many as 100 of these units have been described as "houses of horror" and the "slums de la slums" by the Los Angeles Times (June 9, 1986). I personally experienced one such multi-story facility in which there was no heat, no elevator service, no shortage of roaches and an abundance of gang activity, drug abuse and prostitution.

Roper's (1988) discoveries of the Los Angeles SRO population reflect a similarly younger and nonwhite population. 45% of his sample were under the age of 40 and 47% were Black. 80% of the residents had a high school education or less and 48% indicated poor or fair health. 785 were unemployed, with 52% on public assistance. He states that SRO hotels are the only housing that many individuals are able to afford. Ropers (1988:85) concludes that SRO residents in Los Angeles are "predominantly displaced, disabled, or retired," with the majority of the displaced being unemployed young Blacks.

Gangs

Interfacing with these groups of homeless men and women are several equally distinct subcultures of Hispanic youth gangs. The problems of gangs and drugs in the Greater Los Angeles area has reached crisis proportions. The Los Angeles County Sheriff reports that over 1,400 murders committed within the last 5 years were gang-related (State Task Force on Gangs and Drugs 1989). "Los Angeles is a city of gangs" (Bing 1991:xiv).

There are approximately 250 gangs with a total membership in excess of 30,000 in the city. In Los Angeles County, officials estimate a staggering 600-650 gangs, including between 60,000 and 80,000 members (State Task Force on Gangs and Drugs 1989). Membership is up 100% in Los Angeles since 1985, with the average age of gang members now 13 1/2 years old (Santoli 1991).

Moore and Vigil, in their cooperative study (1989) as well as their individual works (Moore 1978; Vigil 1988), have conducted extensive research among Hispanic (Chicano) gang members in the "barrios" (neighborhoods) of Los Angeles. Reacting to criminologists and law enforcement officials who tend to view Chicano youth gangs as deviant and delinquent, they prefer instead a sociological perspective on gang affiliation, although not denying the frequent lawless behavior.

For Los Angeles law enforcement officials, gang fights, recreational drug use, and offenses such as burglary and vandalism all constitute violations of the law and are perceived as gang-related because they are committed by gang members. Moore and Vigil point out however that to the youthful gang member these acts are viewed quite differently.

Action taken in the name of the gang is not considered deviant, regardless of its nature. The gang is seen as representing the barrio or community and one is required to conform to those expectations. Gang ideology demands a commitment to the welfare and defense of the community. Outside of the barrio, the most obvious manifestation of neighborhood loyalty is inter-gang conflict. Violence in these encounters, no matter how extreme, seems justifiable to them in the same way that war-associated fighting, in the larger society, can be perceived as noble behavior.

The enculturation process among gang members in which the norms, values and lore of the gang are learned, is often complicated by intertwined family traditions. As the gang subculture has become entrenched in numerous Chicano communities, many participants are actually second, third, or even fourth generation gang members. The more traditional view is that the gang serves as a substitute family for its members in that the breakdown of this social unit in society has left a void for young people which is now being filled by this alternative means of affirmation, security, support and protection. In either case, Moore and Vigil conclude that it is extremely difficult for these individuals to become part of the mainstream of society once they have been socialized into the gang subculture.

Gordon McLean (1991), currently ministering to gang members with Metro Chicago Youth for Christ, reiterates the fact that gangs have filled the vacuum left by the crumbling family structure in our culture. He goes further to include the church and the school as also abdicating the hold they once had on youth and their standards of conduct.

McLean (1991:50) portrays gangs as "an illegitimate means of meeting legitimate needs." He sees them as providing protection, action, money, belonging and bridging a cultural gap. He concludes (p. 156), "Gang involvement is more than joining a club; it becomes a lifestyle, even an addiction. The youth surrenders his mind and values to the group and ends up doing things in a pack that he would never do alone. It is a life that starts out with excitement and ends in danger."

STRUCTURE

The research is structured so as to initially unfold the context in which the training of the students take place. The next chapter relays stories of homelessness, gangs, and prostitution as brought to light in my encounters with Green Eyes. These become the milieu for the array of experiences with the students, which constitute the central portion of the study. The last two chapters present the impressions of and impact on the students, as well as a critique of the overall process and suggestions for those seeking to implement a similar endeavor in training students experientially for urban ministry.

The case studies contained in the research are an accurate representation of the activities and conversations of these men and women in their specific environment. As a result, the language used by many is often extremely "graphic." Finally, at the request of some informants and in consideration of privacy and protection for all concerned, most of the names of those portrayed have been changed.

CHAPTER 2

"MY BIG HOUSE DON'T HAVE NO ROOF!":

THE WORLD OF GREEN EYES

The overall cultural scene of this ethnographic exploration is best introduced through the view and experiences of one known on the street as "Green Eyes." During the past 2 1/2 years, this intriguing, caring, and amazingly resilient African-American man in his late 40's has been my passport into the world of homelessness, gangs and prostitution. When it came to awareness of life on the streets, I was the rookie and he the seasoned veteran. I, the would-be teacher, was the naive student, learning from him, my street-wise mentor and instructor. This took place as I chronicled his adventures and interactions while living on sidewalks, in cardboard boxes, hotels, and in jail. In it all he was my sounding board and protector; through it all he became my friend.

This chapter documents my own experiential learning process as I became immersed in his world of unique and diverse acquaintances. These interactions form the backdrop in which the components of experiential learning are fleshed out. Our *experiences* gave me first-hand *exposure* to urban need and often left me overwhelmed and perplexed (*"dissonance"*). I was forced to continually *debrief* those encounters in order to regain my perspective and make sense out of what I was experiencing. Many of those *reflections* are presented at the end of his story and are *applied* in further research and involvement with the students. I have recorded these events somewhat chronologically, but have also collapsed some of the interviews into topic discussions for reasons of brevity. The overall purpose is to recap my own process of discovery so the reader can see how these experiences prepared me to coach a group of students as they learned about similar issues and met many of the same individuals.

THE EARLY YEARS

Green Eyes grew up in a small town in southwestern lower Michigan called Muskegon. He was raised by his mom and step-dad, never knowing his real father. His mom got pregnant at the age of fifteen and married his step dad when Green Eyes was seven or eight-years-old. From that union came a step brother and step sister. The brother is dead, and his sister is living in Tennessee. His step dad died of cancer and he thinks his real father is somewhere in Southern California. He still manages to keep in touch with his mother, calling her on special occasions when he has the money (which is not very often). His loyalty to her stems from the fact that "she was always there. I never doubted her love for me, "'cuz she was all I had."

Life has never been easy for Green Eyes. He spoke of growing up "hungry and poor" and commented, "I got tired of expecting that somebody was going to take care of me, and then you say, 'Hey, I can do something helpful [for the family], I can steal.' What other choice did I have?" His first contact with the authorities came as a mere seven-year-old boy, when he hit his teacher in the belly with a chair. He got as far as fifth grade in school, at which point he succumbed to peer pressure. This was actually the beginning of his experiences on the street, fighting, stealing, and running with gangs. He was sent off to a highly regimented boy's training school in Lansing, Michigan at the age of eleven. While there his bad habits continued. He started smoking and he ran away thirty-eight times. He was always caught and brought back. He lived in a small room with a steel door, a wooden bed, one blanket and two meals a day.

But he seemed to be in the wrong place at the wrong time. Soon after his release at age seventeen, he went joy-riding with a friend in a stolen car. They were caught and he was sent to a juvenile detention center in Ionia, Michigan for the next two years. After being discharged he was soon back in for armed robbery, this time for five years up in Marquette, Michigan. He became bitter and angry during his incarceration and continued to slide. Two of those years were spent in "the hole," which he described simply as "hell." He had gotten in a fight with the cook, who was White. He said that all the prison guards were White and professed allegiance to the Ku Klux Klan. They beat him terribly, until his entire face was swollen out of proportion. He was allowed out of the hole once a week to shower and received one meal one day, two the next, and so on. The only light that seeped in came from the hallway, and there were no bathroom facilities, only a cement bed.

When he was released from Marquette he shot a man in the shoulder with a sawed-off shotgun, and was sentenced to eleven years in Jackson State Penitentiary in Jackson, Michigan, on a charge of assault to commit murder. He talked very painfully about those years. He witnessed people's heads forcibly pushed into toilets, fellow inmates stuck with knives, some even tied up, beaten, and killed. He was raped and could do nothing to stop it from

35

happening. He says he became a survivor in prison and has been one ever since.

"CALIFORNIA HERE I COME"

Green Eyes came to California about eight years ago. He went to Pasadena, completed a 14-week card dealing program, and got a job at a casino in Commerce. But he lost that job after a year and became a night manager at an adult theater, living there as well. He left that job within a year also and ended up in MacArthur Park, which at that time housed hundreds of street people. He then began to notice how people looked at him, and how dirty and disheveled he had become. "So you start to sleep days and roam nights so others don't see you so much," he told me. He left the park because he felt stuck there, roamed around for a while and found an abandoned apartment. He started to fix it up when tragedy struck once more. He was jumped by a group of street people and beaten so severely with a pipe that his neck was broken and 70% of his right side paralyzed. He spent the next year and a half recuperating in the hospital.

Green Eyes has now been in the Westlake area for about five years, most of that time on the sidewalk off Beacon Avenue. The first day I met him, in February of 1991, he had just gotten forced out of a makeshift tent in an alley off 8th Street. Apparently a group of his "friends," other street people whom he had felt sorry for and let stay in the tent with him, had decided to claim the tent as their own. I explained to Green Eyes that I was working on a project for a class, and asked if he would be my teacher and instruct me about life on the street. He jumped at the chance and must have rambled on in

36

dialogue for over an hour! I asked if I could come back once a week to meet with him and learn more. Our relationship had begun!

A BOX WITH A VIEW

The next few visits with Green Eyes were memorable to say the least. I felt like I was watching a movie at times, straight out of Hollywood. I went back to the tent the next week, feeling somewhat intimidated as I walked up the alley. Green Eyes was not there, so I asked some of his "friends" if they knew where he was. "He doesn't live in this neighborhood anymore," I was told quite curtly. One Black man finally told me that I might find him around the corner, on the next block. There he was, seated beside a cardboard box the size of a refrigerator, his new "home."

As we began to talk I could see that he was very distracted. A disturbance was brewing across the street beside an abandoned car, a frequent "rendezvous" spot for prostitutes and their "dates." A White girl and a Hispanic girl named Linda were screaming obscenities at each other. I quickly learned that Linda was one of Green Eyes' "friends." The White girl enlisted the help of a passing Black man to fight Linda and Gus, her seventy-year-old "date."

At this point Green Eyes jumped up, grabbed his walker (a result of the beating) and motored across the street, without even a glance at oncoming traffic. A police car then pulled up, almost as if on script. The two officers, one White and one Hispanic, were extremely physical with all five of them. They frisked them, and forced all but Green Eyes to lie face down on the street beside the car. They found a bag of cocaine on the Black man, cuffed him,

37

and also cuffed and arrested Linda and Gus for priors (prostitution). They let the White girl and Green Eyes go.

As we walked back to his box, he commented about how "stupid" he had been in going to intervene in that situation. "But I had to because Linda is my friend," he responded. He explained that he had known her for a number of years and that she had been "working the streets" since she was a teenager. She is addicted to cocaine as well as "chiba" (heroin) and is bisexual. She began her "career" in Hollywood as a high priced hooker but her drug habit as well as abuse by her pimp soon took its toll and she wound up on the streets downtown. I inquired about Gus (or "Pops" as he is also called) and was told that he watches out for Linda and a number of the other girls. He even has a home in Highland Park that he rents out to several of them. He is what is known as a "sugar daddy," trading drugs for sex with the girls, and has fathered sixteen children, one by Linda. He has been with her, off and on, for over ten years.

DRUGS AS THE "NORM"

Green Eyes generally slept in his box late mornings and afternoons, then roamed the streets at night along with most of the others I met. Many times, seated beside his box, we got into rousing discussions about drugs. One of his priorities was to get "high," which he did most every night. It is the ultimate escape from the nightmare that is life on the streets for him and countless others. He described it as the best feeling he ever has, "better than a woman." He says "it makes you feel light, like you're walking or floating."

Since coming to California his life has been consumed with drugs. He estimates it has cost him about $700,000 over those years. He was doing $700-800 per day the first couple years when he was working and was able to afford it. But since his accident he lives on a grand total of approximately $600 per month disability. It all goes to drugs, plus any other money he can accumulate by selling clothes and other items from the dumpster. He insists that he has ethics, however. He never panhandles for drug money, only for food to survive.

"If you got drugs you can make a livin' in this neighborhood," he says. Drugs are everywhere, on every corner, in the alley, in all the hotels. For most people it's the norm, a way of life. On one occasion he casually informed me of the 24-hour drug house down the street where five guys made about $8,000 per day. At this point I was feeling rather angry at the passivity with which he spoke about such a deadly lifestyle and those who made a comfortable living off them. "Doesn't it bother you that you're such a pawn in their hands?" I blurted out, not meaning to excuse his own choices by any means. He retorted that no one controls him and that he is his own boss. Nobody forces drugs on him, it is by his own choosing.

I asked him if he ever got tired of it all, if he ever wanted to change his life. He responded somewhat fatalistically, almost philosophically, that the streets are his life, his family, and that he's happy out here, even needed. He said he had to make a choice years ago to either be bitter and strike out at people, or to accept life and be happy because what is past is done and cannot be changed. He chose the latter, to look at the good in people instead of the bad. His exact words were, "What is there to be sad about? I'm livin'! There are people worse off than me."

Green Eyes expressed a lack of genuine friendship. "People only like you around here if you can do somethin' for them. They use you." He mentioned that real friends are concerned about you, not about what they can get from you. "Friends are special. You can put your life in their hands." Others are just associates. "Friends are not friends out here. They cross you, and for a rock (cocaine) they turn against you." I asked him if he ever had a "friend." He thought long and hard and finally responded that he couldn't really remember ever having one (by his own definition), except possibly a White girl named Susie who is a prostitute and fellow drug addict. But as he thought about it more, he realized that she pities him and isn't interested in him as a person. As I listened to his honest admissions, I wondered what Jesus would say to him.

THE GOSPEL ACCORDING TO GREEN EYES

I asked Green Eyes about God, and if he felt that the Lord had any relevance to his situation, any interest in his life. He responded that he knows he does wrong, but that "God knows my heart." He reflected on the fact that his mom wanted him to be a preacher and that the family used to go to church back in Michigan. Despite the incongruities of his lifestyle he told me several times that God comes first, and that he puts his faith in him.

Then out tumbled a variety of his religious viewpoints. He said that Jesus was homeless and lived with the poor. He believes "God is in you" and that we are all made like Him. Hell to him is the streets and the wrong things he does. "I know I live in hell," he says rather bluntly, but he still believes in God and feels that hell must not control him. The Bible is "too complicated" and confuses him as do so many religions and denominations. "Nobody is better than another," he continued, "you have to be open minded." He doesn't believe people should be divided by different religions, and that they only separate people and try to control them. "We are all His children," he concluded rather simply. He judges people by what they do, not by what they say, because there are "too many phonies," including Christians.

STAYING IN TOUCH

The Spring semester ended and my weekly pilgrimages downtown to meet with Green Eyes became more infrequent. I was in summer school and had not as yet decided to incorporate this material into broader and more extensive dissertation research. Yet Green Eyes had gladly opened up his world to me as "teacher" and even more so now as my friend. I was committed to keeping in touch with him despite the demands of doctoral study. I made several visits to see him during that Summer of '91, in many instances bringing my wife and little blonde, blue-eyed three-year-old daughter as well. He was still on the sidewalk on Beacon, but had now moved closer to 7th Street.

During the early Fall we lost track of him for several weeks and actually found him quite by accident. It was mid-October and we were giving some visiting friends a "tour" of skid row when we spotted him on the sidewalk beside the Union Rescue Mission! He looked the best I had ever seen him, and we had a happy little reunion, hugging on the sidewalk. He had been staying at the mission and was clean, drug-free, and excited about

41

life and the Lord. He was reading his Bible, and I sincerely believe, had some kind of spiritual experience while there.

A ROOM IN THE INN

We were encouraged by Green Eyes' new-found enthusiasm. He told us of his plans to get a hotel room off of 6th and Broadway, and we arranged to meet him there the next Sunday and bring him to church with us. A week later we showed up, but no Green Eyes. As it turned out, he had ended up in the Post Apartments on Bonnie Brae, between 7th and 8th. I became well acquainted with the clientele of that SRO (Single Room Occupancy) hotel and the neighborhood in general over the next ten months. That dilapidated, roach-infested, five-story building was home not only to Green Eyes, but also to an array of other disenfranchised men and women. It also served as the gang headquarters for the Bonnie Brae Criminals (BBC), and enabled me eventually to meet and build a relationship with their leader, Funee Man.

Since Green Eyes was so newly motivated, and had so few worldly possessions, we were excited about helping him move in and get settled in his room. So we collected food, dishes, sheets, blankets, curtains, pictures, and even a cassette recorder and a small black-and-white television set. We solicited goods from our neighbors and friends in a local church. My wife even recruited a friend and her daughter from that same church to go with her and our daughter on a Saturday to bring Green Eyes all his newly gathered belongings. They spent several hours cleaning and making a home for him out of that barren little room.

We kept up our weekly pilgrimages throughout the Fall, although our visits were much more awkward and often unenjoyable as the needs of the hotel occupants became increasingly real to us. Green Eyes seemed to be a magnet, attracting anybody and everybody who needed help. It was rare to find him alone when we came to visit. My wife was also pregnant with our second child and often felt poorly. The room was dreary and conversation difficult with others generally present. We started bringing folding lawn chairs to sit on, and actually had some of our better visits on the sidewalk below (the irony of returning to the streets in that regard struck me).

This continual barrage of people and parade of need began to wear on Green Eyes. It got to the point where my wife and daughter would wait in the car while I headed up the stairs to his room, past the BBC gang logos scrawled on the walls, never knowing who would greet me at the door. Once it was a Black man cooking rice on the hot plate. Another visit revealed a Black woman asleep on the bed. Still another time a Hispanic man and woman were staying with him temporarily. By now some of the things we had contributed to his apartment had disappeared, including the bed frame. All that remained was a common mattress on the floor.

"WE WISH YOU A MERRY CHRISTMAS"

As the holidays approached, the woman who had come along with my wife and daughter to help clean Green Eye's apartment mentioned him to her daughter's Christian school teacher. What triggered her memory was a book in her child's kindergarten classroom about a cat named "Green Eyes!" The teacher, a former Wycliffe missionary, was interested in a missionary project for Christmas whom her class could "adopt" and buy gifts for. Green Eyes became their "project"!

What followed was a most interesting, but not necessarily out of the ordinary sequence of reactions to homeless stereotypes. There was a hesitancy on the part of several parents toward a Black street person, so the teacher had to check with the principal for approval of the project. Then followed the discussion as to whether or not the class, or select representatives, should bring the gifts to him downtown, or whether he should be allowed to come to the classroom. Neither option seemed to fit, so it was decided that I would bring him to our apartment, they would bring the presents to their classroom, and then the teacher and our friend would bring the gifts over to our house, where we would celebrate with Green. The plan was then to capture it all on video and show it to the class so they could "meet" Green Eyes!

The response of gifts was incredible. Dozens and dozens of them piled up under our tree as we carried them into the house. We were amazed and couldn't contain our laughter as opening them revealed half a dozen pairs of sweat suits, over 20 caps, socks (which he didn't even wear at the time) and numerous toothbrushes and paste (for a very few teeth)! Food was in abundance, and Green Eyes was having so much fun that he wanted to sample every item, from chocolates to Vienna sausages. But upon our return from spending the Christmas holidays with my family in the Midwest, we learned that nearly all of the presents had been stolen out of his room. Someone had literally kicked in the door and made off with the goods.

"HAPPY BIRTHDAY DEAR GREEN EYES"

As Green Eyes' birthday approached, he mentioned his desire to thank the children who gave him the Christmas gifts. In his estimation that would be the perfect way to celebrate his birthday. So with the help once again of my wife's friend and the cooperation of the teacher, we arranged a birthday party over the noon hour in the classroom with all but one of the approximately twenty-five students (her mother chose to keep her home that day). Even the principal made a brief appearance.

Green Eyes was in his glory, outfitted sharply in a bright red shirt and cap. They arranged for us to sit at the front of the classroom and he told them bits and pieces of his life, while I related how we had met. This was followed by a brief time in which the children were allowed to come up single file to Green Eyes and ask him questions. They formed an orderly line and most shook his hand, some gave him a hug. Several, looking intently into his face, inquired sweetly, "Do you really have green eyes?"

Next came a cake and a rousing chorus of "Happy Birthday Dear Green Eyes." By now he was walking on air, and it was a significant "up close and personal" experience for the children as well. Despite his selection as the "token" homeless person and the resultant lavish outpouring of goods now being worn and consumed by others oblivious to the source, the children had come face to face with a person in need, not a mere statistic, and had responded with love and genuine interest.

"HOTEL HELL"

Meanwhile, back in "hotel hell" (as he often referred to the building), Green Eyes' room continued to be a revolving door of activity for a diversity of people and experiences. I knocked on his door one afternoon and he opened it to reveal a Hispanic man lying on his mattress on the floor with a bullet in his arm! Green Eyes calmly informed me that he had been standing on the third floor balcony the night before when a random bullet from a rival gang struck him during a drive-by shooting. Snuggled cozily in his arms was a very scantily dressed prostitute named Tanya. Unlike many I had met, she was very attractive and articulate. I was reminded of the scriptural injunction to make a "covenant with my eyes" as Tanya lay before me, legs spread wide, wearing a loose and revealing halter top and extremely short, cut-off jeans! There were not too many places I could safely look, so I kept my eyes fixed on her face or the wall behind her!

Upon learning that I was not a cop, narc, or potential "date" (the term they generally used for their "clients") Tanya was very willing to talk about her life. Green Eyes had mentioned to her that I was "writing a book," and she responded that she had quite a story to tell. She then began to inform me of things I really would rather not have heard. She mentioned that the general public would be shocked at how many men of power and prestige took advantage of their "services" (i.e. politicians, businessmen, etc.). She continued to relate how she and a number of other girls had been "used and abused" by an undercover policeman. He had supposedly set out to infiltrate their "prostitution ring," but then used the girls for sex and threatened to report and arrest them if they refused. She said they had attempted to turn him in but no one believed them.

As Easter approached, Green Eyes was embroiled in an ongoing "rights issue," as he referred to it. His door still had a hole in it and did not latch. Roaches roamed the room in abundance. The elevator had been broken for weeks, meaning that he and numerous other handicapped or elderly people in the building had to use the stairs, some all the way to the fifth floor. Furthermore, the entire building had been without heat for nearly two years. Since his repeated requests for action continued to fall deaf ears, Green Eyes simply stopped paying rent. Not only that, but he started a chain reaction in encouraging other tenants to do the same!

The people-pressures and depressing environment ultimately caused Green Eyes to want to leave the building. He began talking about trying to get his own place, even if it was just a bare room with no furniture. He wanted a room out of the neighborhood where he could get away from it all and simply eat and sleep in peace. I remember him saying, "Just a box of food is all I need!" We began to encourage him to move out, and he was talking about a place he had discovered just a few blocks away. We offered to come down and help him move on the first of the month when he got his disability check. But the first of the month came and went without any word from Green Eyes. He had decided to stay in the Post Apartments a bit longer, with hopes of getting some movement on the part of the ownership to do some of the desperately needed repairs.

I had the opportunity of getting acquainted with the owner after a visit with Green Eyes during that time period. As I was leaving the building I passed the landlord's office at the base of the stairs. I had never seen his door open before, but on that afternoon it was a jar and, surprisingly, he called me in. I had been looking forward to explain my research to him and ask permission to more fully explore contacts with others in the building. But before I could even utter a word, Martin informed me that he knew from Green Eyes who I was and what I was doing, and that it was basically a waste of time. He proceeded to tell me that Green Eyes has prostitutes and drugs in his room, sells the food and clothes which we bring him for money, and then matter-of-factly pronounced him "a terrible man." I acknowledged that Green Eyes was not a saint by any means, but said I had not noticed him to stick out that drastically from the others I had met in the hotel thus far either!

I began to explain that I was a Christian and deliberately drawn to the people in his building because of the problems he had just described. He immediately retorted that he does what he can, specifically tries to "help Christians and Jews," but that people like Green Eyes "are just trouble". He then made the incredible indictment, stating it twice for emphasis, that for Green Eyes and others like him who are beyond help, "they ought to just kill them!" With that said and repeated, and with no provision for rebuttal, he told me that I was free to leave and ushered me out the door!

FEELING LIKE A "WHITE BOY"

During the Spring of 1992 the riots broke out, and buildings burned within blocks of Green Eyes' hotel. Although I wanted desperately to be down there, I figured that in this case, as a White man, discretion might be the better part of valor! I went to see him the weekend after the uprising, wide-eyed and with my camera in hand. I was shocked at the number of establishments in his general vicinity which had been torched.

As I climbed the stairs to Green Eyes' room I walked into one of the more intimidating encounters of my entire life. Standing just a few feet from his open door were four members of the Bonnie Brae Criminals. They immediately got right in my face. "What the f__ do you want White boy?" They were menacing, angry , and I felt real fear. Were it not for Green Eyes' intervention there was the distinct possibility of my coming out on the losing end of that little confrontation. From inside of his room he overheard our "conversation" and quickly stepped into the middle of my new acquaintances, who had by this time circled around me. He told them I was "alright" and could be "trusted," that I was his friend and was therefore to be "treated with respect." They backed away and I put out my hand to shake theirs. They would not even look at me and ignored my outstretched hand. I was taken aback. The reality of being White and an outsider to their world came home to me profoundly. These guys had never met me before, and yet with the smell of smoke from dreadfully charred buildings still in the air, I was as good a scapegoat as anyone.

I visited briefly with Green Eyes that afternoon and was still pondering my encounter with the BBC when I realized that I would have to confront them one more time. They were standing on the sidewalk directly outside of the front door. I took a deep breath, said a quick prayer, and approached them with a smile. Again they would not shake my hand, but I was able to get some eye contact and told them that I was glad to have met them and would love to speak with them again. Shortly thereafter Green Eyes told me that one of the four had been shot by a rival gang member inside the front entrance of the hotel, and another was imprisoned.

"ON THE ROAD AGAIN"

Several weeks went by before I saw Green Eyes again. My next visit with him during the summer was significant though as he introduced me to Funee Man, who gladly agreed to get together again and tell me his story (a synopsis of which is presented in Chapter 7). By August, Green Eyes' "case" against the landlord had proceeded to such an extent that he had a court date at the end of the month. He asked me if I would be willing to stand with him as a character reference, and I told him that I would. However, we never did get our day in court. His hearing was conveniently pushed back into September. By then, Green Eyes had been evicted from the building.

I attempted to track him down a few days later. I asked around in the building if anyone knew his whereabouts. A young Black prostitute named Ava suggested that I look for him a couple blocks over on Alvarado Street, between 7th and 8th, the place where he gets his drugs. I set out on foot and the sights and smells were amazing. The alleys reeked with piles of garbage. Numerous prostitutes advertised their availability. Many "shoppers" ambled by with their cart loads of goods. Most asked if I could part with a dollar or just some spare change.

Back at the hotel again I spotted Ava on the fourth floor balcony. I called up to her and asked if Green Eyes might still be in the building. Someone else overheard my cry and yelled down from the fifth floor balcony that he was staying in a room up there. As I climbed the stairs I was oblivious to the fact that I would never see Ava again. Just a few months later she was pushed off that same balcony by some gang members and fell to her death on the sidewalk below. She was twenty-two years old.

Green Eyes was walking down the hallway toward me when I reached the top of the steps. He looked tired and haggard, but was glad to see me, and I to have finally found him. He was staying temporarily with a young Black man named Kermit until the end of the month, when the two of them hoped to get an apartment elsewhere. He informed me that during the day I could generally find him either on Alvarado or around 9th and Westlake, where he spent some nights in a parked car.

It was during this search for Green Eyes that I discovered a truly intriguing individual whom I was to get to know much better in the months ahead. Red Dog, so named because of his reddish hair and big bushy beard, actually found me! He stopped me in the hallway and in what I was soon to understand as his typically gruff and profane way inquired, "What the h__ are you doin' around here?" I explained my quest of trying to find Green Eyes, and the broader task of research. To my surprise he immediately announced that he had spent fourteen years living in homeless camps under freeway overpasses and that I should interview him! He enthusiastically proclaimed, "I can show you parts of this city you wouldn't even believe!" Red Dog then named several others with whom he had lived under the bridges, and offered to acquaint me with them as well. They are Big Jed, Lefty, Lenny, Dirty Jake and the Beached Whale (all of whom are introduced in chapters 5 and 6). He showed me his room and I met Billie, his female live-in companion (who is also next seen in chapter 6).

51

AN ENTERPRISING VENTURE

Green Eyes' new venture was trying to sell clothing, which he had piled high in a shopping cart. He generally finds the clothes in the dumpster, washes them, and sells them. I soon realized that most of his "clients" were the girls working the streets. In some cases he would buy various items of clothing for a couple dollars and then turn around and sell them for more. He had several nice outfits in his basket which he proudly showed me. Green Eyes had returned to staying on the streets once again. He was back on Beacon, between 8th and 9th, sleeping on a hunk of foam. Many of the young ladies "plied their wares" in that same general area. Meanwhile, the Post Apartments were taken over by the courts and placed under new management. Several of those I had met, including Red Dog, moved out.

"WORKING SIGNS"

I next saw Green Eyes on my birthday in early October, when we had him over for dinner. As I arrived at his "roofless abode" to pick him up he hastily stuffed some valuables inside the broken down cement wall which runs along the sidewalk. As he hopped in the car he was wearing purple sweat pants and a very dirty gray UCLA sweatshirt with his belly protruding out proudly from beneath it! He asked if we could make a quick stop in the alley (where he had been living when we first met) so that he could exchange that shirt for another.

The condition of the alley was far worse than I had previously known it to be. There was garbage everywhere, wet and putrid, matted down and piled several feet in the air. I waited and watched from the car while Green

Eyes made his way adeptly over the mounds of waste and stuck his head inside one of the numerous shanties. Seconds later an outstretched arm handed him a very nice looking green sweatshirt. Off went the old and on went the new! He was the picture of stylish color, decked out in green and purple. He spoke briefly with those in the tent and returned to the car with a beaming smile!

As we drove I asked Green Eyes about those I had seen holding signs at various freeway on and off ramps. He said that several work together in the area and make as much as $200-300 a day. They then split the take and use it to buy drugs. He described them all as "con artists" and said that the whole thing was "just a scam," and that they have different signs that they use to play off people's emotions. We enjoyed a nice evening together at our home and he slept in the car most of the way back downtown. This was the first time that I was literally dropping him off on the streets instead of at his old room in the Post. I found it hard to do so, even though I knew that his situation in that apartment was not much better than his current existence on the street. Before leaving I watched as he checked to see that his valuables were still tucked away in his "safe" behind the wall.

ANOTHER TRIP TO THE JOINT

A couple weeks slipped by before I had a chance to see Green Eyes again, and it was now early November. He was not at his usual spot on the street, although his bedding, including a half-full shopping cart of clothing, was parked beside the tree. I asked another homeless man named Marty, whom I had previously met, if he knew where Green Eyes was. He said he had heard that "something had gone down" the day before and he had not seen him that day. I drove around his standard hangouts but could find no trace of him.

I showed up a few days later and he was still not around. I noticed that his shopping cart had also disappeared, and it looked as if someone else was sleeping on his foam. I recognized Linda, in somewhat of a daze, sitting inside a small station wagon parked along the curb. As I approached another young woman got out and introduced herself as Denise. She said that she was glad to see me because Green Eyes told her to tell me that he was okay, but back in "the joint" (jail)! She was Linda's sister and a friend of Green Eyes as well. Denise is gay and lives with her lover, Kathy, who, although bisexual, pronounces herself as "straightly gay." Kathy has two children, the younger of which was a crack baby whom she actually bore for Denise, who is unable to have children. They are raising him "together." He calls Kathy "Mom" and Denise "Dad."

I recalled having met Linda while sitting with Green Eyes beside his box. Denise was very talkative about her own lifestyle and that of her lover's as well. Since Linda appeared to be "tripped out" in the car I decided to ask Denise about her sister's activities, too. She spoke of how Linda, now 29 years old, had always been "sex crazy" and has been "turning tricks" since she was 14. Twice she has gotten pregnant with "trick babies," both of whom were addicted to crack at birth. She has been jailed three times for prostitution, the most recent of which for soliciting an undercover police officer. Denise concluded, "She just don't take care of herself. She sometimes don't take baths for weeks...She don't give a d__...She's just really out of it."

Denise and Kathy met Green Eyes through Linda and had brought down clothes for him to sell a couple times during the past few months. Kathy regularly sells items at a swap meet in Cerritos so they had offered to take Green Eyes along with them and the children that Sunday afternoon. As they were leaving they were pulled over in Downey by two White police officers. The reason was simply the suspicious nature of two White women being with a Black man! The officers had tried to make an interracial thing out of it all by badgering Kathy to admit that Green Eyes was her "boyfriend." Denise said that she then blurted out, "That's my girlfriend!" which rather quickly "shut up the cop." She said that the police were prejudiced toward Blacks and were very mean to Green Eyes. They hassled him over his handicap as well (he had progressed from a walker to a cane), taunting, "Come on, you can walk."

The police ran a check on their records and found that each had warrants against them, with Kathy having four. Nonetheless they let her and the children go, and drove Denise and Green Eyes to the police station in Downey. Denise had one warrant for a minor offense and was released a short time later. Green Eyes was detained on a violation of parole warrant dating back to 1985. He was held, finger printed, and placed in a cell. He told me later that he was "messed with" by several White officers who "were all John Bircher's." They "worked him over" pretty well, pushing and elbowing him and repeatedly calling him "Nigger" for being with a White woman. It was nearly identical treatment, although not as severe, as he had received years before in Marquette. They kept him there for five days and then transferred him to the County Jail on Temple Street in downtown Los

Angeles. He was to be arraigned at Superior Court, in the same vicinity, which became my destination as well.

LEARNING "THE SYSTEM"

So began the process of experiencing firsthand the vast bureaucratic machine that is the judicial and penal system. The courthouse was a multi-story maze of guards and security checks, much like the pre-boarding experience at an airport. I had no idea where to go so I asked a guard who inquired whether the charge was a felony or a misdemeanor. Since it was a felony, he directed me to a clerk on the second floor. I went upstairs and got in line. When I got to the counter the officer looked up his name in a large book and announced that I would have to go to another building for his case. I then mentioned a division number which Denise and Kathy had given me and she quickly replied, "Oh, that's up on the 15th floor!" When I finally found the right department, I inquired about Green Eyes and the bailiff said he had been in and out already that morning. I requested the verdict and he replied that he was to be sentenced in two weeks. I asked if he had been released until then and he answered that Green Eyes was being held in the Men's Central Jail on Bauchet and Vignes, and gave me his booking number.

Three days later I drove down to the jail hoping to pay him a visit. The first step involved filling out a form, handed to me by one of two guards at the entrance, before I was allowed into the building. After checking my identification I was "ushered in." I gave the form to another officer, one of several behind a large counter, each with a computer terminal at their disposal. I took a seat on a plastic bench in the large waiting room while they "notified the prisoner" of my request to see him. Despite being seated in a wheel chair, Green Eyes looked in great shape, as good as I had seen him since his brief stay in the Union Rescue Mission over a year ago. He was glad to see me, smiling from ear to ear, and his first words were, "I knew you'd come!"

He had been free of drugs for over a week, and said he did not miss it nor was feeling any physical effects without it. He had not been clean for over a year and was now anxious to make a fresh start. I eagerly spoke of how this could be a real turning point in his life, to which he agreed. He had been speaking with the chaplain and appeared to have a renewed interest in spiritual things. He also wanted to go back and see the children of the Christian school now that he was "clean." He anticipated being released on his sentencing date, the 1st of December, and placed on probation again, because the warrant was nearly eight years old. He thanked me genuinely for coming to see him and expressed his love for me and my family. Then, almost on cue, the phone went abruptly silent, announcing the end of our visit. Through the glass I watched him petition the guards for more time, but to no avail. We waved good-bye as they escorted him back to his barracks.

"HOPING FOR NOTHING"

My wife and I began to get excited about this potential turning point in Green Eyes' life as I relayed the details of our visit to her. We wondered about alternatives to another downtown "hotel hell" existence, such as a Christian rehabilitation facility. We were not fully convinced of his willingness for such a change, nor was it assured that he would be released on probation by the judge. But we decided to press ahead nonetheless, and made contact with a residential rehab program in Pasadena. They were willing to make room in the home despite limited accommodations. The fee was reasonable, even negotiable, and well within his means. They even had a Bible study that night at which time he could meet the other residents. Green Eyes called me collect a few days later, reminding me about picking him up on December 1st. We shared the details of the program in Pasadena, but our excitement was not matched by his. He did say that he was willing to check it out, but we sensed that his acquiescence was as much for our benefit as his.

The big day of his anticipated release arrived and I drove back to the courthouse to be present for his sentencing. The bailiff wheeled in Green Eyes shortly before 10 a.m. He looked around and smiled when he saw me and I responded with a thumbs-up signal of confidence. The judge had his file before him and was perusing it to determine the nature and duration of the warrant against him. He then inquired about his P.O. and Green Eyes responded that he had made an attempt to check in with her, according to the terms of his parole. The judge was sympathetic to his explanation, and asked if he had ever done community service. When Green Eyes replied that he had not, the judge gave him three years of unsupervised probation. He inquired if that was acceptable to Green Eyes, who replied, "Yes, Your Honor," and that was it! Case closed!

WAITING AND WONDERING

At about 3:30 that afternoon another collect call came from Green Eyes. He excitedly said that he was to "go down" in about 20 minutes, meaning that he was to be sent to the release area. He was still quite hesitant about the rehabilitation program, inquiring about the cost and claiming that some "want to take all your money." He finally agreed to try it out for at least that night and I said I was on my way. I was feeling frustrated over his resistance to the program, but even more so, somewhat deflated at the thought of his potentially missing out on a significant step toward real long-term change.

The release area was a cold, sterile-looking room and there was no sight of Green Eyes. On one end was another thick window with a guard seated behind a terminal. I got in line, along with several others who were waiting to speak with him. I gave him Green Eyes' booking number and his computer revealed that he had not yet been released. It was now nearly 6:00. I asked how long it might be until he was actually "released," and he said it might be as late as 1:00 or 2:00 in the morning! He explained that it was generally a very long process in which time they had to gather the inmate's belongings and so on. Taking note of my obvious dismay he suggested that I simply return home and call the information number every couple of hours. I went to bed that night still not knowing when Green Eyes would be released. I awoke the next morning at 6:00, surprised that I had not received a call from him. I dialed the number, gave the girl his booking number, and was told he had been released at 1:22 a.m.!

BACK ON THE MERRY-GO-ROUND

Traffic was thick and it was nearly 7:30 a.m. by the time I was able to reach the jail. I was not surprised that Green Eyes was long gone, although I was curious to find out how. I figured he must have gone to see Moses, his caseworker, at his office on 7th. As I had suspected, Green Eyes was there when I drove up. He was seated on a five-gallon bucket he had found in a dumpster, wrapped up in a coat he had managed to borrow from Marty. An old broomstick, which he found in an alley, served as a cane. He was leaning against the building sound asleep. He smiled at me as I nudged him gently awake. Before I could even ask he told me that he had taken a taxi and that it had cost him $12, which he had borrowed from another released inmate! He had been sitting there dozing off since 3 a.m. He hadn't called because he didn't want to awaken me.

I took him to McDonalds for breakfast as we waited for the office to open at 8:30. Driving toward the restaurant we passed Beacon, and even before 8:00 in the morning two girls were "working the corner." I noticed Green Eyes look intently at them, leaning forward and turning in his seat as we drove by. They must have been "new to the business" because he did not seem to know who they were. I had a sinking feeling in the pit of my stomach, and blurted out, "Aw, Green Eyes, it never ends!" Life on the street seemed to me at that moment to be such a merry-go-round, an unending cycle of desperate people tangled in a web of exploitation and addiction. "Here we go again," I thought, as the lure of the street seemed to be drawing him back into its tentacles.

I was rather quiet as we drove the few blocks back to Moses' office, admittedly feeling disillusioned about the prospects of Green Eyes ever being totally free from the grip of the streets. Sensing my discouragement, he sincerely thanked my wife and I for all our help in contacting the program in Pasadena. He just was not "into it," he explained. For the first time I really understood that the streets were his life, "the big house," as he often described them. As the reality of that prospect was sinking in, he talked with enthusiasm of how he was now finally free to carry on with his life. He even spoke of getting a vendor's license so as to be able to sell things legally on the street. He felt the reason God had allowed this latest stint in jail was to clear up his warrant so that he could now get identification and open up a bank account.

I talked to him again about remaining drug-free and of his need for accountability and Christian fellowship. In response he flashed that wide and charming smile of his, admitting that he was "stubborn" and that "God was still knock, knock, knockin'" on his head to get his attention. He tapped on his skull a few times to bring home the point! I dropped him off and drove away fully expecting to see Green Eyes back on Beacon Avenue in just a matter of days, dependent upon his "medicine" once more.

WEARY, DREARY, AND WORN

Two weeks later I visited Green Eyes once again. I stopped by Beacon, and not finding him there, went to check out his other haunts prior to being in jail. I drove the three blocks over to Alvarado, and spotted him and his shopping cart on the sidewalk. Despite the fact that it was a cold and windy day, the street was packed with people in their usual "business" activities. He hugged me when we met and it was evident by his appearance and the meager belongings in his cart that his newly envisioned business venture had not as yet materialized. He was excited to see me and wanted to know if my wife and I were mad at him for being back on the streets. I assured him that we were not angry, much to his relief. Green Eyes said that he was still based on Beacon and that I could generally find him there when I stopped by.

With the busyness of the holidays approaching, I went down the next week to see him. I arrived at his spot on Beacon and found him hurt and worn down. He had been jumped by some members of the 18th Street gang. His hands were swollen, his good leg sore, and he was concerned about a bruised kidney. It was wet and dreary that day, and the allure of the street and his optimistic vendor ideals had long since disappeared. Despite his obvious pain I was amazed that he was walking around without the assistance of a chair, walker, or even a cane. He had been working hard at it and was proud of his progress. He then said he had already made arrangements to move into the Parkview Hotel on Alvarado after the new year. He was tired of the streets and they were beating him down. He knew he needed to get away and would be moving in as soon as he received his check. He asked if we could help gather some belongings for him once again, and commented that this place was an improvement over the Post Apartments. I explained that I had come to invite him for a Christmas celebration with our family, my professor, and my wife's friend. He eagerly accepted the invitation.

When I picked him up a few days later, he was in much better spirits, both emotionally and physically. He was looking forward to moving back into a hotel and had somehow obtained a matching black outfit for that evening. We laughed, took pictures, ate, and sought to encourage him. Since there were no presents from the Christian school children this Christmas he received far less than last year! He asked us to hold on to his gifts, however, until he moved into his apartment that next week. Remembering last year's fiasco, it seemed like a good idea.

GOING FULL-CIRCLE

I returned in mid-January, expecting to find him in the Parkview Hotel. I asked at the desk and they said he had already checked out, so I drove over to Beacon. I found him on the other side of the street, staying in a rather large "cardboard condo." Since the weather was still miserable, he had managed to scrounge up some blankets, wood, metal and plastic to both insulate and shield the box from the incessant rain. It was actually quite cozy, large enough to hold several people. His "good friend" Little Mousie, a prostitute who I had previously met, was keeping him company inside. It was incredible to realize that when we first met and arranged our "Street-life 101" teacher-student relationship, he was living in a box. Now nearly two years later, one block further down on the same street, Green Eyes was once again back in a "sidewalk shanty." He had gone full circle, and I had received quite an education in the process!

He was pleased that I had tracked him down once more, and explained that he had lasted a grand total of nine days in the hotel room. He had no friends in the building, no one to talk to and nothing to do but sit and stare at the bare walls. So he went back to his "big house without a roof" on the street. I listened with interest as he relayed how his "friends" on Beacon welcomed him back and said how much they had missed him. He spoke with pride of their comments that life on the street "was just not the same without him." He admitted that it was tough out there, particularly in the rain, but at least he had the solace and company of his peers. I gave him his Christmas presents which we had been holding for him, including a gift which had come from my in-laws. It was a box of chocolates which he shared with us all as we leaned against my car in front of his box.

A BIRTHDAY BASH ON BEACON

Green Eyes talked excitedly about his upcoming 48th birthday on February 1st. He wanted to have a party right on the sidewalk. He dreamed of a big sign proclaiming "Happy Birthday Green Eyes" and even a birthday cake. I told him we would be pleased to come and that I would be glad to invite my professor and my wife's friend as well. Only my family was able to attend that prestigious event but we arrived to find his box long gone. The owner of the vacant parking lot behind it had considered it an eyesore and hauled it away. Not only was his shanty in a dumpster some place, but Green Eyes was not around as well. Little Mousie explained that he would be right back, however, and that the party was still on.

While we waited for him, she shared her story with us. Twenty-seven year old Little Mousie came from Mexico with her mother, while her father and all eight brothers and sisters stayed behind. She has been "working the streets" in the vicinity of Beacon Avenue for the past two and a half years. She bears the effects of her trade. Her face is scratched, her teeth decaying, and what used to be long, flowing black hair is now cropped short. She has four children, three of whom live with her mother. The fourth, her twelve year old son, is in the 18th Street gang. She explained that he is "hiding" from her because he does not want her to know of his activities. Interestingly enough, it is to her own son's gang that she pays $10 a day "rent" for protection and security while on the streets.

I asked if she was fearful of AIDS or venereal disease. She bluntly replied that she always "carries rubbers" and insists that her "dates" use them. She admitted that "business is slow" and that she "doesn't make much." She said that she would like to change, but simply "can't kick the drugs." She misses her kids and is "tired of her life," but is too embarrassed to return to her family "a mess" (addicted). She knows she needs detox, and we told her about the women's rehabilitation program at the Los Angeles Mission. She expressed a willingness and we offered to help in any way that we could. But her initial openness soon turned to hesitancy and she opted to remain on the street.

Minutes later the "birthday boy" returned, looking as nicely dressed as we had ever seen him! He had on a bright green shirt and clean white pants, and was getting around nicely without the aid of a cane or a walker. He had picked up some "party supplies," which included a bottle of wine for him and Mousie and a 6-pack of Pepsi for the rest of us. He then announced that he would be staying with a "friend" he had recently met in an apartment in Sherman Oaks. But that was a very short-lived stay as well.

LOOKING FOR LODGING IN ALL THE WRONG PLACES

After a couple weeks in the apartment, Green Eyes longed for the companionship of his friends on the street once again. He returned to pay them a visit but was jumped and beaten a second time by the gang. Bruised socially as well as physically by his "friends" on Beacon, he decided to look elsewhere for lodging. So he shared an apartment on Alvarado with a woman named Deedee, which he rationalized as a "temporary arrangement" until the first of the month when he would get his check and find a place of his own. The first of March came and went however, and that "place" turned out to be the alley off of 8th and Alvarado.

It took me awhile to find Green Eyes' new surroundings, and I had to avail myself of the always-reliable "grapevine" to do so. I asked various individuals milling about on the street and in the process was offered everything imaginable with which to indulge myself. Finally a young Black man, who would not give me his name, overheard my plea of, "Does anybody know where Green Eyes is?" and offered to lead me to him. We headed up the street and it dawned on me how terribly vulnerable I was trusting a total stranger in an area where White faces are few. I uttered a quick prayer as we walked and did my best to mask my uneasiness. He told me to wait for him on the corner and disappeared down 8th Street. Moments later Green Eyes appeared along with my new-found "contact." I thanked the man sincerely and after he affirmed his trustworthiness he was on his way. I inquired of Green Eyes as to his "occupation" and was told he was somewhat of a "look-out," but that his real occupation was as a "second-story man" (a thief who specializes in breaking into multi-story buildings)!

Green Eyes explained that he was living with a "pretty tough crowd" in the alley and that they would not grant me entrance until they knew that I was "legitimate" (not a narc or a cop). I was finally allowed in during my next visit two weeks later after gaining favor with a "sentry" posted at one end of the alley (off of 8th Street). I had been denied access at the 9th Street entrance moments earlier by another "guard" who insisted that Green Eyes was no longer there. Green Eyes showed me his shanty and also proudly revealed his pet dog, which was part pit bull, and had "found" him, he announced. I was immersed in writing and rewriting this study during the Spring and Summer months and was therefore only able to make sporadic visits to see him. On the whole his stay in the alley was not a pleasant one. He looked run-down and did not have the sparkle in his eyes which I had often seen in similarly harsh environments. I reminded him once again of our care and concern.

A NEW BEGINNING

In early September 1993 the phone rang and I accepted a collect call from Green Eyes. He was calling from a skid row phone booth, not far from the Union Rescue Mission, where he had been eating and attending services for the past week and sleeping on the sidewalk across the street. There was life and purpose in his voice as he eagerly spoke of how he had been off of his "medicine" during the same time period and had finally gotten "sick and tired" of the street. He had left the alley after someone had beaten his dog to death and had wandered over to the mission, contemplating for several days as to whether or not the time had come to leave the streets behind. "It's time to change!", he concluded enthusiastically. "I want to serve God 100% just like I used to serve the devil!" He asked about the rehabilitation program in Pasadena and I promised to immediately inquire about its availability. He was to call me back later that night. I was equally excited to discover that they had an opening and welcomed his stay with them. I gave him the news

67

when he called back (at 11:30 no less!) and arranged to pick him up the next morning at 8:00.

He literally glowed as I pulled up along the curb in front of the mission that day. We embraced and he exclaimed, "I told you that when I was ready I would change. Well, I'm ready!" We set out for Pasadena and other than the clothes on his back he had nothing more than a small box of papers and a little tin mail box which he had found in the dumpster. We met with the leadership, filled out some paper work, and Green Eyes was officially enrolled in a Christian residential rehabilitation program! I sat listening in amazement as the director was explaining the rules to Green Eyes. Abstinence from drugs, curfew, restricted mobility, Bible studies, and early morning prayer times were all willingly received. It seemed like a dream, too good to be true!

Green Eyes has been involved in the program now for over a month. He is reading his Bible, cooking an occasional meal, and has even gone out ministering with the staff and residents at a local convalescent home! He even got a job at McDonalds! Our family has gone to see him twice, bringing along my professor and my wife's friend from the Christian school and her family. During our first visit Green Eyes led us in prayer and exclaimed, "I traded in my pipe for a Bible!" Our most recent time with him was attending their worship service, during which he went forward for prayer. At the start of the meeting he leaned over and whispered in my ear, "Did you ever think we would be singing hymns and praising the Lord together?"

I must admit that my faith had wavered, although I had certainly hoped and prayed to that end. I must now discipline my imagination from running rampant with grandiose dreams of his complete freedom from drugs, wholehearted commitment to Christ, and effective ministry to those who remain enslaved on the street! Granted he still has a long way to go, but I am greatly encouraged by how far he has already come in a short period of time. But as I write he is struggling with some issues and considering leaving the program. Regardless of what the future holds for Green Eyes, though, I am forever grateful for his tutelage, guiding me through an incredible world of need. It has enabled me, in turn, to now train others in similar journeys among the disenfranchised and has given me hope as to how the Lord can use us all to impact the lives of the urban poor.

Table 1

A Chronology of Green Eyes' Housing Options: 1991-93

January '91	February	March(start)	March(end)	June
Alley-8th & Union	Cardboard box-sidewalk 8th & Beacon	Budget Inn-7th & Beacon	"New" box-8th & Beacon	Moved box-7th & Beacon

August	September	October	November '91-August '92	
Alley-9th & Burlington	Sidewalk-9th & Beacon	Union Rescue	Post Apartments-7th & Bonnie Brae	

September (start)	September (end)	November	December	January '93 (start)
Parked car-9th & Westlake	Sidewalk-9th & Beacon	County Jail	Sidewalk-9th & Beacon	Parkview Hotel-Alvarado

January (end)	February	March (start)	March (end)-August
Cardboard box-9th & Beacon	Sherman Oaks-apt. with "friend"	Shared apt. on Alvarado	Tent in alley-8th & Alvarado

September (start)	September (mid)-present
Sidewalk by Union Rescue Mission	Christian rehab program-Pasadena

REFLECTIONS ALONG THE WAY

In reviewing the array of experiences with Green Eyes, I came to more fully understand the following fundamentals of urban ministry, which were to prove useful in my subsequent interaction with the students:

1. The priority of networking and the inter-connectedness of men and women on the street.

2. The need of developing a certain amount of "street savvy," namely, understanding and making use of "the grapevine" and learning to overcome one's fears.

3. The importance of caring, listening, trusting, and not judging those on the street.

4. The necessity of persisting faithfully in relationships with the disadvantaged, without necessarily seeking to "change them" in the process.

5. The receptivity of disenfranchised people, albeit in a context of much brokenness and heartache.

6. The fact that despite our utmost efforts, only God can truly "change" a life.

7. The validity of a variety of approaches to ministry among the poor: church, para-church (rescue missions), and the incarnational presence of believers.

8. The reality of discouragement and burn-out necessitates consistent prayer, reflection and overall team work.

9. The vital role of a holistic, experiential approach in reaching out to those in need.

CHAPTER 3

"DON'T JUST TELL US, SHOW US HOW!"

The preceding chapter introduced the reader to the world of a homeless man in downtown Los Angeles. Our interactions formed the basis of my own experiential learning as I was exposed to intense urban need and hurting people and sought to draw meaning from those encounters. Building on those experiences, this chapter recounts the process of designing a structured learning semester for a group of ten Biola University students. Along with classroom instruction, the overall purpose is to expose them to the disenfranchised in the city and acquaint them with various local urban outreaches. The intent is to cultivate within them a burden for ongoing ministry to those in need in similar settings.

So as to better capsulize the array of details involved in initiating the experiential learning project, I have chosen to do so in five broad areas:

Formulating the Approach

The initial task was to identify selected urban ministry models that the students could observe and participate in. Of equal value were relatively unstructured opportunities for them to interact with needy individuals apart from the confines of an established ministry locale. This process involved reflection on my own experiences as well as input from my professor and several urban practitioners who were familiar with specific ministries in the area under study. The following categories and their particular representation were decided upon:

MINISTRY MODEL	LOCAL REPRESENTATION
a. Personal interaction	Green Eyes, et. al.
b. The Christian community	Cambria Christian Community
c. The para-church	Victory Outreach
d. The rescue mission	Union Rescue Mission
e. The local church	Central City Community Church
	First Evangelical Free Church

Although there is some overlap and redundancy in these classifications, it did allow the students to experience and critique institutional approaches to urban ministry as well as those which are more relational and incarnational in their focus. The next step was to meet with key individuals from each organization.

Making the Contacts

Since I had previously established a significant relationship with Green Eyes, and had been introduced by him to others such as Red Dog and Funee Man, the opportunities for one-to-one interaction were already in place for the students. As the semester progressed, these personal encounters grew to include people living under the bridges as well.

I was actually introduced to Green Eyes by a member of the Cambria Christian Community, a small group of believers living incarnationally in the Westlake district. I had made their acquaintance through a personal friend who was at that time living and ministering with them. Their focus in the neighborhood for nearly six years has been building relationships, reaching out to the youth, and more recently implementing home Bible studies toward the end of establishing churches. Although some of their members have come and gone over the years, a handful of dedicated couples and single men and women still maintain residence in a home on Cambria Street off of Union and in the neighboring Cambria Apartments and Beacon Hotel.

Cambria was included in the project as part of our research into incarnational presence in the city. I stopped by the house and met with John, their caring and committed leader, and he gladly agreed to give the students an overview of their lives and activities as a community. John had previously directed the Center for Student Missions (CSM) in Los Angeles, a group which specializes in hosting "urban plunges" for young people. Part of that experience involves a "prayer tour" of the downtown area, providing information about various aspects of the city and its people and allowing for times of intercession at every stop along the way. John was willing to lead our group in a prayer tour, which would then officially commence our headlong immersion into communities of need.

John introduced me to Tim, CSM's new director who was just in the process of moving his office from the Brandon to the Huntington Hotel a few blocks away. As I explained the project to him, including the various categories of ministry models, he mentioned Victory Outreach as an exciting and aggressive organization which takes the gospel directly to the streets. He gave me the name of the director with whom he had a relationship, and suggested that I contact them as well. Upon arrival at their downtown office (22nd and Grand), I was introduced to Paco, their Evangelism Coordinator. A Hispanic man, his arm covered with tattoos, he excitedly gave me a synopsis of his recent dramatic conversion from gang involvement and drug addiction.

Paco spoke of the opportunities that they have as a staff team to minister in those same gang-infested neighborhoods, "evangelizing on the front lines," as he put it. He told of how they go in with megaphones and preach the gospel, paraphrasing the verse about snatching people from the gates of hell, adding that "they even have the smell of smoke on their clothes!" I liked Paco immediately and knew this was an excellent opportunity for our students to not only observe but to participate firsthand in a unique, daring outreach.

Paco showed me Victory Outreach's facility which included an auditorium and a men's rehabilitation program. That same night they were to conduct a funeral for the victim of a drive-by shooting. He invited us to minister with them on a Friday night and before I left asked if he could pray for me. In his prayer he fervently thanked God for bringing us together and asked Him to "light a fire" in the hearts of the students for people who are lost.

Through Green Eyes I had become aware of the Union Rescue Mission on Main Street. I contacted Lorraine, Union's Volunteer Coordinator, and discovered that the diversity of their programs in response to urban need lent itself well to our interaction. We put together a schedule consisting of participation in an evening service and the chance to "mingle" in spontaneous interaction with the homeless. Also included were opportunities for involvement with their youth ministry, which reached out to young people in the neighboring hotels, as well as their off-site residential recovery program for young men.

Lorraine put me in touch with Scott, the compassionate young pastor of Central City Community Church of the Nazarene. He had ministered for several years in one of the missions, but came to the conclusion that what was lacking was a parish mentality, a local body of believers. He noted that there was not a single church in all of skid row to shepherd its estimated 15-20,000 residents. Scott felt it would be more effective to plant a church among them than to incorporate them into existing churches outside of the area. With that in mind, he began holding outdoor services in Pershing Square Park, "worship on the street" as he referred to it, in 1988. After 18 months he had assembled a "flock" of about 40 men and women. They leased some space on the third floor of a 10-story building on Broadway, where they have met for the past three years. They now number over 100 (60% of whom are Black) and, in need of more space, are currently looking for another facility in skid row. We planned to join them for worship on a Sunday morning.

By way of contrast, a more traditional congregation, which was also a part of our study, was the First Evangelical Free Church. At the outset of the semester, the pastor was invited to address the class. He told of his concern for the Pico-Union community in which the church is located and handed out a list of projects which the students could potentially tackle in his neighborhood. These included the needs of a menacing gang population and a homeless camp directly behind the church, under the freeway overpass.

I was intrigued by this opportunity and attended their English-speaking service the following Sunday morning. Although the numbers were small, I was impressed that the church had remained in the city. Its cornerstone revealed that it was founded during the 1920's, but the community is now almost entirely populated by Central American refugees. The church began a Hispanic congregation (which significantly outnumbers the Anglo) as well as extensive ESL (English as a Second Language) and tutoring programs. The presence of gangs in the community was immediately evident as was the homeless tent city not more than 50 yards behind the church. The church's concern for the neighborhood and commitment to leadership development from within the community was impressive. The setting was ideal for doing research, building relationships and contributing to the church's ongoing outreach.

Recruiting the Students

My professor gave me the opportunity of presenting the project to her Urban Research and Ministry class. Each student taking the course was required to do an ethnography over the duration of the semester. I began with the Scriptures which call us to "see" the urban multitudes and "learn" compassion in the context of "the widow, the orphan, the stranger, and the poor" (Matt. 9:13,36; Zech. 7:10). I invited them to join me in Green Eyes' world and spoke of my experiences with him as well as some of those in gangs and prostitution. I highlighted the various ministry models and challenged them to an exciting experiment in exposing and equipping college students in the milieu of disenfranchised subcultures. Ten students (roughly half of the class) responded to that appeal, six girls and four guys.

In addition to the core group from the class, a further unexpected "recruiting" opportunity netted several more volunteers. One of the girls taking the course was the outreach coordinator of the Student Missionary Union (SMU) at Biola. She invited me to share the project with those students who had a particular interest in urban ministry. After doing so a number of them responded, full of interest and abounding with questions. They were eager to be involved, longing for a mentoring relationship, for someone to show them how rather than merely tell them to reach out to the urban poor. I spoke with them all for nearly an hour. They inquired about the gangs and the homeless, specifically asking how one goes about meeting them and wondering about how dangerous it was. All were "raw" recruits, but they were willing and zealous to experience urban need along with us. As it turned out, five of them shared in our experiences with Victory Outreach.

Coordinating the Schedule

Two things surfaced immediately as I began piecing together the perplexing puzzle of matching up diverse student schedules with our available ministry opportunities. First of all, we needed to strive for a fixed routine in which as many of the group as possible participated in regular weekly, or more, time slots. Secondly, since it was proving to be nearly impossible for all ten to be free and available at the same time period on a consistent basis, we had to account for flexible alternatives.

I sat down with the entire team and we looked at every day of the week to see which one received the most "votes" as a convenient time of research and ministry. Compounding the problem was the fact that the group was a mixture of graduate and undergraduate students in a variety of majors. This translated into a very divergent course schedule, spanning both day and night time classes. Even weekends posed problems for most with church, job, family, and social obligations. We finally landed on two evening time slots which worked for most of them. I then arranged the order of our involvement with each of the various ministries, which was driven by a certain extent to their own accessibility and willingness to work within our fairly small window of availability.

The prayer tour with Cambria was to be our "kickoff" activity, followed by two Friday nights of street witnessing with Victory Outreach. Scheduled concurrently was a worship service at Central City Community Church and unrehearsed adventures with Red Dog and Green Eyes. Union Rescue Mission would be our focus during the middle weeks of the semester, and opportunities at First Evangelical Free Church were to conclude the project. The final weeks of the semester would be devoted to writing their ethnography from their field notes recorded during the project.

Reviewing the Technique

During one of the initial Wednesday afternoon class sessions, we discussed the technique of doing ethnographic research in the context of building relationships with needy people while observing and participating in various urban ministries. The students had just read Spradley's *Participant Observation* (1980), and I explained the practical outworking of gathering data in the context of Green Eyes and his network. This review unleashed a barrage of questions. Concerns were expressed about safety, not only on the part of a few students but some of their parents as well. One confessed that she did not want her mom and dad to even be aware of the project for fear they would deny her involvement in it. The off-campus activities release form, which the University required each of us to sign, did not ease their anxiety either (particularly the part about "personal injury or death" which might result from the "dangers and hazards" of our activities!).

A dialogue followed about the nature of spiritual warfare in our urban involvement, the sinful lifestyles of so many people, and its potential impact on us all. We spoke of the priority of prayer and committing ourselves to the Lord. I noted that informants may reveal illegal activities and that we must be wise and sensitive in doing research. I encouraged them to go out in a spirit of ministry, building relationships, and treating their subjects with dignity and respect, not as trophies to be won (i.e. not just using them for their stories). I shared that Green Eyes had granted me his permission to use his story and that I, in turn, had given him a copy of the manuscript and asked for his feedback and critique. I stressed the importance of identifying a key contact into a community or subculture such as a Green Eyes or a Red Dog and I pledged my commitment to assist them in that endeavor.

I felt a responsibility for every student as the project began. I wanted them to have a growing and stretching experience in hands-on interaction with needy people as well as a deeper appreciation for urban ministry and how they could one day be part of it. They were also assisting me in my own dissertation research and their grade for the entire course was heavily dependent upon our upcoming ethnographic experiences. I was stirred by their motivation to know and love the urban poor and challenged by their unlimited potential. I committed myself anew to guide and mentor them and asked the Lord to sovereignly contour the project as a memorable occurrence in experiential learning for each one.

CHAPTER 4

"IT'S A CHRISTIAN THING"

The next two chapters recount in descriptive detail our experiences together in research and ministry over the course of the semester. Writing as a participant-observer, I chose to highlight our interactions and observations with the various ministries apart from our reflection on those activities. This is done so as to unfold in a continuous sequence the diverse contexts and significant individuals that comprised our journey and shaped the students' experiential learning process. Chapter 8 focuses on debriefing those encounters and events to include our impressions, reactions, and discoveries. Each agency or activity that follows is prefaced by its purpose in the overall project and our primary involvement in that setting.

PRAYER TOUR

Overall Purpose - initial exposure to and information about areas comprising the parameters of the study and a spiritual foundation to undergird the semester's activities.

Primary Involvement - prayer, observation, questioning, and limited contact with homeless people.

We initiated our collective adventure by squeezing into the professor's van and linking up with John at Cambria for the start of our prayer tour. As we began, John gave a brief overview of their neighborhood, introducing the city as a place of change and contrast. But he also emphasized that our basis of ministry in the city is God's love for the people not simply their urgent need. He informed us that nearly 1,000 homeless men and women and nearly 20 different gangs are within a half mile radius of MacArthur Park, where we made our first stop.

Our second destination was an abortion clinic on Westmoreland, where 1,300 abortions are performed annually. Many of their clients are the neighborhood prostitutes who are tragically exercising one of their few marketable skills in exchange for money and drugs, carelessly discarding the occasional by-product of their numerous trysts. We interceded not only for the unborn child and parents but also for the many children who were spared but are trapped in destructive lifestyles nonetheless. As we moved on he probed our thinking by inquiring, "What is the 'good news' the church has to offer to a prostitute, a gang member, a drug dealer? We are good at telling them to turn from, but what do they turn to?"

Our next stop was a detention center on Alvarado in the Pico-Union district, a densely populated Hispanic region which contains nearly 100,000 people in a mere square mile, and a significant amount of drug trafficking. The facility is in essence an INS ("La Migra") holding tank for illegal aliens, caught and awaiting deportation. John lovingly reminded us that the majority of these men and women are not criminals and have few rights or advocates on their behalf. In prayer we were convicted anew of our biblical injunction to love the alien as we love ourselves (Lev. 19:34).

We continued our journey through the core of downtown Los Angeles, passing through the financial and commercial districts as well as the heart of skid row (John referred to each area respectively as "make bucks, spend bucks, and no bucks!"). The stark contrast between rich and poor was brought home to the group as we spent a few minutes wandering through the prestigious Biltmore Hotel on Grand after having just caught a glimpse of some of the thousands who literally make their home on the streets.

Thinking that our experience had drawn to a close we settled down on the steps of a large bank in the financial district that bordered on skid row to pray and debrief our tour of the sights and sounds of the city. Yet God in His sovereignty chose to bring across our path several street people who tended to "interrupt" our formal time of reflection but in doing so confronted us first hand with the opportunity to put our prayers into action.

John had just finished a discussion about the nature of those living in poverty on skid row. He explained that some truly are desperately poor and unable to escape the cycle of poverty, while others may have actually chosen the lifestyle for various reasons. For some it may have been convenient, but now, having made that initial decision, at what point do they become victims, addicts, prostitutes, the sinned against?

He was speaking of the priority of incarnational presence, "hanging out" and getting to know and understand people's needs when almost on cue a Black homeless man strolled up to us, introduced himself as T.J., and took center stage in our discussion! I had to suppress a smile as he exhorted us to "look deep down within yourself for the answer!" He rambled on for several minutes about loving us all and how he was keeping a good attitude despite

83

being "screwed around" on the street, and unable to get a job. Not withstanding, he claimed to be a "kind, friendly person" and unprejudiced because "no matter what skin color, we bleed the same blood!"

I looked around at the faces of the students and it was obvious that T.J. had managed to grab their attention. So he finished strong in high hopes that his "presentation" to this obviously rookie crowd would be rewarded financially. He concluded, "I never shot dope but I smoked pot. You all understand what I'm sayin'? But I still need help. I'm stuck out here with only one person I can call, my grandmother!"

T.J. did manage to accrue a bit of spare change from the group and happily exclaimed, "Hey, I can eat for two days on that!" He then wandered off down the sidewalk as John sought to regain our attention. But already it seemed that the word had gone out that we were "easy prey" for panhandlers because momentarily another individual approached. A Black woman this time, but as emotionally distraught as T.J. was lighthearted. She was clutching a handkerchief, visibly upset, and simply blurted out that she needed help.

It was obvious that we were getting nowhere in a reflection mode and yet the opportunity to interface with these men and women was a tremendous one and an equally pertinent learning experience. To enable John to continue interacting with the students I took the woman aside to listen to her story and was joined by Brenda, one of the graduate students.

How much of what she related to us was true we may never know but it certainly was a very sad story. She had just come to Los Angeles from Texas with her little girl (who she said was being looked after by someone nearby) and was hungry and homeless and in need of money. She listened attentively as we encouraged her toward the Union or L.A. Mission, explaining that the latter had a program for women like herself. I gave her a couple dollars for which she thanked me sincerely as she wiped the tears from her eyes.

I sensed that we had just witnessed one who had legitimate need while T.J. had most likely taken advantage of an unsuspecting audience. Brenda, who had been listening attentively as I shared with the woman, was really struggling over these two encounters, unsure whether she should have helped out financially or not. She had given $5 to T.J., all that she had, but was feeling badly about it. She wished that she had shown more discernment, supposing that the woman may have been more deserving and in greater need. I replied that discernment in these matters is born in the trenches, in encounters such as these where we learn to hear and trust the Holy Spirit's prompting as to how we should respond. I related to her times when I had been taken advantage of but reminded her that ours is not to judge worthiness, rather to give "as unto the Lord." I commended her for being sensitive and willing to even wrestle with the situation as to how the Lord Jesus would have her respond.

Another street woman approached the group as Brenda and I were talking, but soon came our way after making little headway with them. A grad student named Sandra did speak with her for awhile, but by now none of us had any cash left or were wary of dispensing it to what seemed like an endless supply of willing recipients! It was getting late and with classes in the morning we decided to call it a night.

The mood in the van as we returned to Biola was one of perplexity and unresolution. Although uncomfortable, it was a healthy condition on the whole in that we had not only been exposed to overwhelming need but had seen firsthand how "messy" and subjective interaction with the urban poor can be. Our debriefing had been abbreviated but we were able to go back and reflect and tie up some of the loose ends in our next class period together. In addition, the entire event, and particularly their vulnerability to being solicited, had brought to the surface numerous issues which were fresh on their minds for our next activity together.

INTERVIEW WITH GREEN EYES

Overall Purpose - face-to-face contact with a street person in a safe
environment so as to diffuse stereotypes, promote dialogue, and
establish the basis for an ongoing relationship and further interaction.
Primary Involvement - questioning and extensive personal interaction with a
homeless individual.

While the prayer tour provided an overview of the dimensions of urban ministry, our next activity together enabled the students to personally interact with a homeless individual. I armed them with a list of questions by which they could potentially glean pertinent information from Green Eyes. As I was picking him up and driving him to my house I also tried to coax him toward a relevant presentation of his situation to their own! I gave him a copy of our "agenda," which I hoped would steer him to cover his background, prison experiences, life on the streets, and how Christian college students could better understand his world and respond accordingly.

As I suspected we immediately got off track, yet it proved to be an informative and very worthwhile evening. Green Eyes quickly diverted from our "list" by asking one of the students about his perspective of skid row (Green Eyes knew we had just seen it). The student replied that it was a place where people were trying to survive, to which Green Eyes responded to the group, "Everyone should have to scrounge around in the garbage for food to better understand." Sandra inquired about how he keeps warm on the street at night and he explained how he currently was using a large trash bag with holes poked in it for his arms and legs to stick out! He climbs into it at night and it works surprisingly well to ward off the chill of the wind.

Brenda asked whether or not Green Eyes wanted to change his life or if he was happy with it. He answered that he would change "nothin'," that he was not miserable at all and that "material things do not make a person happy." He elaborated somewhat and in doing so revealed his own perspective on giving to those in need on the street:

> A man is known for his word. Material things go, but your word is priceless. It's all ya got. If your word's no good ya better check in because nobody, even the lowest in the ghetto, can live without it. A lot of people can't understand that...I don't put much principle in money even though I'm on the street. I may be hungry but if I see someone who may need it I give it to them because I've been there. If I got it I can't in my heart say no. Some people say I'm a fool. I say, "Why not? Do you want me to smoke it all up on myself?" At least I think that I feel better by doin' somethin' to help somebody else... Smokin' is the most unuseful thing a person can do with their life. I would never recommend to anyone to use the pipe. It's the most degrading thing you ever do to anyone or yourself, smoking cocaine.

This rather candid revelation of his drug problem surprised the group somewhat and sparked interesting dialogue about the nature of drug usage and the effects of cocaine and heroin. He was pressed about whether or not he could or would kick the habit and admitted that he enjoys it too much to stop now. "I love it," he confessed unashamedly.

Green Eyes then shifted the focus off of himself and back on the group in what turned out to be a very pertinent interaction for the students with respect to their frustrations of a few days past. He asked them all to try and "think and deal with life the way it is if you were in the ghetto." He then inquired about what they would do if someone asked them for a quarter for "something to eat, a piece of bread." I listened with interest as Brenda replied that she probably would give him a quarter if she really believed that he would use it to buy bread.

Green Eyes, with a twinkle in his eye now, replied, "Did I sound as if I wanted some bread?" She then speculated as to whether or not she should take him at face value and Green Eyes launched into a lengthy response which proved to be most helpful to the group:

> Why wouldn't I ask for a donut? If you're asking for money then I have to make a judgment. Are you asking for money, for food or drugs? If I were in a supermarket, where would I go to get some bread for a quarter? How many fools have I asked for that same quarter? For that same piece of bread? If I was hungry why wouldn't I go into a bakery and ask them if they had some bread for the homeless? But the hustle game and the con game is not to ask for a whole lot of money. People will give quarters and dimes and not think nothin' at all. But if you was givin' me a quarter today, before the week's over you'd give me $5. Because I see that I hit that soft spot where I can get you to believe what I want you to believe by the tone of my words.

He was interrupted by the question, "So are you saying that we shouldn't give money when people ask, that it's just a hustle?" Green Eyes continued:

First of all, 90% of the people on the street get income. G.R., S.S.I., or Social Security. They make five times as much as their income by hustling, more than their check every month! The average smoker is going to smoke maybe five rocks a day - $50. That's $350 a week and $1,400 a month. Where is he ever gonna get that kind of income? That's for only a $50 habit! Panhandling can get you maybe $25. Washing windows, maybe $15. Maybe finding clothes in the alley like I do and selling them for a few dollars. So you know what I mean? What kind of a job are they going to get to make that kind of money? A homeless person! Are you going to pay him $1,400? Then you got some that even dare to come out here [the suburbs]! You all so generous out here! They catch the bus like going to work! It's a job, you know what I mean?

One of the students inquired, "What would you say they need more than money? He responded in an eloquent and very "Christian" manner:

Food. Don't give him nothin' he can sell. "Are you hungry? Wait here." Then go buy him a sandwich. "That's what you wanted money for isn't it?" It's not wrong to do good deeds. Sometimes it's wrong to give a person the opportunity to use the money. Sure they're clothesless, they're hungry. They need the money. But hey, don't give 'em money 'cuz that's what they're doing. I'll help to support your needs if your needs are clothing and food. But other habits, like smoking and drinking, don't. That's not my humane obligation to another human being to support that extra activity. For a person who loves God, you should help with their necessities if you can.

Green Eyes reiterated the destructive nature of drug abuse, referring to it as a "suicidal environment" and claiming that "nowhere in the drug culture do you find happiness." To this remark one of the grad students astutely challenged him, "But you said you're happy!" Green Eyes, thoroughly enjoying their interaction, answered, "Me? I'm happy. But that don't mean that I'm happy, happy, happy always. Because when I'm down

I'm just as much depressed as anyone else... But who wants to be miserable? If I get miserable I go to sleep. When I wake up I be alright!"

Another female student then asked, "Have you ever thought that you're maybe not happy, that the drugs are deceiving you?" "Sometimes," he admitted. She continued, "Would you say then that people on the street are like prisoners?" "They are," he answered. "And maybe they're not even aware of it?" she persisted. "They are," he agreed, "but they don't want to admit it." "Do they have a name for it?" she asked. "Confinement," was his reply. "That's what it is, confinement." He continued in more of a subdued manner:

> Do you know how how far I've been in the years since I've been living where I'm at, in this city, in my little world? About three blocks each way. That's as far as I've been. It's sad to say. I don't know about California. I know somethin' about these blocks though. I know every square foot of it. Every person that be's in there, every drug addict, every dope fiend, everybody in that area and they know me, and that's my world.

I then sought to steer him back to a discussion of his daily existence on the street and that led to his sharing extensively about his accident and resultant life of constant pain, which he seeks to anesthetize with the drugs. He spoke in images of being "married to pain," having to "embrace and understand her and talkin' to her like you're talkin' to your mate" (all very interesting concepts to a group of attentive, single students)!

One of the girls then asked quite out of the blue if he feels sorry for them at all. Green Eyes smiled and answered, "Not sorry, it's just that you're missin' somethin' because you let society push you away, to not even get close to other people, to be friends. Instead you let society make you selfish and make you protect yourself. 'Oh, I don't want to get too close to her,'" he mimicked in a high voice!

To that she acknowledged, "Most of us here are taking this class because we want to get out there and learn, I mean we want to meet people and not take from society but give." His response to her captured the essence of relational ministry:

> To go out into society and give is a beautiful thought and a beautiful theory. I'm not doubting what you believe, but don't go out and expect to give somethin'. Just be there. If there's somethin' to give it'll come, because when you go out into the ghetto to give somethin' you're expectin' feedback, even though you may think that you're givin' from your heart. It's best to go out there to be, to expect nothin' in return. You can be an influence by bein' an example and not sayin' nothin'. You're very interested, and your interest is good. But you have to be able to put yourself in another person's place.

A thought-provoking dialogue then followed about prostitution and the role it plays in generating income for women who have few alternatives. Green Eyes stated, "There has to be acceptance [of the individual] cuz it's there [prostitution], we can't erase it. Regardless of whether or not we think it's wrong and against God's law, it's there."

His further comments were particularly relevant in the context of Christians seeking to "minister" to the girls:

> Don't go out just to give God's love and all the goodness in the world... because they been hearin' that all their life. But the only thing they don't have is the friend that they can count on without no opposition. To count on somebody to be there. Period! Being there to talk. Hold hands. Cry. Without judgment. Without criticism. People in those kind of situations got more hurt to get out, but they're chokin' on their feelin's. And some of that stuff that they got to bear you wouldn't even be able to listen to because if some of those girls told you the real thing it's so unbelievable. You wouldn't imagine what another man could do to a girl and still be in existence and live. The girl cannot go no place. They're trapped.

A discussion about sin and its consequences followed. Green Eyes was asked, "How do you define sin?" He replied, "Breaking God's law, but a sin is a sin, one is no different than another." I then interjected the scriptural example of Jesus and the woman caught in adultery. He showed acceptance and forgiveness of her as a person without excusing or minimizing her sinful activities. I reminded them of how we have to constantly work at separating the sin from the sinner. We need to love and accept the prostitute for who she is as one worthy of God's grace and pardon, yet maintain that the lifestyle in and of itself is a violation of the biblical standard.

One of the grad students then posed the question to him, "What do you think God made you to be?" He answered philosophically:

> I believe I got my own purpose in the world. Things happened in my life where I shouldn't even be alive and have this opportunity to speak my opinions. I believe that my purpose is where I'm at [on the street], that's where I belong. I could've got off the street, I tried, but there's a purpose for me to be there.

Doug, one of the undergrads, wanted to know Green Eyes' perspective on the underlying cause of the Los Angeles riots less than six months earlier. He suggested that "boredom" was the issue, speculating that "the people in the ghetto needed some excitement, so they used Rodney King's situation for an excuse to let off some steam." "It was fun," Green Eyes continued, "rip and run. Somethin' for them to do, a form of recreation. Afterward they all went to bed." One of the girls then queried, "Did they think it was fun to hurt and destroy their own people and families and businesses?" "But they didn't," Green Eyes corrected her. "The police thought that Hispanics and Blacks was going to fight against each other because they let Hispanics in Black neighborhoods. But Spanish people didn't own them stores. They wasn't owned by Blacks, or Whites, but by Koreans."

Doug asked once again, "But the question still remains, 'Why did this "entertainment" manifest itself across racial barriers, against Koreans?'" Green Eyes postulated the following hypothesis:

> Because you don't have such a racial or cultural barrier between Spanish and Black. You got two strong forces in the ghetto that aren't gonna give. One's been tryin' to make the other fall for years. They done killed already how many of their own homeboys? Pretty soon they're not gonna have anyone of their own left! Rodney King was an excuse. Gangs didn't want to beat themselves up no more so they turned on others.

Questions for Green Eyes on a variety of topics ensued while we transitioned into an informal meal together. As we concluded the "interview" and students were beginning to leave, he teased Tammy, one of the undergrads, about having said very little during the course of the evening. She smiled and sheepishly admitted that she was "just takin' it all in." I had spoken with Tammy after the prayer tour a few days earlier, however, and knew this was a whole new experience for her and that she was working through a great deal of fear and uneasiness toward the city and its peoples. Little did we know that our next ministry encounter would force several of the students to face their fears in an even deeper way!

VICTORY OUTREACH

Overall Purpose - appreciation for an aggressive inner-city ministry that is effectively reaching diverse subcultures and the opportunity to join with them in supervised on-the-job training.

Primary Involvement - worship in a multi-cultural context and observation and participation in street-witnessing.

Two carloads of us, including several SMUers, joined forces with Victory Outreach (V.O.) in their street witnessing efforts on successive Friday nights. We met for prayer each evening at Biola at 5:30 and did not get back to the dorms until 1:00 a.m. Our second experience with V.O. also included one of the grad student's wives as well as two members of a local church's college youth group (Kyle, one of the undergrads, was a youth director).

Both nights, when we arrived at their facility, Paco had arranged an orientation for the students in their conference room. It consisted of an overview of V.O.'s history and philosophy of ministry as well as dramatic testimonies of several staff members. These proved to be highlights for the group and a few of the students were able to develop friendships with these young men. I was impressed with the fact that the organization is deeply committed to evangelism among the gangs and actually traces its roots over 25 years ago to David Wilkerson and Teen Challenge (who led their founder, Sonny Arguinzoni, to Christ in New York City). There are now more than 100 V.O. sites across the country and around the world.

Paco welcomed us warmly, explaining that although many churches have moved out to the suburbs, "turning their back on a lot of people, Jesus Christ is here in the barrio, in skid row, with the gangs and the prostitutes, the addicts and the homosexuals." He shared with us the first week, summarizing his "B.C." (before Christ) years as one who was "busted, disgusted and couldn't be trusted!" But he now gives his loyalty to the Lord and the ministry of V.O. as he once did to his gang not long ago.

He related how his father was a drug trafficker and his mother a dealer, the latter of whom was shot six times. With them as role models, he, his brothers, and even his sister all became "gang bangers" and addicts. His younger brother is in prison until the turn of the century and his older one was shot. Paco spoke of how he used to get jumped and beaten up on the way to school, ultimately dropping out. He joked about knowing even the dogs in his neighborhood alleys from having to run and hide in them so often! As a young person he finally joined the gang for protection and as he put it "inquired an inheritance" that comes with the territory.

He ended up in San Quentin followed by a stint in Soledad. After his release he met someone from V.O. who invited him to one of their services. He laughed about how "everybody looked like ex-gang members and even the pastor sounded like Cheech and Chong!" He further joked about watching his wallet for fear that it would be stolen, but then added, "people hugged me and that had never happened before." But nonetheless he resisted their message of God's love and forgiveness and went on home. Later that same night he was stabbed repeatedly and left for dead by a rival gang. God spared his life and after he recovered from the wounds he gave his life to Christ and joined V.O. to reach out into the same communities from which he had come.

It was clearly evident that his burden was for evangelism. He quoted the Apostle Paul's exhortation to Timothy to "do the work of an evangelist" (II Tim. 4:5), adding his own paraphrase to "not just warm up the pews and be spectators." He also referred to the Prophet Jeremiah's "all consuming fire in his bones" (Jer. 20:9) to proclaim God's Word and related how we would have the opportunity to "be like Good Samaritans" in ministering to needy people!

His "homemade" evangelistic illustrations continued as he exhorted us to "be like the U.S. and Iraq, 24 hours of bombing the enemy" putting us on the devil's "top 10 most wanted list!" He further likened the ministry of V.O. to a recent incident where a baseball player ran out of the dugout to stop a person in the stands from burning a U.S. flag while the crowd and his teammates did nothing but watch. "Victory Outreach is like that baseball player," he proudly proclaimed, "taking action while many sit by and do nothing."

Two more members of the street witnessing team gave their testimonies the following week. The first was 18-year-old Tomas, who very articulately and with maturity beyond his years read Matthew 28:19 to us, announcing that God wants us in obedience to reach out to gang bangers too. He continued, "If Jesus were here He would go out to them... We gotta make it happen and put our hands to the plow... It's not a V.O. thing, it's a Christian thing."

He alluded to running with a gang in the past but emphasized, "Now I'm faithful to God and to my wife and little girl." Rob, one of the students, asked if he still had contact with his old friends. He replied, "When I did I kept messin' up. I couldn't serve God and hang with them. So I decided to go all the way for God instead of the devil...Now they see the change big time...that this is for real." Another question was posed by Kyle as to whether or not he is still recognized by rival gang members and in any danger. He answered that in certain places he is vulnerable and has been surrounded and confronted on more than one occasion. "But I tell them I'm with V.O. and my life has been changed," he explained. They respect that allegiance enough to not harm him.

Tomas then gave way to his older brother Alberto, who is as large and socially awkward as Tomas is slender and charismatic! Unlike his sibling he shared more details of his struggles and those of his family prior to his conversion. Their father was an alcoholic and the mother left the home. As a result "family time" was non-existent and the void was quickly filled by his "homeboys." Alberto joined the gang when he was 14 and by 17 was addicted to PCP, crack and alcohol. Not satisfied he turned to heroin, but testified, "That drug, like the others, messed me all up. I was helpless and hopeless and unloved." He tried several times to get off drugs but always fell back and was in and out of jail for "robberies and crazy stuff."

Finally, at only 21 years of age, he was facing 20 years "in the joint" when his father got saved and Alberto first came in contact with Christianity. But he said, "I thought Christians were wimps, hiding under the Book. I didn't know Jesus has the power to change lives." Miraculously the evidence and the witnesses who were to have testified never materialized and 14 counts against him were reduced to only one. He was left with only a one-year sentence which V.O. arranged for him to serve in their program.

He described that experience for us:

I heard people praying and singing and I freaked out! 'I'm in the wrong place!' I called one of my homeboys to come get me and told him, 'These Christians are tripping me out!' But then I had a vision on the bus bench and started crying out to God. So I came back and gave my life to God. I started praying and God took the prejudice out of me and put love in my heart. It was all God. It's been two years since I committed any crime or drank or smoked. Now God uses me to hit the streets.

He challenged us all as he continued, "I believe every Christian needs to be a fisher of men. It's the hardest thing I ever done. It's easier to be a gang-banger and do drugs. Anybody can do that. I praise the Lord for keeping me in His power. Don't worry if you're not an ex-gang banger. Just give 'em the Word and you' be okay."

Toward the conclusion and prior to our going out on the streets, Paco stood before the congregation asking for volunteers to join us. He exhorted them, "If you're not fishing you're not following Jesus," beckoning them to reach "the outcasts, the rejects of society." In the services that followed the worship time was extensive, with a small band leading the congregation in numerous choruses. Most of the students participated freely and were not intimidated or offended by the expressiveness of the audience. I watched Kyle and Rob clapping joyously and raising their hands in praise.

Preceding the message the second week, Paco again stepped forward to drum up enthusiasm for street witnessing that evening. I had to smile as he pleaded, in his own unique way, "Get yourselves dirty! Get contaminated for God! We're going to go out there tonight with Biola University and give the devil a couple of black eyes, make him look like Rocky Racoon!" Alberto followed closely on his heels, exclaiming, "The devil is going wild out in the world, so we Christians need to go wild too! Be violent for Jesus! The Lord is working, so we need more workers to come out with us. God is not asking for volunteers, it's our job, our obligation."

The sermon that second evening was superb, in my estimation. It was given by one of the pastors who was himself a former PCP addict and a product of one of their rehabilitation homes. He preached on Ephesians 2 and contextualized the passage marvelously to his audience. He began, "Once you were gang bangers, pipe smokers...But God...pulled us out of it all! Now we've been called to be a light, His workers. God is stirring us up. The enemy is shrewd, a liar. He wants you back in the spirit of the world, the carnal mind...This city desperately needs Jesus Christ!"

During the prayer time which came next, nearly three quarters of the church went up to the altar. About all who remained in their seats were Biola students! While many knelt in prayer, others began to lay their hands on them. I watched with interest as Rob went forward and placed his hands on the shoulders of a couple. Moments later one of the SMUers, a freshman named Nick, also moved to the front in what was obviously an impromptu and inaugural experience in the laying on of hands! A Black man soon rested a hand on him, and Nick in turn put both of his hands on a man for whom the pastor was sincerely interceding. Within seconds the man was flat on his back and Nick, quite puzzled by the experience, made his way back to his seat! I suppressed a smile as Rob, seated beside him, greeted Nick with a high five! I was pleased with the group as I observed several jotting down notes during the service and entering into conversation with many on the rehab program afterward.

The blaring wail of a bullhorn, in the hands of Alberto, signaled that we were about to hit the streets! So we gathered in the middle of the parking lot, clasped hands and formed a circle. He then led us in prayer, asking for boldness and protection and binding of the enemy. In total we numbered 25 men and women in a five-vehicle urban commando fleet! Paco cautioned everyone to remove their jewelry and secure their wallets and purses , and with that rather sobering admonition we were on our way!

A young Black man named Lewis, on V.O.'s rehab program the past 7 months, climbed into our car with us and shared of his life on the streets and cocaine dependency. We drove only a few miles, parked our vehicles on the edge of skid row along 7th Street, and once again circled with hands held as Alberto interceded for us all right on the street corner. Paco then dispensed tracts and V.O. leaflets to each of us. They were written in both English and Spanish and gave details of their services and rehab programs.

We had purposely "landed" in the middle of transvestite country. Many were strolling along the sidewalk and plying their wares to passersby. A liquor store on the opposite corner seemed to also be a strong attraction for numerous homeless individuals. Alberto immediately gave everyone within range (which was easily an entire city block!) a "blast" on the bullhorn. He identified us as being with V.O. and having literature for them which spoke of Jesus Christ and His love and death on their behalf. Many others gave brief testimonies through the loud speaker, emphasizing Jesus as "the answer" and "only hope." Each related how they too had been "all tore up" on drugs or on the street, but that "God did a miracle" in their lives.

Several of the students took their turn behind the bullhorn. It was a first for most everyone of them, especially the SMUers. Nick was rather timid, but his roommate (a sophomore named Josh) aggressively passed out the literature. Most of the girls were hesitant and remained in the middle of the pack on the corner, although two shared on the megaphone. I did notice a few of them conversing with an elderly Black man and woman at one point.

We spent nearly an hour milling about on that corner in numerous conversations with the homeless. Several of us linked up with V.O. staffers to better observe and "learn the ropes." Nick and Josh and I were privileged to participate with Tomas in praying for a frail, lonely Hispanic man. He had come from Mexico looking for work, leaving his family behind to do so, and ended up on skid row. I sincerely believe that he gave his life to Christ in that encounter.

Around 11:30 p.m. we piled back into the vehicles and drove a couple miles west on 6th to Bonnie Brae, in the heart of 18th Street territory. Despite the hour it was alive with activity, a curious mix of street people, Hispanic immigrants and gang members. In the midst of this intriguing yet intimidating context we parked our cars, disembarked and prayed once more. I counted a dozen shopping carts along the curb in front of the corner liquor store, each bulging with an assortment of people's belongings. It was truly a sight to behold, much like a "drive-in" for homeless people! Many sat or slept on the sidewalk, wrapped in blankets, and several huddled underneath a large blue tarp. Nick and I noticed someone light what was obviously a cocaine pipe through a hole in the tarp. It was ironic to witness the occasional police cruiser pass by, seemingly oblivious to all the illegal activity around them.

We followed Lewis as he approached a young Black man fertively pushing his cart up the sidewalk. In it was a large black plastic garbage bag which Lewis later explained was full of cocaine. We then understood why the man was so hesitant to speak with us and obviously preoccupied! Lewis mentioned that he was probably dealing for some of the Hispanic "heavies" in the community, in exchange for "all he could smoke." We watched him sit down and light up, in fact, as we walked away.

As we mixed with the multitudes on that corner, Alberto continued to blast away on the bullhorn and gave the students an opportunity to do the same. A few of us had an encouraging talk with a Hispanic man who had suffered through many hard situations in that same community over the past 25 years. He related how he had lost his wife and two young children in a tragic accident and had ultimately turned to drugs to cope with his resultant despair. A V.O. staff member shared his own testimony of drug addiction and despondency with the man and how he had been delivered in Christ. We then prayed that God would draw this man to Himself as well. I sensed a release in his spirit and he thanked us warmly for coming out that night, claiming that he was going back to his room to read his Bible and go to sleep "with a clear head."

A group of V.O. staffers was forming to target a specific gang hangout around the corner so Nick, Josh, Kyle, Rob, and I eagerly joined in. As we approached the parking lot where they were gathered we were struck by the intimidating nature of their presence. There were easily 30 or 40 young people dressed in gang attire and they eyed us suspiciously as we drew near. We all knew we were literally in the heart of enemy territory and we could feel the oppression. Tomas, the ring leader of our group, sensed that it was too risky for us to confront them and turned us all around. The students were quite disappointed with his decision as we had been looking forward to interacting with gang members. I wondered if we might return later that night with the entire V.O. and Biola group, but that did not occur. Although we did not know it then, it was the following week that we would make extensive contact with them.

Paco finally shut things down around 12:30 a.m. despite the fact that the area was still abounding with activity. It was inspiring to watch him and his teammates in their appointed roles and how they functioned so well together. Paco served as crew chief, Tomas as the point man, and Alberto the fearless bullhorn operator! Their command of the street and sensitivity to the Holy Spirit's leading was a real challenge to the students. Paco and Tomas later explained that the situation with the gang kids "was just not right" for our group and needed to be brought before the Lord in prayer before we penetrated their world. Paco also said he was thrilled that we had come to "sow the seeds" with them that night and I assured him the feeling was mutual and we would be back the next Friday. He was proud of how many of the students had gotten behind the bullhorn, noting that it was a great way "to stir up the gift" (of evangelism) in them! We all had a good laugh as he beckoned us back to the vehicles through the bullhorn, exclaiming, "Last one here is a rotten egg!"

We gained several more students for the following week's "evangelistic assault." Only one, an undergrad, did not return, although I was not surprised at her absence. She admitted afterward to being very uncomfortable and had found it difficult to share with people in that environment. She had questioned its effectiveness, so I recapped for her the two Hispanic gentlemen as examples in particular of those whose lives God had seemed to touch that night.

The guys were especially eager to make contact with those gang members we had seen the week before and I was also curious as to how or even if V.O. would go about it. I noticed that students' Bibles, very conspicuous the first night, were noticeably absent in our return engagement! We had come with a "traditional" witnessing methodology but had since been introduced to a much more rugged "take it to the streets" approach!

At the sound of the horn we gathered in the parking lot for "round two." Paco asked me to lead in prayer as we joined hands in our accustomed circular position. He then informed us that we would be only making one stop that night, that being the now infamous locale of the 18th Street gang. This time we all squeezed into two vehicles; they in a large purple van and we (all 11 of us) into one of the student's station wagon.

Enroute we drove through skid row again, past the incredible sight of "transvestite row." Always the opportunist, Alberto was blasting away with his megaphone through the open window of the van ahead of us. We disembarked and prayed one last time across from the familiar shopping cart-lined liquor store. It was nearly 11:00 and business was brisk so we passed out numerous tracts while waiting for our "orders" from Paco. Soon he split the group in half, and all of the guys from Biola were to accompany him and Tomas and another V.O. staffer named Joseph into an encounter with 18th Street.

Anticipation and a bit of uneasiness mounted within us as we walked up the sloped sidewalk toward their gated territory. We witnessed several younger kids running in and out as we drew near as well as a few older guys who seemed to be literal sentries at their posts. We waited as Tomas spoke with them briefly and we were granted access to enter. We slipped through the opening and in doing so felt as if we had entered another world! A quick head-count revealed about 30 young people, male and female, in addition to at least half a dozen kids who were tossing a football in the parking lot. Music blared from a large "ghetto blaster" in what was a scene that would have lent itself well to a Hollywood script. We were truly in "the hood!"

Some low-income apartments formed the back-drop behind the parking area and most of the young people were in guy-girl clusters, seated on broken down picnic tables underneath some trees. Others were standing and milling about and almost everyone of them had a 40 oz. bottle of malt liquor in hand. Many of the guys had shaved heads, while some wore their hair in a long, tight tail. A few sported backwards baseball caps and several had on dark sunglasses. Most were outfitted in the "traditional" baggy pants and white t-shirt. I glanced at several of the students, who were taking it all in wide-eyed, and commented, "Well guys, here we go! This is the big leagues!"

For what seemed like minutes, but what was in reality only seconds, the Hispanic gang members looked us over dubiously. Then a few guys approached as we stood in the parking lot. One was very cynical, bordering on menacing. He looked squarely at Tomas and Joseph and asked if they were "Mexican". Receiving an affirmative reply he then fixed his gaze on us, the Biola "White boys," and spit out the words, "You don't know nothin' about us!"

Nick answered that we were there to learn and I suggested that we did know something about the Lord Jesus Christ and we wanted them to know Him as well. He backed off somewhat at this point and another stepped forward and began to share what he dubbed as his "own philosophy" with us. He rambled on and on, occasionally touching on God, but it did serve to break the ice somewhat and allow us the opportunity to explore spiritual matters with the others.

Some of the guys started playing football with the younger boys. A few of us, booklets in hand, headed toward the tables, realizing later that we were somewhat vulnerable in doing so. A guy named Bullit walked toward us, wearing his sunglasses backwards on top of his shaved head. We talked briefly and he accepted a tract in the hand that was not clutching a beer. Nick began speaking with a guy named Yogi, who said that he got his name because he talked like Yogi Bear! Meanwhile, I zeroed in on a nearby table of several guys and girls. I began a conversation with Oscar who spoke of how they were just out "kickin' it on a Friday night." When I explained to him that we were all Christians he immediately responded in a guilty manner, much to my surprise!

A girl who was seated beside him chimed in about how she used to go to a Pentecostal church but had not attended for quite some time. Oscar in turn admitted that he was a backslidden Christian and although he knew better was unable to get out of the gang lifestyle. He then related that less than two months earlier he witnessed his own brother shot and killed on that same sidewalk. Oscar had even dropped to his knees and prayed for him while he was still breathing in hopes of insuring his brother's salvation. He died 20 minutes later.

Oscar spoke further of how he used to go to a little church nearby but now lives in fear. He described how he actually prays, gun in hand, when the gang goes out "blasting" (shooting), that he won't have to shoot anyone. He sighed with relief as he acknowledged that as of yet he has not had to pull the trigger. I reminded Oscar of God's love and forgiveness shown to the prodigal son in the Scripture. I emphasized that it was not too late and that God had enabled our paths to cross that night for a reason. I encouraged him to go to Victory Outreach that Sunday and then motioned to Paco, who was nearby, to come over and meet him.

Paco shook hands with Oscar, the girls, and several other "homies," who were beginning to gather around him. His presence was magnetic and he spoke as one having been there, commanding their respect. He shared his background with them and told of how Jesus, through the ministry of V.O., had radically changed his life. He then prayed with the whole group - Oscar, Bullit, the girl seated on the table, even "the cynic" and "the philosopher" who had been eavesdropping on his testimony.

By now it was well past midnight and he signaled that it was time for us to head out. As we were leaving he winked at me and with a broad grin and exclaimed, "Pretty good, huh?" He explained that we had witnessed a very realistic Hispanic gang setting and that the women and kids were all very much a part of it, "like a family," he concluded. The younger boys ("peewees") were literally being conditioned for a life of gang activity by what they heard and observed from their older "role models." Nick, walking excitedly at our side, then shared how one of those same boys, age twelve, had told him that it was the first time that the gang had ever let any "White boys" into their territory other than the police!

As we rejoined the other half of the group the guys eagerly recapped for the female students our encounters with Bullit, Yogi and the others. I was encouraged to see Susan and Sandra seated on the bumper of the van, faithfully making notes of our experiences. It was equally rewarding to overhear one of the students ask Paco if he could bring out a group from his own church one night, and Kyle and Rob make plans to meet with Tomas and Joseph of V.O. at a later date. Finally Nick's strong desire to come back for a third time and to haul Josh along with him was most satisfying of all. He had caught the "ministry bug" and was now contagious to his peers!

CHAPTER 5

"GOD WANTS TO USE US TO TRANSFORM THE CITY!"

UNION RESCUE MISSION

Evangelistic Service

> Overall Purpose - acquaintance with and appreciation for the
> traditional rescue mission approach to urban ministry and its
> impact on the lives of men on the street.

> Primary Involvement - observation, interaction with staff and street
> people, and limited participation in a chapel service.

Our next corporate adventure was at the Union Rescue Mission.
Although not nearly as dramatic as our experiences with Victory Outreach, it
did prove to be extremely valuable and provided impromptu, unexpected
encounters with numerous street people and staff members alike. We
gathered for prayer at Biola late in the afternoon and took two carloads of
students. After creeping along through the heart of rush hour traffic as well
as skid row we managed to arrive simultaneously with both cars in their
downtown parking lot on Main Street. We walked up the sidewalk, passing
several men and women seated and lying on it, with a few camped out in
"cardboard condos."

The group met and briefly spoke with Union's newly appointed street
chaplain, who was out mingling with the masses as we approached the

entrance. A sharp young man, he explained how he is just "learning the ropes" of his job description as he had only been at it for the past few days. He anticipated being able to walk the nearby streets and alleys to share Christ with their occupants as well as to invite them into the mission. We were encouraged by his own commitment and that of the mission's in commissioning him to do so.

A program resident then escorted us to the tiny, cramped office of Bernard, the chaplain of Guest Ministries. We were intrigued by that title and he explained that the street people are all their "guests" to which they render such services as feeding, clothing, counseling, chapels, and a bed for the night. Since it was 5 p.m. and none of us had eaten, he introduced us to Russell, one of the cooks, who was also on the rehab program. We followed him into the dining room where we "wined and dined" on the traditional rescue mission cuisine of beans and wieners.

After the meal, Russell proudly toured us through the kitchen on our way back to Bernard's office. There we met a dear little 63-year old Black woman named Ruth, whose face simply radiated the presence of the Lord Jesus. She had been the head cook for the past few years, the fulfillment of her "life-long dream to be a missionary." She had been unable to go overseas, had no education or training, but loved to cook. So when the opportunity "to serve the Lord at the mission" opened up she was ecstatic. She claimed, "God has blessed me so," and spoke of how much she loves working with her assistants, the young men on the program. She announced, "I encourage them to live the rest of their years for God," and bubbled over about how "God always provides the food, more than we can ever use."

The students were deeply challenged by this saintly woman and her joyful service to Christ. When asked the secret to her longevity she quickly replied, "Jesus!" What was equally impressive was the fact that her "mission field" was a small, aging, steamy kitchen with water on the floor, and the aroma of life on the street wafting through open windows. It was located in the very back of the mission and out the door we could see the rear parking lot which had been converted into an area where their "guests" could wash up at outdoor sinks and use the bathroom. It was a very wet and rather messy area with the smell of unwashed bodies hanging heavy in the air. But it certainly was well used as several men were washing their hair and brushing their teeth in the sinks. Some had even shed their shirts and were scrubbing away at the dirt with soap in hand.

We rejoined Bernard and by now it was nearly 6:00. Most of the group was able to squeeze inside his office and Tammy and I listened in through the doorway as he began sharing his testimony with us. No stranger to the needs of the men, he emphasized that he himself had gotten saved at the mission six years earlier. A short, stocky 56-year old Black man, Bernard had been an alcoholic for 35 of those years and a cocaine addict the last 14. He described himself as having come to the mission much like many others have done, "totally wasted and drugged out" and in desperate need of the structure that the program offered to reorient his life. He acknowledged that God began changing him the very night of his conversion and has not let him down since. He later married a Hispanic woman and they have several children together. They are currently living in Bethel Haven, which is Union's multi-residence facility for families in recovery. As evidence of God's goodness to him he related that he has never done drugs again. He knew he had gained victory over them when only a few months after entering the program he found a bag of cocaine, worth about $2,000 on the street. He poured it all down the drain.

While Bernard was sharing with us, scores of men were assembling in the chapel area outside of his office for the evening service. He referred to those despondently finding their place in one of several hundred chairs set up for that purpose as "lonely, hopeless, and unloved men who never thought they'd end up in a mission." He exclaimed, "I want you young people to realize that, with all your hopes and dreams and zeal for doing good." He continued, with wisdom and understanding, "People who set out to serve the poor have a good heart. But along the way we often get off track. It's rather how much capacity do I have to bear with insults and anger and threats. You must be able to look past all the turmoil, inside that shell of a man or woman, to their heart condition."

We were challenged by his insight and caring perspective as what he shared was extremely pertinent to the group. He concluded, with shades of Mother Teresa, "Our service to homeless people is a service to Christ. He comes to us as a dirty, stinking drunk. How do we respond? 'Get him out of here, he's dirty and has bugs!' Will Jesus say, 'Depart from Me! I don't know you?' Is there an element of compassion in what we do?"

Throughout this meaningful discourse Bernard was frequently interrupted by the questions of various staff members and the needs of noisy street people congregating in and outside the door. At one point a young Black man off the street approached Tammy and me as we were partially protruding out into the hallway. He evidently perceived us to be an easy mark and related a tale of woe about his desperate need of money for a bus ticket. When we attempted to decline his request as graciously as we could, he quickly turned on his heel and stomped away. This interaction prompted a question along similar lines to Bernard after he had finished sharing with us. He stated that he has learned in most cases not to give money to people but rather to seek to direct them to places like the mission where they can receive help. But he added knowingly, "If you do give money, don't worry about what they do with it. Be free in your giving, 'as unto the Lord'!" My eyes met those of Brenda and we nodded in agreement. She later confirmed the helpfulness of his answer to her struggle in that regard.

Bernard took us upstairs and showed us around the dorms. As we walked Doug inquired, "What do you do with those who are homosexual?" Bernard responded that they don't "harp on it" but do occasionally discover a few who are gay. Some are then dismissed from the program, but others may be dealt with through Bible study and counseling. He revealed, "I'm more frightened by the big, strong guy who doesn't look like it than the effeminate, more obvious ones. The big ones try to mess with the others in the shower sometimes."

We headed back downstairs as the time for the evening service drew near. Part of our experience was to observe and assist in any way that we could. In the interim we watched with sadness as two women and a child were informed at the door that there were no beds for them and that their meal time had come and gone. The one woman appeared resigned to her plight, while the other grew increasingly frustrated, raising her voice in anger over "the run around." The young Black man who had given them the ̲̲̲̲̲̲ kindly replied that he was sorry and Bernard intervened, suggesting to the woman an alternative shelter facility for the night.

It was quite a powerful illustration for the students as we were reading Lupton's *Theirs is the Kingdom* (1989) in class together and had just finished the chapter entitled, "The Referral Game." It dawned on us that we had just seen it take place before our very eyes. We spoke briefly with the nicely dressed man seated at his post just inside the entrance and he heaved a long sigh as he explained that those encounters are all too typical. He commented, "We refer people and try to help them and they don't even take advantage of it. They just come back again. It's frustrating."

As the meeting was about to begin, the first of several spontaneous occurrences befell us! Despite the presence of a half dozen church members from a congregation in the suburbs, who had come to do the service that night, Bernard invited us, their "guests," onto the stage with them! Preferring to go incognito and find a seat in the crowd, we deferred. But we were quickly overruled, paraded onto the platform, and introduced along with the church group to the sparse applause of those gathered before us.

Then as Bernard welcomed the real guests in the chairs, impromptu episode number two unfolded. One of the church members hastily made his way across the now heavily congested stage toward us with a look of panic on his face. Their piano player had apparently gotten sick that afternoon and they had been unable to find a replacement for her. Would one of us be willing to step forward and fill the gap? We all looked at each other with a mixture of amusement and disbelief. Finally Brenda agreed to do so amidst

114

helpless cries of being "rusty" and "out of practice". All smiles, we immediately affirmed her ability to rise to the occasion (truthfully Doug, seated beside me, was doing his best to contain outright laughter over the whole situation on the platform). Still petrified, Brenda recruited me to sit beside her on the piano bench for moral support and we laughed about how this was real "participant observation."

Meanwhile, Bernard was wrapping up his rather lengthy but well-meaning introduction. He announced, "We're here to serve you, if you need a shower, clothes, or a bed for the night. If you have a drug addiction, don't give up. There's always one more chance. Take advantage of your opportunities, we're here for you to talk with us. We love you." In response, a voice from the crowd called out, "God bless you," and another, "Oh sure!", to which Bernard cautioned the latter that he would either have to quiet down or be ushered out.

The church group then sprang to action with a rousing chorus of that traditional rescue mission favorite, Amazing Grace, followed by a very nervous gentleman who read from Scripture. Next came a testimony and then another hymn, Trust and Obey. More Scripture reading ensued and already half of the audience was asleep! Fortunately, Bernard came to the rescue with the offering. He explained that this was an opportunity for them "to give back to God, like the widow's mite," but warned them against thinking that they could "buy God." Just as he began to pray a man in the chairs stood up and began cursing profanely. He was quickly led away while Bernard assured the crowd that they still loved him and that it was "really not him but the demon in him" who had lashed out in such a manner. He then thanked the Lord in prayer for everyone in attendance, asking God "to touch them."

Special music was next on the program and we looked down in amusement at what was in reality the sad sight of several in the congregation who jokingly raised their hands in mock worship. One enterprising young man made sweeping mannerisms with his arms as if he was conducting the singing! Only a handful clapped routinely after the song and Bernard chided the group for their lack of enthusiasm. They responded with somewhat more vigorous applause and Bernard encouraged them to rouse those asleep beside them prior to hearing the message. Almost on cue two guys immediately got up and walked out. The church group leader spoke on prayer and as he did so my eye caught the verse of Scripture from Isaiah 54:10 inscribed on a large plaque on the back wall. It read, "Though the mountains be shaken and the hills be removed, yet My unfailing love for you will not be shaken, says the Lord who has compassion on you." The sound of a man belching loudly brought me back to attention as did the sight of another man getting up and walking out. The speaker then thanked them for letting their group come and closed the meeting with "I Need Thee Every Hour."

Bernard returned and asked for all those who felt God had "touched them" and needed prayer to come forward. Six men responded, to the polite applause of the crowd. He inquired a second time and two more approached the stage. He interceded for them all as a group and announced that he wanted to speak with each one individually to ascertain their specific needs and determine whether or not they are ready for or interested in the program.

As Bernard spoke with the eight in another room the remainder of the crowd stayed seated and were served sandwiches by some attendants. Shelley, one of the undergrads, had to leave for work so I walked her out to her car. There was a large number of street people milling about on the sidewalk and when I got back to the front door it was locked! I tried calling through it to the door monitors on the inside, who also doubled as bouncers. They automatically answered with the standard, "We're closed, you'll have to wait" routine. I finally had to yell, "I'm with the church group!" to be heard or even taken seriously! They sheepishly apologized as they opened the door and let me in and we had a good laugh over it! Looking back, however, I realized that I had begun to feel what it must be like for so many on the street to be helplessly on the outside and powerless to do anything about it.

Having been restored to my position as an "insider" I was very pleased to see that the students were all engrossed in conversations with several in the chairs. Brenda was speaking with a Hispanic man who agonized over his life-long drug dependency. His mother had sold drugs and now his entire family was involved in dealing. He had lost everything and wound up on the street. But Brenda was encouraged by the fact that he was committing himself to "start a new life" and was taking the necessary steps to get on the rehab program.

The mood in the car on the way back to school was lighthearted and enthusiastic. The entire group claimed to have benefited from the experience. It was particularly significant in that after being together for nearly a month I sensed that we had begun to gel as a group both in ministry as a team and enjoyment of one another.

117

Youth Ministry

Overall Purpose - acquaintance with the needs of children growing up in skid row and an understanding of a youth ministry strategy to reach them.

Primary Involvement - observation of the outreach program and the hotels in which the young people live, as well as leading the singing during the club.

With a smaller group we returned the following Sunday afternoon to participate in Union's youth ministry. Upon our arrival we met with Leslie, Union's youth ministry director, who had been on their staff for the past 6 years. She did a short orientation for us, giving us an overview of their outreach to disadvantaged children and teens living in several of the downtown hotels as well as in a nearby low-income housing project. She explained that many of the kids have already come to Christ and encouraged us to meet and build a rapport with at least one that afternoon as part of their ongoing relationship with them. Most of these young people are Black and Hispanic, but like those around them in skid row are a product of fractured and very transient families. The lure of gang activity is also a very real temptation for the kids, so Union's youth outreach to different age groups on various days of the week is also very much of a "rescue" operation.

Additional volunteers from local churches and universities were gathering for that afternoon's kid's club while we accompanied Leslie and the other staff members to pick up the kids at their hotels. Sandra and I jumped into the vehicle driven by Leslie and were off to the Brandon and Huntington

Hotels. The other students left to pick up young people from the Frontier Hotel and Aliso Village projects. Many of the kids were waiting on the sidewalk as we pulled up to the curb and the van was quickly filled with excited little bodies.

We saw and met very few parents in the process. We waved to one who was calling out the window of the Brandon and chatted briefly with a couple others in front of the Huntington. One Black mother had forgotten and we waited as she hurriedly ran upstairs to collect her children. I had previously been inside buildings in meeting with Tim of CSM, and much like the Post Apartments neither were very conducive to raising a family. I had earlier witnessed prostitutes flagrantly meeting dates right in the lobby of the Huntington. Now seated in the van we had a clear view of what were in all likelihood pimps and dealers hanging out in the entrance, returning our inquisitive gaze with stony stares of their own.

As we drove the eight or so blocks down Main Street toward the mission the appalling lack of healthy role models in the neighborhood for these kids was starkly evident. The vast majority of what we passed on that stretch were a mixture of street people, addicts and winos set in a disheartening context of dirty, smelly streets, dilapidated buildings, and cardboard condominiums. What a heritage those children were bequeathed! What an indispensable influence, by contrast, Union's youth programs were providing!

The children tumbled out of the vans and were herded downstairs to a large club room which had been nearly filled with folding chairs by the other volunteers while we were away. We counted 32 young people once they were

119

all seated and Leslie and the others began the program. We had fun helping lead the singing for the first ten minutes or so with a guitar and choruses projected overhead. Children quickly found their way on the students' laps as we took our places among them. Leslie led the group in Scripture reading, prayer, an offering and special recognition for visitors and those children who were noteworthy in their weekly club achievements.

They were then dismissed to their classes by age group so we made our way from room to room to observe and participate. Sandra joined in with the younger children and several of the others with the older young people. They had a Bible lesson, led by one of the volunteers, and then worked on a craft in which the students entered in and conversed with the kids at the table. Refreshments followed for the entire group in the dining area, or more accurately, a fairly substantial meal, consisting of sandwiches, beans, and a drink. We chatted some more with Leslie while they ate and she explained that part of their ministry is to provide one of the more healthy meals that they get all week long.

We inquired if there were any other of the numerous missions downtown who were ministering to kids in the hotels and she replied that there was one other, the Fred Jordan. I asked about overlap and she replied there had been some in the past but that now they are trying to coordinate their efforts and synchronize schedules with a new youth ministry staff member at Fred Jordan. Shelley then made plans with Leslie to return on upcoming weeks and ultimately chose to focus her ethnography on this aspect of the project.

Crossroads Rehabilitation Program

> Overall Purpose - awareness of the rehabilitation component of rescue
> ministry, including those who staff the program and the
> residents in it.

> Primary Involvement - preparing a meal, sharing testimonies, and
> worshipping with the staff and residents.

Two nights later we came back downtown in our accustomed two
vehicle procession, having regained most of the group. Our destination was
Union's young men's rehabilitation residence called Crossroads. It is actually
a large, old Victorian house which has been beautifully restored and is located
in the Pico-Union community, only a few miles from the mission but in the
heart of an 18th Street clique. We were greeted by Paul, the program director,
who led us to his office in a small building adjoining the house. He spent the
next half hour or so describing the program to us and fielding our questions.

They minister to men between the ages of 18 and 25, most of whom are
addicts and have gone through detox at Union. Their capacity is twelve men
who generally complete the program in about a year's time. Its focus is three
dimensional: spiritual, psycho-social and vocational. The first component
involves Bible study and discipleship. The second is based on the Twelve
Step model and includes counseling and recovery issues dealing with
addiction, family problems, poor self-esteem, etc. The third element helps
them identify gifts and talents and actually land a job. It is the last phase of
their recovery and usually consists of off-site vocational training.

Doug asked if the younger men are open to the gospel. Paul replied that many are but in reality some just want to get through the program. He commented, "Most claim to be Christians, but the proof is over the long haul." He explained that they worship together mid-week and Sunday evenings and attend a local church on Sunday mornings. They are all required to participate in a church and he acknowledged that their relapse, or lack thereof, is often tied into that involvement and inherent accountability.

We inquired about discipline problems and he answered that it is an ongoing challenge but not as much of a problem as it used to be. Several guys left two months ago and another was kicked out. He noted that on the average, four or five are excused over the course of a year and that one "walks" about every two months. Paul did mention that in the past they had dealt with some rather severe situations, such as an attempted suicide at 3:00 in the morning when a resident slit his wrists. But he admitted that as the staff increased, both numerically and experientially, they are now better equipped to handle the residents. He cited the example of learning how to deal with the occasional man on the program who is gay. He claimed that the problem is "widespread in the homeless community" and that they have had "to grow and become more sensitive" to the issue. His wife, Andrea, now handles the counseling with these individuals and is dealing with one on the program currently.

In addition to Paul and his spouse (he is Black and she is White) there are two single young men on staff, one Hispanic (who is also engaged to be married) and the other White. They all live on site and Paul and Andrea have a one-year old boy (their "home" is above the office). Interestingly, their ethnicity is akin to those on the program, which is a similar mix of Black, White and Hispanic.

Doug asked about Paul's personal struggles in leadership and he mentioned the challenge of administering the program, the danger of the neighborhood (there was a shooting on the corner the week before) and the stress of living on the premises as a family with little opportunity to "get away from one's work." In response to a further question by Shelley, Paul acknowledged that he would ultimately like to be ministering in an urban church in order to "see the church get more involved in this kind of ministry."

He then walked us through the massive two-story residence and we were enamored by its ornate wooden banisters and stained glass windows. He explained that it was formerly owned by Catholic nuns and showed us their upstairs chapel complete with communion table, pulpit, pews, and a closet, which was at one point a confessional booth! During our tour we met and spoke briefly with many of the residents, some of whom were engrossed in computer games upstairs. Then we set out on our assigned duties for the evening, that being to help prepare a spaghetti dinner to feed all 20-something of us!

We thoroughly enjoyed ourselves in the process, laughing and joking as we prepared the meat and literally cried our way through the seemingly endless task of slicing onions, peppers and tomatoes! Adding to the festivities was the mischievous tendency of the guys to succumb to the irresistible temptation of literally "tossing" the salad in the direction of the girls as we were creating it! As an exercise in group dynamics, it was an extremely healthy undertaking and when we were finished we hoped the same could be said for the food!

As it cooked, two of the students, who had been asked to give their testimonies in the service that was to follow, made last-minute preparations while the rest of us mingled with the residents and staff members. A few of us spoke with Andrea who also related the pressures of living in constant proximity to the guys and the particular challenges of having a child in that environment.

We split ourselves up as we sat down to eat at a large dining room table and it was a delight to see the students in conversation with various ones. Two of us sat beside Manuel, the sharp, young Hispanic staff member who does much of the counseling and was to be married that following week. He and his new bride would then share a room upstairs which he was presently fixing up for her. I was deeply impressed by the incarnational values shared by the staff as a whole. In the course of our conversation he revealed that he used to work at the Fred Jordan and we mentioned our involvement with Leslie (whom he knew) at Union just two days earlier. He spoke very passionately of how "the kids in those hotels need all the love and attention they can get." His burden for them still was very evident as he told of the deplorable "dark, dingy, dirty rooms" in which they lived. He concluded, "they don't get anything positive but what they get from the missions."

Dinner completed, we gathered in the spacious living room for a service together. Paul led the group in the singing of several choruses on an overhead, accompanied by another staff member on the piano. First Doug shared his testimony about growing up as an M.K., followed by Sandra, an

Indonesian, who related how she had been led to Christ by a missionary. Both stories were well received by the residents and certainly helped to broaden their horizons.

Paul then shared briefly and we concluded with a time of prayer, after which we spoke personally with many of the residents. That kind of firsthand contact was invaluable to the students but it was also uplifting for me to see the encouragement they were to the young men and of how grateful they were that we had come. We left with full hearts (and full stomachs!) at having been able to affirm them in their recovery as well as their relationship with the Lord.

CENTRAL CITY COMMUNITY CHURCH

Overall Purpose - exposure to and appreciation for church planting among the homeless, specifically, the uniqueness of contextualizing worship to that audience.

Primary Involvement - observation and participation in the Sunday service, meeting and interacting with church leadership, and membership off the street.

The Sunday following our initial experience at the mission, so as to gain a contrasting perspective on ministry approaches among the homeless, we attended Central City Community Church of the Nazarene. Other than those of us with overseas experience, we commented that it was one of the first times in our lives we parked in a multi-story garage and rode an elevator to get to church!

It was an enjoyable adventure just to find the high-rise building off of 4th and Broadway, sandwiched in between a number of Hispanic shops, including a beauty salon on the ground level. But as we made our way to room 309 we were warmly received by many of those who had gathered for worship, in particular a big, bearded man who introduced himself to us as Jack, the designated greeter.

A very diverse crowd were seated in folding chairs aligned in staggered rows to form a rather crude half circle, broken by an occasional aisle. Most in attendance were Black, some White and a handful were Hispanic. Several were elderly with quite a few women and children. But of the approximately 75 people there that morning the predominant membership were young Black men on the rehab program at Union.

Scott, dressed casually in jeans and a t-shirt, welcomed everyone and opened in prayer. Bernard was at his side with guitar in hand, and he waved to us in friendly acknowledgment of our visit. He and Scott then led the group in several familiar choruses on overheads and a Black woman joined them up front with her tambourine.

One of the more meaningful aspects of the service followed the singing, a substantial and highly participatory testimony time. The following are some excerpts:

-Pray for my ex-wife, she's on the street.
-Praise the Lord, my daughter came home to me.
-I thank the Lord that I haven't smoked for 3 months.
-I'm struggling to come back to God. I feel good. I'm feeling peace. I'm glad I'm here.
-I just rededicated my life back to Jesus Christ. I thank the Lord for bringing me back to His bosom.

-I thank the Lord for helpin' me not to fight back and cuss but to say
'God bless you' instead!

-This is my third time coming back to Christ. I've got the fire in me
goin' again and I ask you to pray that it'll keep goin'.

-I'm grateful today God is workin' with me and hasn't forsaken me.
It's a relief to know God is real. I've been all messed up for 40 years.
I'm happy today.

All those in attendance clapped politely after each testimony and there
were tears in my eyes as I listened to their stories and sensed the very real
presence of the Holy Spirit in our midst. Scott then acknowledged one other
woman in the audience whom he felt should also speak to the group. She
had been conspicuous to all in that she was coughing and hacking almost
constantly, a raspy, bark-like sound that was quite irritating. In a most gentle
and accepting manner Scott lovingly explained that she had come to him for
counseling earlier in the week and he had encouraged her to be part of their
congregation. He had her stand and she related her tragic tale, much to our
conviction at having been "bothered" by her "annoying hack."

She shared, "I praise God that I'm alive. I was in a coma for three days.
I was beaten by bats and raped. I praise God that the bandits didn't kill me.
They cut my arms and made me swallow a bunch of pills but they didn't kill
me. I'm also an AIDS patient. I've had AIDS for eleven years." Scott prayed
for her and included a plea for the others that God would help them to
"overcome the barriers blocking them." Bernard also led in prayer, thanking
God that they "could come and worship in the midst of adversity." Included
in his petition was a request for those "who want to come but the cares of the
world keep them away."

The woman who had earlier played the tambourine then popped up
and was identified by Scott as Josie, whose duties included managing the

prayer box (which sits on a small table in the back of the room beside the offering box. Scott later informed me that the offering averages $27 a week, $20 of which comes from one man who has a job!) She proudly exclaimed, "I'm tellin' you this prayer thing works!" She then enthusiastically related how God had been answering her prayers and urged everyone to fill the box with their own requests, promising to pray faithfully for each one.

Announcements were next as Scott reminded them about their very first adult Sunday School class which was to follow the service. The initial theme was to be that of evangelism so as to instruct them in reaching out with the gospel to their friends who were still on the street. He also prompted them on the Wednesday night meeting (on how to study the Bible) and their Thursday night relapse prevention session (which Scott had told me is attended by two-thirds of the congregation!). Scott's wife Beth also put in a plug for the women's support group and Bible study which she leads on Saturday mornings.

The kids were then dismissed to their own classes in small rooms down the hall and everyone laughed as a little Black boy called out "Bye Daddy!" as he ran down the aisle toward his class. Scott had everyone turn to Isaiah 61, explaining that "it's in the middle of the Bible some place, before Jeremiah and after Psalms and Proverbs!" When he mentioned that he would be reading the entire chapter several people groaned and one exclaimed, "the whole thing?" "Yeah, the whole thing!" he replied with a laugh. Another guy then called out, "We're with ya!" and Scott began to read.

After doing so Scott recalled that this Sunday was the five-year anniversary of when the church had first begun in the park and he felt it was appropriate to give glory to God by briefly reviewing their heritage. When he finished he asked if any other members of the congregation wanted to share memories of their journey together. A woman named Sarah stood and said how much she appreciated that the church is "real and down to earth" and that "you don't have to wear no fancy clothes." She concluded, "People can share their hardships, no matter what race you are."

Bernard then got up and rather emotionally relayed how he didn't know where he would be if it were not for his association with Scott and the church. He claimed that God had first begun to soften his heart, prior to his actual conversion at the mission, during one of the initial services he witnessed in the park. As he reviewed that episode, Sarah nodded her head and voiced her agreement. Scott had been preaching in the open air when a homeless man, yelling and screaming, came up to him and spit in his face with disgust. Bernard was deeply moved by the fact that Scott responded with compassion to the man while he "wanted to kill him," he acknowledged. But he added, "I had a warm feeling at that moment and felt that God was beginning to change me." He knew that he needed to be a part of what God was doing in that venture and asked Scott if he could join them, bring his guitar and become an "active contributor" in the fledgling church. He challenged those in attendance to get involved as well.

As Scott began teaching his style was interactive, much like an informal Bible study rather than a sermon. He frequently asked questions of the group, encouraging them to respond and participate in the learning process with him. His comments focused on the first four verses as he compared those addressed in the passage as "broken-hearted" and in despair to many in the congregation. Yet he spoke encouragingly that God wants to use them as the "rebuilders" of not only the "ruins " of skid row but all of Los Angeles! He held up some broken pieces of wood as an object lesson, emphasizing that those materials could be restored to usefulness as they once were much like the way God longs to bring healing and "gladness" to their lives, to raise them up as "oaks" from the ashes of crumbled ambitions. "God wants to use us to transform the city!" Scott announced yet again. He acknowledged that the Lord can bring revival as they become "agents of change and love" and are willing to return as ambassadors to many of the same dilapidated hotels in which they had previously lived lives of sin. Citing verse 9 he claimed that when others see their lives being changed they will take notice that God is at work and will choose to follow Him as well. He added that the reason he wore a t-shirt that day with Martin Luther King, Jr. pictured on it was because he too "has a dream for revival in this area, that overcomes racism."

Scott closed in prayer and as he finished everyone recited the Lord's Prayer in unison, adding their own unique, motivational conclusion, "Keep comin' back! Jesus works!" Afterwards we thanked Scott and Bernard for allowing us to participate with them. We met their wives and children as well and each had a new baby. Scott and Beth live nearby in an apartment on 6th and Spring, which was a further testimony to the group. As we were filing out a poster on the back wall caught our eye. Pictured was Martin Luther King, Jr. and the caption read, "The Church must be reminded that it is not the master or the servant of the state, but rather the conscience of the state."

FIRST EVANGELICAL FREE CHURCH

Overall Purpose - awareness of the issues involved in an existing church's attempt to contextualize its urban ministry focus within a changing and diverse low-income setting.

Primary Involvement - limited tutoring and sports outreach in the neighborhood and the opportunity to make contact with a homeless community behind the church.

Toward the middle and latter weeks of the semester we focused on the final component of the ministries under investigation, the First Evangelical Free Church. As it turned out, the graduate students in the group tended to have the greatest interest in gaining a deeper understanding of the local churches' perspective on and involvement in urban research in their own community. Thus those three individuals and I ended up with the majority of the group's experiences with that church and its leadership.

After the pastor had spoken to the entire class, our group was especially interested in the homeless community living under the freeway overpass behind their building. In addition to that dilemma the church was also faced with the pressures of the young people in the area toward gang activity (18th Street), as well as an urgent need for tutors and ESL teachers for the throngs of Hispanic immigrants that have descended on their neighborhood. The grads and I arranged an initial gathering with several of the church's significant lay leadership who were actively engaged in extensive ministry within the neighborhood and had developed strong relationships with many community members as well. Jeff, one of the students, had been attending

131

the church for quite some time and therefore had already established a rapport with all those individuals.

Prior to our brainstorming session we listed on a sheet of paper some items which we had hoped were pertinent to the needs of the church as well as the students. These included the aforementioned ministry opportunities as well as time constraints of the students, available laity who could put us in touch with key people in the community, and the potential longevity of outreach beyond the confines of the semester. When we met at the church it was evident rather early in our discussion that both of our agendas were somewhat more aggressive in scope than was feasible to tackle within a few short weeks. They referred us again to their own list of 13 research projects which the pastor had mentioned to us in class and although each merited serious consideration most were simply too much for our limited time frame.

All in attendance from the church then shared their specific ministry involvement and needs for volunteer assistance. Kim, a single White woman, mentioned the ongoing opportunity for tutors. We were challenged by her commitment as she has lived the past nine years a block away from the church and coordinates the tutoring and E.S.L. program. She also suggested a rather pioneering venture of rounding up the junior high-aged boys on her street and playing some basketball with them on the court in her driveway. She spoke of the urgency to reach the twelve and thirteen year-olds in their community before they become immersed in gang activity.

Hector, in his mid-20s, concurred with the vulnerability of these young people to the gangs, mentioning as well the prevalent drug dealing in a nearby parking lot. He had grown up only a block away and now, as a contractor, lived there still. As a result he knew the ins and outs of the neighborhood and its people and offered to act as somewhat of a spokesperson to put us in touch with key individuals. A further opportunity with the young people was posed by the Anglo youth pastor, who along with his Hispanic volunteer assistant, admitted to being in need of "crowd control" on Saturday nights, when they generally have over thirty junior highers and high schoolers assembled at the church. They were also interested in gaining a better understanding of a relevant strategy to reach Hispanic-American kids toward building a successful youth group.

At this point the grads gave their feedback. Jeff agreed with the uniqueness of the Hispanic-American young person in that area as a product of El Salvador, Guatemala, Panama, and Mexico. Brenda felt as if tutoring might work for some of the group and I thought that the opportunity to play some ball with neighborhood kids would appeal to some of the undergrad guys. We agreed that we would go back and present the options to the students and allow them to decide on which, if any, were possibilities. Sandra then brought up our interest in making contact with the homeless community. I had sensed that we may have been more strongly motivated to that end then they and my suspicions were confirmed when they paused to answer. Finally Hector cautioned us that they were a "tough bunch, mostly all drug addicts" and it was evident that they did not have as strong a burden for the homeless as they did for the youth and immigrant families in the vicinity.

Concerns were expressed about our safety, especially the females, and we explained that we had already been involved in fairly extensive interaction with a wide variety of the homeless on the street, under the bridges and in the mission. We offered our efforts to build initial relationships and assess their needs in an effort to assist the church in what could become a longer term outreach project. This met with approval and Hector agreed to accompany us and assist in the process. Sandra and Brenda were especially eager to be involved in that endeavor and we agreed to return and meet Hector the following Tuesday night.

He was waiting out front as we pulled up to the curb and led us to the heavily fenced area under the freeway overpass which appeared to contain about a half dozen tents. The only access was through a narrow opening near the road and it was obvious that Hector was not about to walk right in uninvited. So he called through the fence and two Black men approached, Freddie and Buster. We all stretched to shake hands over top of the enclosure and I explained that we had come in hopes of meeting them and offered to be of help if we possibly could. Freddie, quite disinterested, walked away but Buster chatted with us in quite a friendly manner (although not inviting us in).

He suggested that we come back later because he and Freddie were the only ones around at that moment. We inquired about how many lived under the overpass and he replied that there were about twelve in all. Brenda asked if any were women and he responded in the negative. I mentioned that we were part of a larger group of students and would love to come back and get to know them whenever it was convenient. We asked about another evening the following week and he agreed to spread the word in advance of our arrival.

Our initial efforts stymied, we were somewhat disappointed but now more aware of the challenge before us. We resolved to continue to make it a matter of prayer and return that next Tuesday night with additional reinforcements as well as some food, which we hoped might at least get us inside their fortress. Since we still had some time that evening we asked Hector to show us around the neighborhood and he drove us by numerous graffiti-scarred buildings in front of which hung out a number of the local 18th Street gang members.

We dropped in on Kim, who was just leaving her house to walk over to the church (which came as quite a surprise to Brenda as by then it had gotten dark). She was about to lead an E.S.L. class for thirty people and asked us to join her. Although homework demands were beckoning the students back to their dorms we stayed long enough to assist Kim in arranging piles of clothing on a table for those who were soon to arrive. We greeted many of the Spanish-speaking women as they entered and took their accustomed places at several large folding tables. Kim welcomed them all and began the session as we slipped out. But before beginning the meeting she made another request for tutors and E.S.L. assistants and we promised to petition our group on her behalf.

The following afternoon in our class session we assembled the whole group during a break and gave them an update on our interactions with the church thus far. Everyone was excited about returning the following week and attempting to make further headway into the homeless community. The guys were also eager to play basketball with the youth but there were no takers for tutoring or E.S.L. Three of the female students were interested but it was simply not conducive to their schedules nor to the overall focus of the project.

We arranged to take two carloads for our second trip. The guys, in my car, would leave earlier and seek to round up some kids and play ball for an hour or so prior to the girls arriving at the church in another vehicle at around 6:00 (the time Buster had suggested that we return). Hector met us at Kim's house but only a couple of the neighborhood youth were around. They mentioned that most of their peers were down the street playing basketball at the rec center. So we headed that way and found a game in progress with a number of young people. We introduced ourselves and they welcomed our participation with them.

We split ourselves up and played several games for over an hour. Although we did succeed in winning their approval, there was little opportunity for any kind of extensive rapport or interaction. We offered to come back the following week and play at Kim's so as to have a greater degree of control and possibility for sharing. But as it turned out Hector got sick, one of the students was completing an exam and none of the kids showed up. We chalked it up to experience, realizing that the potential was there but that it required a greater degree of time and physical proximity than we were able to give.

We drove back to the church, arriving just before the carload of girls. Shelley immediately blurted out that her car had been stolen so we included that request in our prayer on the sidewalk for God's sovereign intervention in our evening's activity. Since there were eight of us in all we made the spontaneous decision for half of the group to approach initially so as to not overwhelm them with our enthusiasm. Hector, the grads and myself would lead the way, food in hand, and would immediately beckon the others if we were invited inside.

Hector got their attention once more and a Hispanic man named David hesitantly approached the fence. We explained who we were and that we had come the previous week and spoken with Freddie and Buster. He cautiously remarked that they were not around, in fact, only one guy other than himself was there at the moment. David was initially resistant, but noting our sincerity he agreed to talk with us for awhile, although once again we were forced to remain on our side of the fence.

Forty-two year old David shared how he had just lost his job and had been living under the overpass for only a month but was already tired of being on the streets. He related that his parents had died and that he had no other family. He had resorted to panhandling to get by, admitting that he had really "screwed up" and that his biggest problem was drugs. He confessed that although he had been able to stop doing cocaine he was helpless in his efforts to kick the heroin craving. Hector intervened, explaining that he had "been there" and that it was also possible for David to be set free from his addiction. He urged him to give it up, calling it a "matter of life and death." David related that he had already tried detox and even gone "cold turkey" during a recent stint in jail. But he referred to that experience as one of "the worst of my life" in which he had "hardly slept at all" and was therefore unwilling to go through the pain once again.

He seemed out of place, as if he didn't really belong in the homeless camp, and appeared to be relatively friendless. He spoke of several under the bridge who had mental problems and that most were newcomers to the camp. The longest anyone had been under there, as far as he knew, was about a year and a half. He stated that they all needed a job and "a decent place to live," as well as food and blankets in the immediate future. We gave him all the food that we had (in hopes that he would dispense some to the rest of the guys as well) and told him of our affiliation with the church, to which he responded rather indifferently. We also mentioned the availability of Victory Outreach's rehabilitation program, but he was once again very resistant to that prospect.

As we were talking with David, Buster entered the fenced-in campsite. We called out to him but he brushed us off coolly, claiming that he was "too busy" and didn't have time to talk. He mumbled something about needing a dollar and left again shortly thereafter. Moments later two other residents, one White, walked by without even acknowledging our presence. Suffice it to say that they were not exactly rolling out the red carpet for us! David then said that he had to go, so the four of us were left on our own, more or less rebuffed in our efforts at penetrating that community. I felt badly for the other four students who had been waiting to join us so we walked back to the church, only to find that they were all inside, helping out Kim with E.S.L.

While we waited for them we shared our frustration in being unable to break through with the homeless men, contrary to our other far more positive experiences with the likes of Green Eyes and Red Dog. After another twenty minutes or so the other students poured out of the church, excitedly recapping their cross-cultural opportunity. One of Kim's E.S.L. teachers had not showed up, so when she spotted them waiting for us she put them right to work! They had assisted with the lesson (Doug and Tammy knew a little

Spanish) as well as giving individual attention to some in their reading skills. Kim had even had a couple share their testimonies. Overall it was time well spent and I was extremely pleased with the maturity shown by the group as well as their initiative and spontaneous participation in whatever ministry opportunity presented itself.

THANKSGIVING DINNER UNDER THE BRIDGE

Overall Purpose - encountering the homeless in their own
environment so as to observe and more fully understand their
context and begin building relationships.

Primary Involvement - sharing a meal under the bridge with homeless
men and engaging in conversation with them.

One of the last corporate experiences we had as a group was toward the end of the semester when we shared Thanksgiving dinner with Lenny, Lefty, Big Jed and Tony, alias the Beached Whale, under the Figueroa Street bridge, between Temple and Sunset. I had done extensive interviews with each one of them earlier in the semester and stopped in to see them about a week and a half before the holiday. I initially invited them to join us for dinner, thinking that it may have been a treat as well as a change of scenery. They graciously admitted to being somewhat "uncomfortable" with that prospect, however, preferring rather that we join them. Lefty then confessed that they "always drink on holidays" and I could sense that they did not want to be an embarrassment to us. Jed also chimed in that they "don't go anywhere on the holiday" and that "it's a family thing." I replied that we would then do our very best to fill that gap and be their "family" for that afternoon.

I double checked with them again a few days before Thanksgiving. They were really quite excited about our coming. Jed exclaimed, "We're even going to clean up the place a bit!" I did my best to suppress a smile as he also promised that they would try not to use profanity out of respect for "religious people!" They also pledged to "try to be sober" and I laughed as I committed to supply them with all the soda they could possibly drink. We then discussed the logistics. They had some old dilapidated chairs they would attempt to resurrect and I would bring along a portable folding table. I also checked in with Tony, who was living in the bushes nearby, before leaving. He declined the invitation to our "dry" celebration under the bridge, but said he would gratefully accept a plate or two of food if I would bring it over to him.

Because of family commitments several of the students were unable to participate. However there were still six of us who made the excursion in two vehicles, including the professor. As we rolled in around 1:00 p.m. and parked along the curb under the bridge, Jed, Lefty, and Lenny all came down to greet us. We exchanged pleasant introductions and handshakes as Jed in particular was in a most gregarious mood. With a wide sweeping motion of his arms toward the bridge he announced merrily, "Well, come see my house!"

All three of the guys are hardened veterans of the streets. Forty-eight year old Big Jed grew up in Alabama. His parents divorced when he was only a year old, leaving him to be raised by his grandparents. Jed was "in trouble"

140

from a young age and has spent nearly half of his life behind bars. He came out to Los Angeles to stay with an aunt but as an ex-con he was unable to get a job and ended up on welfare. He soon turned to the streets and eventually gravitated to the bridges, where he has remained for the past nine years. Like the others, Jed is a chronic alcoholic.

Lefty, so named because he lost his right arm in a childhood automobile accident, is fifty-years old and grew up in Texas. He too was raised by his grandparents because his mother and younger brother were killed in the same car crash. His father died a few years later of alcoholism and Lefty admits to being a "drunk" since he was twelve. Like Jed, he dropped out of school in junior high and "hit the road" as a mere fifteen-year-old. After a failed marriage he attempted to take his own life but the gun misfired. On a whim he headed for California and wound up on skid row, where he has spent the last twenty-five years of his life. He discovered the bridges about four years ago. He initially drew support from "passin' bills", which he explained as handing out advertising fliers. But he lost that job and ultimately came to rely on his handicap as a means of soliciting finances. He boasted that by panhandling he can make $30-40 in an hour or less simply by holding out his dirty old baseball cap "and not sayin' nothin'."

Lenny, fifty-five years-old, is a native New Yorker and the senior-statesman of the group, sporting a long gray beard. Abused and abandoned as a child, his grandparents took him in, but "used me like a slave," he recalled. He too left home at fifteen after two stints in reform school, which he described as "an alternative to prison." There he earned the nickname "Cat Man," due to his propensity for burglary. He married and found work in a

141

bakery, but the marriage crumbled when his wife began fooling around with another man. That coupled with a warrant for his arrest motivated him to go west. A temperate climate drew him to Los Angeles, where the streets soon laid claim on him as well. But he tired of the bridges, preferring rather to be "out in the open." Although he joined us under the bridge that afternoon, he currently stays in a cluster of bushes on the other side of the freeway. In contrast to Lefty's purely emotional appeal for aid, Lenny "works a sign" on the Grand Street off ramp as a source of income. But alcohol has been his constant companion too and consistently saps his funds. He recalled, "My father was putting whiskey in my bottle before I was a year old."

The three of them helped us haul the food, coolers and table over the short wall along the sidewalk, through the hole in the fence, and up the grade to their campsite area. But as we began to set everything up, we discovered a huge, half-eaten ham sitting in a large pan over the fire. Jed and Lefty immediately apologized for the fact that they had already gorged themselves and weren't hungry.

Jed explained that a few hours earlier someone had literally driven up in a car and offered them the ham. They simply could not refuse it and had initially planned to save it for the next day, or at least later that night. But it "smelled so good" that their resistance soon weakened and they "pigged out" shortly before we arrived. Compounding matters even more, and shedding light on their "happy" demeanor, was the fact that their "pork present" also included a substantial jug of wine. Thus their promised sobriety had also gone by the wayside as they had been sipping away on the brew (out of styrofoam cups no less!) for quite some time before our arrival.

The whole situation actually hit us as being rather humorous. Here we were, in such typical Thanksgiving-season fashion, intent on dutifully feeding the homeless and hungry, and they were full! In fact many of us had not eaten anything yet that day and I, for one, was starved! But the most amazing and significant thing of all was Jed's next comment. Referring to the fact that they were already "stuffed" (without having eaten our stuffing!) he exclaimed, "That's alright! Let's just talk!"

It dawned on us so clearly that what they valued far more than food was fellowship, companionship, relationship! They didn't necessarily want or even need something to eat, they wanted us! What an indictment this was to us on our typical response to the homeless, on Thanksgiving and Christmas in particular. We give them everything except ourselves! My mind flashed back to how, although entirely well meaning, Green Eyes had been lavished with presents from the Christian school children last Christmas. We realized anew how much more pertinent and tangible it is to give the greatest gift of all, our lives.

So we served ourselves generous portions of turkey dinner (actually Lefty took a plate full as well) and sat down on broken chairs and spare corners of their well-worn mattresses. It was fun to watch the students enter into conversation with them. Kyle began interacting with Jed about his prison experiences and Brenda, although hesitant at first, soon joined in as well. Another sat beside Lenny and Sandra continued her familiar routine of pulling out her camera and capturing the moments on film!

I served Lefty a soda and sat down beside him. He had previously told me that he no longer drinks wine because it nearly killed him a few years ago.

143

Lenny was also much more in control of his thirst that afternoon, sipping just a small amount of the fruit of the vine. But it was Jed who made up for the other two, increasingly becoming more and more the "life of the party" as the day wore on. His other resolution, to avoid the use of profanity, also became a thing of the past the more he drank. But every time a "bad" word escaped his lips he politely covered his mouth and begged to be excused! Once again he told us not to feel bad about all the food we had brought which was sitting relatively untouched. He assured us that they would give it away to "the bums" who pass by. It was of interest to us that he did not include themselves in that category.

I broke away from the group and made my way down the trail to drop in on Tony, the Beached Whale, under his bush. Big Jed had previously explained to me how Tony had derived his street name, claiming, "He looks like a beached whale, just layin' up man, that's all he ever does!" Red Dog, prior to introducing me to Tony, had described him as "a big guy who just sits there on his a__ and panhandles." In his mid-40's, Tony is the youngster of the group, although the streets have been his home since the late 70's. He professes to be a Buddhist because "the Christian Bible condemns homosexuals" and he is openly gay, claiming that he was "born that way." Because of that fact his family disowned him and ultimately kicked him out of the house. He has not seen them for nearly 20 years, commenting, "I hated them for an awfully long time."

Because of his lifestyle, Tony met a man in Hollywood "who was into boots and whips and bondage" and turned him "into the ultimate speed freak." But when his new-found "friend" committed suicide, Tony attempted to do the same. To his chagrin, however, he explained, "What I mainlined wasn't enough to kill me." So he tried again several months later by slashing his wrists, but once more to no avail. He ended up in a psychiatric hospital and then skid row upon his release. The drugs have given way to gin and vodka to which he devotes all his resources. He eventually found his way to the bridges, but chose his current camp in the bushes over a year ago, explaining that "nobody hassles me here."

As I had found Tony on previous visits, he was reclining on one arm in his "beached" position. I greeted him, inquiring if he wanted a plate of food. His answer struck me as being almost as ridiculous as the ham episode. He replied, "What have ya got?" So much for being taught all along that "beggars can't be choosers!" So after "taking his order" I said I would be right back and asked if I could bring a couple others with me. Not in the best of moods that afternoon, he said that we could only stay "for a few minutes." I returned shortly with Sandra, the professor, and his lunch.

We approached through the adjoining parking lot this time so as to avoid the feces along the trail. I handed Tony the plate of food and couldn't help but laugh as he thanked me for it and then set it aside for later (you guessed it, he wasn't hungry at the moment)! We made small talk for awhile after I introduced him to the others. He apologized for how messy his place was, reminding himself that he needed to clean up a bit. He also described for them his plastic roofing arrangement and how he sets it up to keep dry in the rain. We chatted a while longer with Tony and then bid him farewell. We were eager to get back under the bridge and rejoin the rest of the group. They were all still engrossed in conversation to which we entered in once more. I watched with amusement as Lefty had a small pile of cigarette butts beside him which the guys obviously had saved or collected and were now passing around between the three of them, puffing contentedly away on an after dinner smoke.

Finally, with homework and other commitments beckoning, we began to pack up the leftovers, leaving everything with them except the jello, salad and gravy (which they said they didn't want!). As we were doing so another homeless man passed by and, since he was an acquaintance, they flagged him down, sending him on his way with a plate piled high.

One carload took off, but before the rest of us left we went across the street to check in on Dirty Jake, who was stationed at his accustomed spot beside a concrete bridge support. Red Dog had introduced me to Jake weeks earlier and I had been able to glean excerpts of his life from him in a succeeding visit. He had literally been "shunned" from the bridge community because he "has bugs" and was "banished" to live on his own. He had also tried to commit suicide several years ago by jumping off a building, leaving his legs permanently damaged and making it difficult for him to ascend the incline up to the bridges.

"Dirty" Jake's nickname is certainly apropos. The dirt is literally caked on his cracked leathery feet. The day we spoke he was shoeless, seated on a dirty blanket beside the pillar, surrounded by crawling vines and his own discarded garbage. I inquired as to why he chose not to shower or get deloused in order to live under the bridges with the others. He claimed to prefer his privacy and to "make more money panhandling looking this way." Fifty-eight years old, Jake never married, has no children and both of his parents died long ago. He was raised in Minnesota, moved to California and ultimately came to Los Angeles because he "heard they had good missions." But he claimed to have gotten the "pests" (lice) there and opted rather for the streets. They have been his home for the past 25 years.

I had hoped to give Jake some food and to introduce him to the students, but he had obviously been drinking heavily and was in quite a sullen mood, liquor bottle in hand. He looked rough, and waved me off with a sweep of his hand. He bluntly said that he was not at all interested in food or visitors so I wished him well and told him I would stop by again another day. All in all it was not a traditional Thanksgiving Day setting, but the consensus of the group was unanimous in affirming that our last experience together was a most valuable and satisfying one.

CHAPTER 6

MAKING THE MOST OF MENTORING MOMENTS

In the midst of our experiences as an entire group during the semester I attempted to seize every opportunity for time with the students individually or in pairs. This always occurred in the context of the project, but generally lent itself to dialogue on various aspects of the student's walk with the Lord, personal struggles, and ministry aspirations. Our discussions often took place in the car, as we were driving to and from ministry sites and times of personal interaction with various men and women. These fifty mile round trip "commuter conversations" proved to be invaluable to my relationship with them and enabled me to monitor their spiritual and emotional highs and lows throughout the semester. I was able to share in significant mentoring opportunities with eight of the students, excerpts of which are recapped on the ensuing pages, along with significant observations of our interaction.

TOURING WITH BRENDA AND SANDRA

Early in the semester, in their enthusiasm to get started, Brenda and Sandra asked if they could tag along with me one day while I was making contacts to at least get a glimpse of what they were getting themselves into. Always eager to oblige, I gladly agreed to give them the whirlwind tour.

As we exited on Pico off of the 10 Freeway, the girls were enamored by an extremely haggard looking man with long, matted blond hair. He was standing alongside of the off ramp holding a cardboard sign on which he had scrawled a nearly illegible message. We were able to discern part of its plea for aid to read, "Crime Victim. Hurt. Please Help." The girls commented numbly on how he certainly looked the part.

We stopped in at First E. Free and one of the lay leaders walked with us through the neighborhood, telling of its diversity and opportunities for ministry. We passed large murals depicting Jesus and the Virgin Mary as well as a huge store-front caption reading, "We do not have generations, we only have 15 years in which to save our planet." The girls got their first real glimpse of the menacing and defacing effects of graffiti, announcing that we were "trespassing" on another's turf.

Next we went by the Post Apartments and happened upon both Red Dog and Funee Man. Red was on his way down the street, while Funee was hanging out with a few of his "homies" on the sidewalk. He warmly greeted the girls with his traditional, "Hey, they call me Funee from Bonnie Brae!" Brenda in particular could hardly believe she had just shaken hands with a gang leader. We drove by Cambria and as we turned the corner back onto Union we noticed a Hispanic man on his knees on the sidewalk in the heart of the Orphan's territory. It looked as if he was praying before a small altar or artifact of some sort. We all got out of the car and walked over to investigate. It turned out to be a candle with some kind of incense sprinkled around it and had obviously been there for a few days. Then we noticed a handwritten note on a torn, white piece of ruled paper, attached to a support wire from the telephone pole nearby. It was smudged and dirty, but we were able to make out the following message: "In memory of Eager Edgar. I will miss you always. Love, Wanda the Witch." Sensing that this may been a gang-related situation I asked the Christian Community about it the next day when I was back downtown. "Eager Edgar" was actually the gang name for 15-year-old Daniel, who had been killed in a drive-by shooting a few days earlier. "Wanda the Witch" was one of the girls in the gang (unknown to the Cambria people), and the candle had served as a quiet memorial to one whose young life had been snuffed out so violently.

We wound up in skid row and at this point all that Brenda had seen in the past couple of hours seemed to erupt within her at once. Sandra seemed to take it all in with intrigue, jotting down notes, and clicking one picture after another with her camera. But Brenda needed a sounding board. She expressed real fear as we passed literally hundreds of men and women congregating in alleys and milling about on the streets. She related how despite the fact that she had spent time in Calcutta, working among the poor with Mother Teresa, she was still afraid of those she had seen that day.

Brenda continued to insightfully contrast the two, and we noted how they basically fell into the categories of absolute and relative property. Those she had come to know in India had broken her heart, especially the teaming numbers of poor women and children. But she sensed that those here on skid row had power over her and she perceptively labeled it as a "poverty of violence." She elaborated on how she feared being "shot and killed" if she walked on her own in gang areas or through skid row. She never felt that way in Calcutta. She wondered what would happen to a woman who would go among the American urban poor to help them as Mother Teresa did in India and was unsure if she could ever do so. She was struggling with the sinful nature of many of their lifestyles and sensed the oppression and spiritual warfare in communities we had visited.

We talked about absolute and relative poverty and of the incredibly violent nature of the American inner city. We admitted the very real dangers of working among gangs, drugs addicts, and prostitutes, particularly for a woman. But we also spoke of the willingness to be vulnerable so as to build their trust and respect. However we sought to bring a balance to that zealous, pioneering approach by acknowledging the importance of linking up with veteran staff members at the nearby missions who have already made significant inroads into those communities and have the expertise in ministering to them.

This discussion led to a consideration of the urgency of the task and the pressing problems of urban subcultures within the United States, which are too often overlooked (yet are arguably more violent) compared to the needs of the mission field overseas (which have traditionally been presented as the greater challenge). But we agreed that the same historical commitment to front-line ministry and the "regions beyond" which required such selfless, sacrificing service is still in vogue and certainly the need of the hour today.

Significant Observations:

Mentoring - Enthusiasm and intrigue is an initial propellant into the city. But that eagerness and naiveté is easily overcome by fear and

151

disillusionment. The mentor acts as a "sounding board" for those emotions and consistently monitors the students' efforts at overcoming their anxieties.

Ministering - The presence of gangs, prostitutes, and volatile men and women heavily drug dependent and milling about on the streets reflect a "poverty of violence" within Los Angeles' skid row. Despite its "relative" nature of poverty (in contrast with "absolute" poverty in numerous third world urban settings), there is a strong sense of oppression and spiritual warfare. One feels vulnerable to its "power" and fears being "shot and killed." This is particularly true of women who would set out to minister in these settings. What ramifications does this have upon our incarnational witness? The Christian gospel has always gone forth in a self-less, sacrificial manner. Should this not be the case as well "at home" in our inner-city communities?

MOVING EXPERIENCES WITH DOUG

A week later the opportunity arose to help Red Dog and Billie move from the Post Apartments to their current room on Union Street, between 8th and 9th. That venture was an excellent occasion to bring a couple of the guys along with me and to acquaint them with Red and Billie in the process. Of all those I met on the street, forty-two year-old Red is far and away the roughest and gruffest of the bunch. He is a survivor extra-ordinaire, a fourteen-year veteran of the streets, bridges, and bushes, with the scars and harrowing tales to prove it.

Red closely resembles the proverbial hillbilly with his pock-marked face, bushy red beard (which at one time was down to his chest), and flowing hair. He even grew up in the hills of Tennessee! But like the others, his early years were also unguided. His father left the home when Red was a year old. Red commented, "I was twelve when I first started getting in trouble and I've been in trouble off and on for the rest of my life." Drinking, fighting, and carousing became his forte, landing him in reform school. Soon thereafter it was attempted murder for which he went to prison.

Upon his release he married, fathered two children, and promptly left them all behind, running from them and a misdemeanor charge which would have sent him back to jail. He bounced around for a while and finally settled in Los Angeles, where he remained and found work driving a truck. He remarried but his wife left him shortly thereafter, tiring of his drinking and temper. He then quit his job and ended up on the streets, which is where he first met Billie eight years ago. Despite the fact that she is seventeen years his senior, they've been constant companions ever since.

A crude, tough woman, Billie epitomizes the classic "bag lady" stereotype with her weathered features, raspy voice, graying hair, and a grand total of three teeth. She was raised on the East coast and while still in her teens married unknowingly into an Italian family strongly connected to the Mafia. Thirty-five years and five children later, after confronting her husband about his repeated infidelity, she set out on her own and headed West. She wound up on skid row in downtown Los Angeles, "living" in a refrigerator box on the sidewalk in front of one of the missions. She met Red in Pershing Square Park and they soon found their way to the bridges. Together they made quite a team on their early morning "can runs" and Red developed a flair for "dumpster diving" for their meals.

Their daily routine consisted of pushing a shopping cart from dumpster to dumpster and scrounging around for whatever they could find. In addition to extracting aluminum cans they were often rewarded with various assortments of meat, potatoes, cheese, eggs, and bread. Red commented, "Everybody under the bridge would find a little bit here and a little bit there...then we'd sit down and feast!" But a "banquet" such as that was not complete without something to wash it all down. Red continued, "Ya go back home with what ya got in your cart. Then ya get yourself a few six-packs. Come back and drink until ya get so plastered that ya pass out. That's everybody's life under the bridge...that's about the only way you can cope with reality, stay half drunk."

After several years of that lifestyle they were able to transition from the bridges into an S.R.O. This was made possible by Red's persistent effort to qualify for S.S.I. (disability). They ended up in the Post Apartments, because "this place didn't ask for any credit reference or run a credit check." Four months later, Red had a major heart attack. He has had five more plus a stroke in the past two and a half years. Because Red's health continues to be poor, Billie is now paid by the state to act as his nurse. But after another encounter with gang bangers, in which Red claimed to have been shot, they decided that it was time to seek new lodging (true to form, however, Red assured me that the wound "wasn't serious" and the bullet was easily removed by a doctor!).

I had offered to lend a hand with their relocation but Red had downplayed the need of my assistance, assuring me, "I can manage!" This despite his multitude of ailments, including the fact that he was not to lift anything heavier than 10 lbs.! But I persisted and once he did accept my proposed aid he certainly held me to it. He phoned me on a Sunday night a few days later, announcing that the following morning was moving day! He asked how many I was bringing with me (I had mentioned that I could maybe take along a student or two), as well as if I could scrounge up a truck. I laughed and explained that I didn't have a truck, nor did I have the means or access to get hold of one. It was also news to me that he was moving the very next day, but I promised to do my best to round up as many bodies as I could! Not only did I call all the guys in the project but I tried the SMUers as well. But because it was a school day none were available (a little more advance notice wouldn't have hurt either), except for Doug, who had just the morning free. We agreed to meet at Biola at 7:30 a.m. and to have him back on campus in time for his 11:30 class.

I phoned Red and he said that he now had a lead on a truck which we could possibly use on Tuesday morning and asked if I would check on it. It belonged to Henry, the manager of the building that was soon to be their new home. So I gave him a call, oblivious to the fact that he, like Martin, shared some rather strong opinions about various members of the human race! Obviously he had no idea who I was, so I quickly aligned myself as a "friend" of Red Dog and Billie, calling on their behalf to borrow his truck. He immediately replied, "What's your angle?"

I explained that I was a Christian college student working on my dissertation and doing research among the homeless, gangs and prostitutes. Those comments seemed to "stir a sleeping giant" because he recounted my list of subcultures, added "drug addicts" and "illegal immigrants" to it, and

155

then incredibly proclaimed that "we should kill them all!" I could hardly believe it and nearly dropped the phone! It was dejavu, "open season" on the disenfranchised once again! I was beginning to have serious doubts about the mental well-being of the landlord population! I regained my composure and replied that despite the dysfunctional nature of many of those people I personally embraced somewhat of a more rescuing and redemptive world view!

Henry scoffed at my softness and naiveté, recounting how he had shot an intruder in his building three times in the chest and killed him 2 years ago, and had "no regrets whatsoever" about it! He explained that he was a veteran of both Vietnam and Korea and believed in "taking no prisoners." He continued by laying blame on the "d___ Central American refugees" for the problems in his community, even more so than the "gangsters" and street people. I listened with amazement as he revealed further animosity toward "niggers, homosexuals and child abusers." Referring to my earlier statement about being a Christian he bluntly suggested that "churches need to be put to the torch!" He particularly disliked Pentecostals "for their tongues" as well as Fundamentalists and Baptists "because they interpret the Scriptures wrongly."

I had rarely heard such outspoken bigotry and distorted ideology and strongly suspected that something was at the root of his dogmatic and callous assertions. It was getting late and I had been on the phone for quite some time so I asked if we could continue our conversation during the next day or two after moving Red and Billie. He agreed and commented that he had only just begun to divulge the many experiences of his 60 years!

I picked up Doug in the morning and as we pulled up to the building on Bonnie Brae I introduced him to Funee, who was out front with several other BBCers. He greeted Doug in similar fashion as he had done with the girls, exclaiming, "Wha's Up? They call me Funee from Bonnie Brae!" We promised to come back and chat with him after helping Red and Billie for the next few hours.

We trudged up the stairs to the third floor and found the two of them in the smoke-filled room. They had managed to pack some of their things into boxes so Doug and I began hauling them downstairs (the elevator was once again out of order) and loading them into the small confines of the trunk of my car (which doubled as our moving van since the truck was not available until the next day). It was quickly filled to overflowing and the four of us piled in and drove the few blocks to their new abode. Enroute Billie commented on how much "nicer and safer" their new location would be. She continued, "The people there really want to change and help make something of themselves. Not that I'm against any kind of people you know, but some people just don't care or even try." We did discover the place to be a definite step up from the Post. Their room actually had a small kitchen as well as a walk-in closet and bathroom, making it a veritable mansion in contrast to where they had been! We unloaded their goods and returned with a second trunk full, leaving only the larger items which exceeded the capacity of my "moving van."

Henry was not around but apparently had agreed to let us use the truck the next morning to transport those items. I promised Red that I would return and had high hopes of bringing another student along with me as well

157

as finishing my conversation with Henry. Red mentioned that an elderly woman on the fifth floor, named Martha, had wanted us to stop by her apartment before we left. I had a sneaking suspicion that she had gotten wind of the service we had provided for Red and Billie and was desirous of the same. We knocked on her door and as she let us in we learned that was exactly what she had in mind. She wanted out of the building as well, and Doug and I laughed about how we had quickly become the Biola moving crew! She wanted to move in a couple of weeks and was eyeing the room next door to the one now occupied by Red and Billie. I graciously explained that we just did not have the time, manpower, or transportation to assist her. I encouraged her to inquire with Henry about the use of his truck which he was providing for Red the next morning. She said she would do so and then proceeded to talk non-stop for the next half hour, giving us the condensed version of her life history.

Martha is 60 years old and has had muscular dystrophy for the past 25 years. As a result she has to be hooked up to an I.V. 12 hours a day and have her blood drawn every two weeks. But she said that the nursing attendants were too fearful of entering the building any longer so she was forced to take a taxi to the hospital to receive her treatment. Apparently one of the nurses was robbed during a recent visit which put an end to their in-home service. She shared about twice being widowed, her first husband killed by a drunk driver. She moved to California from the Midwest to escape the memories of his loss but soon after contracted the illness. She had spent the past three years living in fear in the Post, locked away in her room in virtual isolation.

Martha commented with disgust on the persistent presence of gang members, drug addicts and prostitutes in the building. She spoke of the constant fighting and screaming in the hallways at night and of people being shot. She also expressed her sadness over how many children ran around unattended and how many were abused and neglected. She cited one example of a father who would lock the younger children out of the room so he could have sex with his older daughter. She had tried to intervene in one instance where she observed an 11-year-old girl being seduced by a 25-year-old man. She warned the child who later returned with her mother and hit Martha repeatedly with a trash can lid. She called the police, but no charges were filed. She rambled on and on about her terrible anxiety during the large earthquake last summer when she stood under the door frame pleading, "Dear God, make it stop!" Finally she shared how exciting it was that some "college students" had come to visit her. As we were leaving we commented on how sad it is that so many people exist in such lonely, shut in settings as these S.R.O. hotels.

We spotted Funee on the sidewalk outside of the building and walked over to talk with him for a while. Just weeks before I had done a two-hour interview with him and he had freely shared his story with me. He is a 17-year-old Hispanic who moved from East Los Angeles to Bonnie Brae Avenue when he was two-years old. His earliest memories are of gang life or violent activity in the community. He spoke about the high visibility of drug dealing in the neighborhood ever since he was five or six-years old. He recalled one incident when he was eight and his mother had sent him alone on an errand to the liquor store to get a gallon of milk. He said he was just trying to mind

159

his own business when he overheard two dope dealers arguing over what he described as a "20 (dollars) of chiba (heroin)." Suddenly one stabbed the other twice in the stomach, and Funee cried out to the man at the counter, "Call the ambulance, a 'Vato' (homeboy in the "barrio" or neighborhood) got stabbed!

Before his 11th birthday he and his friends had officially formed their gang. They picked the term "Criminals" because they would "shoot or stab people who mess with them" and Bonnie Brae, of course, was their street. However he did say that their "territory" actually extended from Wilshire to Olympic and Westlake to Beacon. They began "mostly with tagging," writing BBC all over the walls of their turf to announce their presence in the area. Soon however they bought a .25-caliber automatic pistol from some drug dealers who sold it to them for $55. Everyone pitched in a few dollars to get it. Little by little their arsenal increased and drive-by shootings became an integral part of their activities. He spoke with no remorse of how many rivals were hurt and killed in the process, some by his own doing.

There are two "cliques" or groupings of the BBC and his has seventy-five members. I inquired as to why he was chosen to lead them, and he explained it was because he was "the oldest and knows what's up with everything." He also said it was due to the fact that "people always come to talk to me about their problems." They "jump in" new members, upon the request of the would-be initiate. Three of those already in the gang then beat up (punch) that individual for seven seconds. He is allowed to fight back, but if he can't take the beating he is then "jumped out" for seven more seconds.

I listened with intrigue as he described the hierarchical nature of the gang's infrastructure. Funee and four others comprise the upper echelon of the gang's "brain trust." His fellow "officers' are Negro, Cholo, Boxer, and Dundee. They are each responsible for the supervision of 15 other gang members, "to see if they have problems," I was told. This management group meets together weekly to discuss any "problems" which have been brought to their attention by their subordinates. Taking action on these matters generally consists of planning and ultimately implementing "paybacks" against rival gangs, something Funee said they simply "must do." The entire gang gets together every third Friday night to discuss issues of concern to the whole group, and weekend evenings generally provide the opportunity for more informal "social" get togethers.

Toward the end of our interview he confessed being "upset with himself" and "ashamed" that he's a gang member. He acknowledge that it was "stupid to join a gang" and that "gangs are bulls__." He continued to say that by choosing gang life, "you're showing your guts to your homies. You don't have to do it, but you're pressured if you don't." He admitted that he "needs to get away from his problems," but he feels that "he'll never get out of the hood." Most of his time is spent "claiming the barrio," morning, afternoon, and night. He defined that to mean defending or guarding it against intruders, stating that "he would shoot any other rivals who come by." He explained that "if rivals don't see anybody (standing guard), they aren't afraid and might come in and kick it (hang out) and cross them out." That is the ultimate insult to a gang, writing their own logo over top of another and "dissen" them (showing disrespect). He bragged that he had not been shot "yet" while at his post because he's "quick" and "always watching" whenever a car drives by and a "gun sticks out the window."

As I thanked Funee Man for his openness with me that day, we had laughed over our attempt to shake hands, mine the traditional approach, and his much more extensive and a unique reflection of his "hood." He showed me the official BBC handshake and smiled at my awkwardness in seeking to master the various stages of clasping hands, wrist, and forming the letters BBC with my fingers. Now, with Doug, I did my best to recall that greeting, much to Funee's delight. He immediately began to speak of how "wild" it had been on the street on Saturday night, how they had been drinking and that "lots of Vatos" were mingling about. Doug and I had seen broken glass everywhere as we arrived that day, a testament to their "good time" over the weekend. He explained that there had also been some shootings and they had retaliated with a couple drive-bys of their own.

He then looked at Doug and launched into somewhat of a "machismo," tough guy act. He addressed himself and all his homies as "crazy a__Vatos," and admitted that "gangs are f___ up." But he emphasized how deeply committed they are to it, so much so that they would actually die for it! He spoke of how they "will go down claiming the barrio" and then struck a pose with his head back, chest puffed out proudly, and BBC formed distinctly on the fingers of both hands. The one rule they live (and die) by is that "you must always be true to the barrio." Before we could say anything by way of response, Funee told Doug that he trusted him because he trusted me and would allow me to "hang out" with them because I was "a good guy." But then he continued, very seriously, to say that he (Doug) could never break that trust or "it would be trouble" and they "would be after him." He then stated emphatically that "no one could ever betray them to another gang."

He illustrated his bravado and loyalty by recounting that BBC had done a drive-by shooting the weekend before, the same night that one of the Orphans, who are their rivals, was shot and killed. The police then brought over another member of the Orphans that same evening to Funee's neighborhood. He spoke with disdain about how "the cops'" would-be "informant," when faced with the presence of "the enemy," denied that BBC was responsible. It was the young man's fear and intimidation toward BBC which was particularly galling to Funee. He stressed that "you always have to be true to your gang and never back down to another, even if that means dying for it." As he spoke I found myself wondering how I could interject Christ into such a world view. I felt though that my relationship with him warranted that I at least give it a try.

I commended him for such strong loyalty and commitment to a lifestyle that he so strongly believed in. But I responded that there were greater and far more eternal things to "claim" and give your life to beyond the barrio, which was found in allegiance to Jesus Christ. I spoke of how He wanted such sacrifice and longed for fearless "soldiers" to join his "army" and fight against His great "rival," the devil, who already had laid claim to Funee and his homies. He listened attentively as I spoke, and I sensed an openness on his part that belied such a tough exterior. He simply replied that he "hoped to get out" of the gang eventually and to "settle down" somewhere else.

We bid farewell to Funee, climbed into my car and had turned the corner onto 7th when we passed by Green Eyes. He was at the intersection of Westlake, wearing a big, floppy white hat and carrying a bag full of clothes which he was trying to sell. We pulled over to the curb and he hopped in, grateful to see us, and in need of a ride to Moses' office just down the street. We were glad to oblige and equally thankful for the opportunity to gain his perspective on our little chat with Funee Man!

We asked Green Eyes about the violent nature of gang activity and the incredible loyalty to his clique which Funee had expressed, even to the point of giving his life for it. Green Eyes, hailing back to his earlier experiences with gangs while growing up, commented that along with acceptance into the gang comes "responsibility." He continued, "cliques have laws that if you don't do it then it's done to you." You cannot simply "walk away" from someone who "disses you," or your homeboys, because "your people don't let you walk away." But if you have a "piece of metal" (a gun) on you "it makes you feel strong, like superman. So why walk away from danger if you have something to solve it with?"

Seeing that we were working hard to process it all, our "teacher" sought to further enlighten his "students" in the psychology of "gang banging." He spoke of how, in the gang, "everybody had guns," that you simply "got to have one." He explained that it's all "part of having a reputation." He stated that it was "like putting on a shirt or a coat," carrying a gun was a "part of your dress, period."

His further comments provided more insight into the gang mentality:

You have to understand the state of mind of a 15-year-old. Bein' in a gang and doin' drive-by shootings gives recognition and respect. Those [who are] gang bangin' and drive-by shootin' and patrolin' this avenue and hangin' out are not more than 19, they're 14 and 15 [years old]. They're stayin' up all night and partyin' in the hotel room and in the hallway, and they're 15, 16, 17 [years old]...[Funee Man] isn't more than 17.

As we made our way back to Biola, Doug was really challenged by what he had seen and with those whom he had met. He recapped our morning as being "very good" for him and claimed, "I've never seen anything like it!" He had a pad of paper in hand as we drove and was hastily making notes of our experiences. He spoke of being such a "rookie" when it came to understanding the city and its people and thanked me sincerely for bringing him along. He asked if I ever felt "burned out" by working with "these people" and we talked about the demands they often put on you and of their intense need. I mentioned the priority of prayer and accountability as well as team-oriented ministry, all of which are practiced by Cambria as a local example.

Doug was enamored with Funee's assurance of his trust simply because he trusted me. He commented that Funee seemed to view trust as "a commodity to be dished out." He referred to Funee's incredible, though extremely misdirected, willingness to die for the barrio and we pondered the sobering realization that it may require such as us to give of our lives sacrificially to reach those like him who are so entrenched in that lifestyle. But Doug honestly and openly acknowledged that he was struggling with "kingdom values" and God's call on his life. He sensed God leading him toward missions but likened himself to Moses in his puzzlement over why God had chosen to call him for the task! He stated his desire for a relationship with a girl and yet admitted that so few share his calling to ministry. He asked about how my wife and I had met and I recapped how both of us had sensed God's calling and burden for the city while we were single, prior to God bringing us together in marriage. I emphasized the priority of deeply cultivating his walk with God and trusting Him to divinely orchestrate the choice of his life partner.

Those were hard words for Doug and his voice choked as he related how he knew that God was asking him to "put his all on the altar" in the area of relationships as well as his vocational dreams (engineering) and interest in material things. But he determinedly repeated the phrase that if the Christian life is worth living it is worth living 100%. I really encouraged Doug to press on knowing that God would honor him, fulfill his desires, and make his plan for his life evident in His time (Matt. 6:33). As we pulled into the Biola parking lot we prayed together and committed his future into God's hands once again. I drove home extremely grateful to God for that experience with Doug, which was arguably one of the highlights of the semester for me as far as personally interacting with the students is concerned. It was a delightful privilege to be a part of that tender-hearted young man's spiritual journey and I knew that God had allowed us an invaluable moment together.

Significant Observations:

Mentoring - Ministry issues are a significant part of the students' journey in experiential learning. But mentoring is a holistic endeavor which incorporates their "spiritual journey" as well. That role includes guidance in the area of relationships, vocation, and the broader arena of "kingdom values" and God's calling on their lives.

Ministering - Countless elderly men and women exist in slum-like SRO hotels, locked away in virtual isolation. Many are starved for conversation and relationships, presenting a strategic opportunity for the church to channel its outreach efforts.

- Most organized gangs function according to set rules and "ethics," to which one must be wholly committed and loyal, even to the point of death. This is a powerful analogy to Christianity and should be a part of the message we share with gang members. To do so, however, we first must earn their trust.

DODGING BLOWS WITH ROB

Rob was free to accompany me the next morning to finish moving Red and Billie. He also had to be back on campus by the noon hour and I picked him up at 7:30 as well. Traffic was horrendous and it took us an hour to get downtown. But it did allow for fruitful interaction with Rob as we talked of smog and congested traffic as a very real part of the city. He commented how he so much preferred the trees and the mountains but that he was growing in his appreciation for the city and its people. This led to a discussion of the ultimate motivation for urban ministry being the Word of God as it reveals His heart for "the widow, the orphan, the stranger and the poor." Many of those scriptures were unfamiliar to Rob and I encouraged him to investigate them as well as to take notice of the numerous biblical references to the word "city."

As we drew near Bonnie Brae, Rob observed the proliferation of graffiti, in particular the BBC tagging, which seemed to be scrawled on every

167

unclaimed surface. I could sense that he was intrigued by the gang subculture as he recalled our involvement in 18th Street territory the previous week with V.O., commenting, "It really got me thinking." I hoped, for Rob's sake, that Funee Man would be out that morning, and was excited to see that he was as we pulled up to the curb in front of the Post. He greeted Rob with "Wha's up, Homes!" as we shook hands, but because Red was peering down impatiently upon us from the second floor balcony we were unable to talk with Funee. We told him that we would be free in a couple of hours, but by that time he was no longer around (much to Rob's disappointment).

Even though the truck had not yet arrived, Red Dog was raring to go and called down to us to wait for him by the car. He joined us momentarily, made Rob's acquaintance, and we drove over to their new apartment where the truck was parked in the lot. In order to use it we first had to empty it and then drove it and my car back to the hotel. Billie was waiting in the room for us and greeted Rob cordially. He and I hoisted up their rusty, grimy, roach-infested stove and hauled it toward the elevator, which we were pleasantly surprised to find in working order. We propped open the door and made several trips until it was packed full with a dirty, ripped love-seat, a small, badly scratched table, a chair with a broken leg, an old dresser and a tiny night stand. We managed to squeeze ourselves inside and shut the door, all the while clinging to the belief that we would not be forced to spend the rest of our lives inside. We pushed the button and it actually began to descend, much to our relief!

Rob insightfully noted that most all of Red and Billie's prized possessions would be classified as "junk" by the average middle class

American and donated to Good Will! We were reminded that "one man's junk is another man's treasure," particularly when you've spent a great deal of your life under a bridge! Those "treasures" filled up the truck and we made other trips for smaller items which we piled into the trunk of my car until the room was empty. We transferred their belongings into their new residence and they acknowledged that they were thrilled to be there and grateful for our help.

Rob found himself "at a loss for words" after we met Henry, the Mexican-American landlord, in the hallway as we were leaving. He immediately launched into his war stories and once again Rob was dumbfounded at his claim that "human life has no value to me" and that "it was a pleasure to kill people." Referring to our conversation on the phone a couple days earlier, I asked if he would talk about his background. He proceeded to relate a tragic tale of abuse, gang violence and drug usage. His parents were killed in a car accident on his fourth birthday when they were hit by a drunk driver. He spent the next decade in a Catholic orphanage where he was repeatedly abused both physically and sexually by the nuns. He graphically recalled how one in particular would "lift up her dress and push my face between her legs." He claimed that he "became an atheist" as a seven-year-old because no one responded to his prayers for protection or deliverance from his abusers. He ran away at the age of 13 and ended up in California. He soon was caught up in gang activity, brought before a judge, and opted for military service in lieu of California Youth Authority. He proudly dubbed himself "a h___ of a good soldier" and seemed to relish the opportunity as a means to get back at all those who had so cruelly taken

169

advantage of him. After numerous "successful tours" he returned to Los Angeles and got involved in the garment industry. But his health began to rapidly deteriorate, including several strokes and a heart condition which left his right side partially paralyzed. Medical bills piled up and he wound up heavily drug-dependent and on skid row for nearly a year. He was finally able to get into apartment management, with which he has now been occupied for the past several years. As we were leaving Rob commented, "I've never met anyone else like him!" I had to agree.

As with Doug, I drove Rob around the neighborhood for a while to show him the sights. He was enamored by the persistent calls of "Wetto" (White boy) which were addressed to us by the numerous and flagrant Hispanic drug dealers along Alvarado. We went through 18th Street territory and were surprised to see a number of the guys congregating on the sidewalk. On our way back to the Post to try and find Green Eyes, we had an interesting encounter in the middle of 7th Street. A homeless man, wearing a hooded sweatshirt, was stumbling across the street in a drunken stupor. We slowed the car to a mere crawl to allow him to cross in front of us when he suddenly lunged toward my open window and tried to hit me. The punch came nowhere close to landing and we drove on by, but it certainly startled both of us! We laughed about how we had each flinched and Rob had even ducked out of the way! He shook his head and exclaimed, "I still can't believe he took a swing at you!"

We found Green Eyes in Kermit's room on the fifth floor. On the way up we met the new landlord who, in place of Martin, had been given the responsibility by the courts of turning around the facility. He was obviously not in the least bit enamored by his job as he barely acknowledged our presence and could care less about our activities and relationships with those in the building.

Green Eyes was glad to see Rob and grateful for the food I had brought him. He suggested that we go outside and have a picnic at nearby MacArthur Park where we could sit and chat for a while. This turned out to be a highlight of the semester for Rob. We picked out a spot under a tree and I bought a few sodas from a Hispanic vendor across the street. While Green Eyes munched away on his lunch we watched the world go by, interpreted for us by our street-wise "translator" (a term Rob later used to describe him).

We sat facing Alvarado and Green Eyes pointed out young Hispanic girls who were "boostin'" sweaters (which he explained as stealing them from local stores and selling them for less on the street). He then exclaimed, "See that Black guy, how fast he walks? He doesn't live here! If he did he'd be walkin' slower and enjoyin' the area. He's in a hurry, on business." Rob was fascinated! A nicely dressed Hispanic man walked by and he identified him as a "big drug dealer." Rob really took notice when Green Eyes focused our attention on what we thought was a woman passerby, but who was in reality, according to our "translator," a transvestite. He calmly described how "she" was really a "he", dressed in "drag" (women's clothing, including heels). We had seen several others in skid row while ministering with Victory Outreach, but Green Eyes proceeded to enlighten us with inside information as to the tell-tale sign of whether or not one was witnessing a male or female! He instructed us to take special notice of the Adam's apple, claiming that "what God gave them they can't change."

171

Green Eyes then recalled that he had just received a letter from Tanya (the one whom I had "covenanted with my eyes" against) which he thought I would be interested to read. As he pulled the crumpled correspondence out of his pocket he informed me that she had been jailed for prostitution toward the end of the summer. She wrote that she would be getting out in the fall, but had no place to go, and asked if he could help her with food and clothing. She mentioned that she knew many other prostitutes in jail, and even listed their names, familiar to Green Eyes but not to me at that time. Then she matter-of-factly related how she would "turn tricks again" after her release, "because she needed the money." Green Eyes commented that she generally made $300 a night, due in part to her attractiveness, but also to the fact that she, unlike most that I had met, was not a drug addict. But the note ended with the tragic admission that "men only want me for my p__ or my money, not for myself as a person."

Rob's "real" class back at Biola was quickly approaching, so we had to put an end to this "extension course" conducted by "Professor" Green Eyes! He wanted to sell a few clothes so we dropped him off on Alvarado and went on our way. Rob was bubbling over with enthusiasm for all that he was learning about gangs and homelessness from our experiences that day and the week before with V.O. He commented on how street-wise Green Eyes is and how he himself was so naive. He admitted that he didn't "see things the way Green Eyes did," meaning that he was oblivious to so much of what went on around us. But he was encouraged by the fact that his own eyes had been opened to "lots of issues" and he was eager for his next opportunity to learn more.

Rob was especially intrigued by the way Green Eyes had managed to "turn the tables" on him. When I had run across the street to get the sodas Green Eyes had asked him why he had come. Caught quite off guard, Rob had replied, "To learn, I guess!" He realized how Green Eyes really had taken the role of his teacher and of how dependent he (the "educated" one) had been on him to make sense of what we had seen. He wondered how long it would take before he or anyone else would be able to understand and reach the people in that community. I commented that Cambria had been in the area for over five years and they were still building relationships and struggling with lives that seemed resistant to change. We acknowledged the limitations of a semester project, especially our commuter approach to doing so, admitting that urban ministry is ultimately a test of endurance that warrants faithful persistence regardless of the obstacles.

Significant Observations:

Mentoring - One of the greatest contributions of a mentor is to point the student toward the Word of God as it speaks to His concern for the city and the disenfranchised. This lays the foundation from which the students' motivation for and perseverance in urban ministry is ultimately derived and maintained.

Ministering - In order to really "see" the needs of the city and become effective in urban ministry, one should seek out the assistance of a street-wise "translator."

UNDER THE BRIDGES WITH JULIE AND SUSAN

Two of the undergraduate females in the group, Julie and Susan, had a class every Tuesday night preventing them from participating with us at Union and First E. Free. As an alternative, they both were interested in spending time with women who had been on the street. I asked Billie if she would oblige and as it turned out, with Martha living in the apartment beside her, the girls were able to develop a relationship with both of them over the duration of the semester. I arranged to take the girls downtown to meet with Billie initially on a Saturday morning. On the way I recounted a bit of her life and experiences under the bridge for them.

Red and Billie had been drinking quite heavily before we arrived and were both in very good spirits. In fact, in the hour or so that we were in their apartment, I counted five beers that Red alone drank. There were also three empty cans on the table when we walked in. They found a place for us on the couch and offered us each a soda, which they had picked up for just such an occasion. We had to smile when Red announced that he had done a little baking for us as well. Some jalapeno corn bread no less! But our smiles quickly faded upon first tasting that concoction. It was incredibly hot and we needed every drop of our sodas to choke it down.

I asked Red and Billie to describe for the girls their "home" under the bridge. Red had previously bragged to me of how their "showcase" dwelling had attracted coverage, complete with a photograph, in the May 16, 1988 issue of *Insight Magazine!* He proudly recalled their site for us:

> I had my camp set up just like an apartment! I had wall to wall carpet.
> I had a T.V. and a refrigerator, run off a car battery. Powered them by
> getting a generator and hooking it up to the refrigerator, then ran a wire

from the generator to the car batteries to recharge them. Even used it to run a little plug-in cigarette lighter.

Billie expounded in great detail on some of the feminine touches she gave to their elaborate bridge dwelling. She mentioned a grandfather clock which Red had found and fixed and she had hung up on the back wall, complete with a chime! She spoke of "cleanin' my house and sweepin' the rugs every mornin'," and of a certain spot in the back of the bridge called "the hole" where they stored their wood on a skid. She described how they actually made walls under the bridge to separate the various "rooms!" Red would find sheets of plywood which they would stand on their side and wedge between the ground and the bridge "ceiling." She explained, "So when we had a fire in our kitchen we had our wall so smoke didn't go on our bed!" In addition to their "kitchen" and "bedroom" they also had a "washroom" where she did their dishes and laundry and a "living room" with a couch "where guests come and stay." Red ingeniously, if not illegally, managed to hook up a hose onto one of the sprinklers set up by Cal Trans on the side of the bridge. This provided a consistent supply of cold water at regular intervals and did away with having to lug jugs of water up and down. Red also dug stair steps into the side of the hill to make the ascent an easier one.

Billie then blurted out in frustration how the state had just cut back her monthly pay check. This hit a sore spot with Red, and he chimed in about how his S.S.I. had also been reduced. He continued, visibly upset, in what was somewhat of a tirade against the perceived injustice of it all. Red concluded his little diatribe with quite a succinct and sobering challenge to the three of us:

I just been back in the hospital with more strokes and stuff but they said they still have to cut me back...So what d'ya think people gotta do? People gotta live on the g__ d__ street if they keep f___ with their g d__ money like that! I qualify for that g__ d_ money! Why can't I get it? And you think I don't have anger built up? You think that's right? Now what d'ya think we're on the street for? You college kids that are comin' up. Look what they're doin' to us now! I hope to h__ you can do somethin' about it! I may not live to see it, but I hope you can help the people behind you.

I had hoped that Red would be willing to take us for a quick trip under the bridge because both Julie and Susan had been unable to participate in our Thanksgiving celebration with the guys. Red enthusiastically agreed to do so. In fact, he was honored to show the girls his old stomping grounds! Julie and Susan arranged to come back and see Billie (as well as Martha) in the weeks ahead and we all climbed into my car (except for Billie, who did not indicate even the slightest bit of interest in joining us).

We drove away from their apartment and Red bragged once again, "I can show you parts of this town that would blow your mind!" We passed a large dumpster and he revealed that just the day before he had found "14 fish patties, 20 hamburgers and a bunch of McNuggets" in the dumpster behind McDonalds! I glanced over my shoulder and grinned at the girls in the back seat. Their faces registered looks somewhere between amazement and amusement!

As we neared the bridges, the girls commented on the numerous panhandlers along the freeway off-ramps. Red then revealed three categories of panhandlers, who he labeled as the sitters, the walkers, and the ramblers! The sitters do just that, they sit with their hand out at their accustomed spot each day. The walkers are a bit more mobile and generally patrol a certain street or sidewalk, or even an intersection. Finally, the ramblers "go all over the place" seeking handouts.

Table 2

A Taxonomy of Panhandlers

Category	Description
Sitters	Confined to a specific locale - i.e. storefront, freeway off-ramp
Walkers	Patrol a certain street, sidewalk or intersection
Ramblers	Wander at random seeking handouts

We parked under the overpass and began the ascent to the bridge. Big Jed saw us coming, and he and Red exchanged derogatory greetings from afar. Lefty was also lounging on his bunk and Red boasted to the girls that he had known these guys for years. Jed mentioned that he had just gotten over a bout with pneumonia but nonetheless he and Lefty each had a beer in hand. Despite all that Red had drunk earlier that morning he talked Lefty into giving him a deep drag from his bottle. He looked our way and commented, "See, on the street we share." Red then told of his own recent ailments and hospital stays, stating that his latest stroke resulted in his left leg being "all f___ up" and forced him to use a cane. But he also managed to brag a little about his "big kitchen and everything" in their new apartment.

Conversation ensued about "the good old days" under the bridge and the many others who had shared those experiences with them. Mechanic,

Moustache Moe and Mexican Jose were mentioned among others. Tiger, their cat, sauntered by and they joked about how he was more afraid of rats than they were of him! Lefty started to tease the girls about how big the rats were and even claimed that one had recently bitten him. "They're hungry and they'll bite ya!" he warned with a chuckle. They all nodded their heads in agreement. The guys then instructed us on the proper etiquette to be used the next time we came by. Red revealed, "You don't just walk into a man's camp, you got to give them warning first!" He illustrated his point for us by calling out, "Yo, enterin' camp!" or "Yo, comin' in ta camp!" Lefty then affirmed, "Yea, Comin' in!" [Although this sounded most impressive and so very official I found that I never needed to use it on any of my return visits!]

Red took one last, long swig out of Big Jed's bottle and we were on our way. Back in the car once again he launched into his peculiar political positions and we had all we could do to contain our laughter this time. He emphasized his democratic affiliation, because "the republicans say, 'To hell with the g__ d___ poor man!'" But Red lamented the fact that he couldn't vote because he had been in prison. His next statement however is where Julie in particular nearly lost it! He exclaimed, "The republicans put all the democrats in prison and then they can't vote for eight years!" "So that's their strategy!" I replied with a grin, winking over my shoulder at the girls. "Yep," he answered, "that gives the republicans eight years freedom!"

We drove by the Performing Arts Center, which was only a couple blocks from the bridge. The girls both commented that they had just recently seen a play there and were amazed at the contrast between the two entirely different worlds. "It's the difference between daylight and dark," Red confirmed authoritatively! We also crossed Hope Street, mentioning that it was the former location of Biola a generation ago. We found ourselves pondering whether these bridges had provided a home for the homeless back then and wondered if our response to them would have been any different had we lived only blocks away. The girls were a bit intimidated by the constant calls of "Wetto!" as we drove from 3rd to 6th along Burlington. "18th Street country," Red announced. "Any White person come down the street here you're gonna have that all the time. They're tryin' to sell ya a rock. That's why I never walk the street here. They'll kill ya in a heartbeat!"

We dropped off Red and the girls thanked him sincerely for opening up his fascinating world to them. As we returned to Biola they were amazed at all they had seen and the diversity of so many lives. They mentioned how friendly and personable everyone was to them, so unlike the stereotypes they had previously held about the homeless. They commented on their unique street names and their hearts went out to their tragic stories. Billie especially was on their mind and they were eager to develop more of a relationship with her.

We also discussed and reflected upon a categorization of the homeless which Red had spontaneously shared with us as we were driving from the bridges through skid row and back to his apartment. As we contemplated his unintentional "taxonomy," we found it to be quite accurate and very useful in understanding the world of homeless people.

He had lumped them into four basic groups, distinguished primarily by location: bridge people, bush people, street people and highway people. We had already met several who fell into the first two categories and Red defined the last one to include the traditional hobo or tramp, always on the move, hitchhiking or riding the rails from one city and its missions to the next. The third classification, although extremely broad and arguably overlapping, is illustrated by Green Eyes and his choosing to literally live on the streets (i.e. cardboard box, abandoned car, tent in the alley, etc.) Green Eyes himself had further broken down this category for us when he had spoken to the students earlier in the semester. He had mentioned two additional clusters, set apart moreso by lifestyle, namely skid row and the drug culture.

Skid row, in his terminology, includes those who frequent the missions and remain in a somewhat passive and transfixed state, anesthetized primarily by alcohol. As he put it, "They're stayin' in themselves by drinkin' and just bein' content and die." Panhandling is their primary source of income. The drug culture, of which Green Eyes by his own admission is a part, consists of those addicted primarily to cocaine and heroin. These individuals however are generally more desperate in their efforts to obtain their next "hit," even at times preying off of each other. Such activities include prostitution, dealing, robbery, gang affiliation and a variety of "creative" sources of income (most of which are illegal).

Table 3

A Taxonomy of the Homeless

Category	Representative	Descriptions
Bridge People	Red Dog, Billie, Big Jed, Lefty	Live under freeway overpasses
Bush People	Beached Whale, Lenny, Dirty Jake	Live in clusters of bushes near freeways
Street People	Green Eyes, et al.	Live in boxes, alleys, abandoned cars, sidewalks
-Skid Row		- frequent the missions, alcohol dependent
-Drug Culture		- cocaine and heroin addicts; often resort to prostitution, dealing, robbery
Highway People	N/A	Traditional "hobo," hitchhiking or riding the rails from city to city.

Significant Observations:

Mentoring - Walking with and coaching the students in face-to-face encounters with the homeless helps dispel their stereotypes, diminish their fears, awaken their concern, and build confidence in their abilities to continue reaching out to the poor.

Ministering - Receiving gifts from the poor deepens their respect for us and cultivates a reciprocal relationship rather than one that is paternalistic and condescending.

- Homeless men and women take pride in their ability to survive on the street and are honored by our interest in their lives.

- Many of those who are veterans of life on the street have a great deal to teach us about their world. They possess keen insight into its inner-workings and we do well to draw from their experience.

LOS ANGELES MISSION WITH BRENDA AND SANDRA

Toward the end of the semester I had one additional opportunity to accompany Brenda and Sandra on their initial trip to the Los Angeles Mission. Regretfully, it was not until we were well into the project that I learned of its unique and extensive rehabilitation program for homeless women. It was brought to my attention, of all things, by a fund-raising appeal which I received from them in the mail shortly before Thanksgiving. It proved to be very timely for Brenda and Sandra in particular, who were anxious to establish personal contact with women who had been on the street. I passed on the information to the girls and they set up an appointment.

I drove by the building a few days prior to our visit in order to check it out. I had gathered from the brochure that it was a modern, state-of-the-art facility, but upon first glance it was still a sight to behold. It rose like a palace in the heart of skid row, rimmed by lavish iron gating and consuming nearly half of the block along 5th and Wall. I described the impregnable nature of the facility to the girls as we were enroute and Brenda was actually quite relieved that she would be safe. We recalled our conversation at the beginning of the semester about her fears and she admitted to making progress in that area. But she was still wrestling with a compassionate response to those whose lives were so riddled with the vices of sex, drugs and alcohol.

She found drugs to be particularly loathsome, stating bluntly, "I hate them!" and calling them "a tool of the devil." She blurted out very honestly, "How can one have compassion on people who are so bound? It's like having compassion on the enemy!" I agreed with her that it's very difficult and acknowledged that Victory Outreach among others had shared the same perspective. Satan does have a stronghold in these communities and we alluded to the problem with alcohol and drugs that both Red Dog and Green Eyes have. But we also noted how God had so marvelously released Bernard and Paco and so many others from their addictions and that V.O.'s entire approach was that their truly is victory in Jesus' name to overcome the enemy. We recalled the admonition of Matthew 9:13 to "go and learn compassion," mused on the activities of the Good Samaritan in Luke 10, and reconsidered Jesus' gracious dealings with prostitutes and sinners in John 8.

She admitted that her struggle was due in part to the insecurity she often feels in ministering among the poor. She too was wrestling with her gifting and God's calling in this regard. She acknowledged that the Lord seemed to be drawing her in that direction but was grappling with the ramifications. One of those was a developing relationship with a student in a different major who, she confessed, did not seem to share a desire for missions, to say nothing of involvement with the poor. I sympathized with her plight and encouraged her that she was not alone in her yearning for "the man of her dreams" nor was she the only one in the process of discovering

God's calling on her life. I mentioned similar conversations with some of the other students and reminded her of God's faithfulness and promise "to do exceedingly abundantly beyond all that we ask or think" (Eph. 3:20) as we trust His purposes in our lives.

We rolled into the mission parking lot, past a security guard and were met by a female staff member. She guided us through a maze of doorways until we arrived at the office of Marsha, the founder and director of the women's rehab program. Martha shared her burden of how the needs of homeless women are often overlooked in favor of the needs of men on the street. With that as an impetus she began the ministry five years ago and runs it entirely separate from the men's program in the other end of the building. She identified it as "closed," meaning that the women are unable to come and go at their leisure for an initial six-month time period. This is due in part to her claim that women who have been on the street need much more attention, nurturing, and affirmation than do the men and take longer to recover. She pointed out the differing personality composition of women and men, such as their "nesting " tendencies which require a more "homey" atmosphere. Thus they shy away from the "barracks mentality" of housing and have a very limited capacity. They also provide numerous on-site activities and will occasionally bus the women on outings to parks, concerts, or the beach.

Despite their efforts, however, Marsha related how difficult it is to keep the women from leaving the program. She described the "huge turnover" of losing 50 during the first half of the year. Many simply long for male companionship and go back to staying with men on the street, despite being used and abused. She acknowledged having no choice but to isolate them from men during the early stages of their recovery. The staff discourage romantic relationships during the 18-month program since it "distracts" them from getting their life back together. But the lure of the streets is powerful and literally right outside their windows. Marsha mentioned a case in point where just two weeks earlier they had been forced to dismiss five of the women from the program. The group had tested positive for drugs, which they confessed to obtaining by attaching a sock to a string and lowering it out of the window to the street below!

As we drove back to school we were encouraged by all that Marsha had presented to us and Brenda and Sandra were eager to get to know some of the women on the program. Marsha invited them to be involved on a weekly basis and they chose to make it the primary emphasis of their research for the remainder of the semester.

Significant Observations:

Mentoring - The mentor must help the students continually work through the "sin versus sinner" dichotomy when ministering among individuals who are bound by various addictions.

Ministering - Christ alone can ultimately deliver those who are trapped in destructive lifestyles and can give us the grace to love them despite their shortcomings.

- In seeking to reach and restore women on the street, an approach that is nurturing and affirming seems to be more effective than one that is highly programmatic and impersonal.

CHAPTER 7

"IT'S A MELTIN' POT OF MISERY!":

A NIGHT ON "WHO-STRO"

Green Eyes had been after me for months to spend a night on the streets, to see for myself what really went on so as to gain a deeper understanding of his world. He actually felt that I should spend several nights on the street so as to get the full experience of being tired and hungry and disenfranchised. I had been impressed by Grant's (1986) insights and encounters during his three day plunge into life on the streets of New York City and had desired to do the same here in Los Angeles. The timing never seemed to be right during my coursework, but as dissertation research approached the opportunity presented itself in a more realistic and strategic framework.

MAKING THE ARRANGEMENTS

As the semester began and the project was being initiated with the students, I began to think through the feasibility of taking some of the guys along with me. After a few weeks I bounced it off the group as a whole, and not only did all three of the young men respond with enthusiasm, but one of the female students did also! This caught me a bit by surprise and I was uncomfortable with bringing a woman on the street, so I thought it wise to seek advise from the "streetwise" man himself, Green Eyes. He too felt that it was "asking for trouble," so much to our brave female colleague's disappointment we decided that it would have to be only a "men's night out." Green Eyes was ecstatic at not only my willingness to "finally do it," but that others would be joining us as well.

In giving thought to exactly how much we should focus and structure this evening excursion, I spoke with a friend and former staff member at the Union Rescue Mission. He cautioned us against just launching out impetuously, and suggested we limit our parameters to "safer sections" of skid row in proximity to the missions. He also suggested the possibility of spending an evening "in the chairs" at Union, which accommodate several hundred men every night as somewhat of an "overflow area" when all the beds are taken. He had done that himself during an urban internship while a student at Biola and had found it to be a good opportunity for interaction.

As a foursome we then discussed the options, as well as a specific date, as the midpoint of the semester approached. Finding a time in which all of us were free proved to be quite a challenge however. My schedule was actually the most flexible, while the other three were immersed in a full load of classes and extra-curricular activities. Weekdays therefore were excluded, plus the fact that Green Eyes had told me that the street were often more "alive" on weekends. But even those days were quite congested for the students.

It soon became evident that schedules would only allow us to do one night, and we finally zeroed in on a Sunday evening, after church. Complicating matters still was the fact that midterm exams were scheduled for that same week. One of the guys had a test at 8:00 Monday morning, and another had an exam that afternoon. But since no other date for weeks to come was feasible for the whole group, we chose that night nonetheless.

The group's preference was for as much of a "street experience" as was possible, so we decided against an evening in the chairs at the mission. We also felt that since our stay was now an abbreviated one, we would prefer to spend it on the streets with Green Eyes, following him around, gaining his perspective and getting to know his "acquaintances." The ground rules we set included dressing in old jeans and a sweatshirt or jacket, no food (preferably skip supper) and no money. But we were not to "leave home without " pen and paper and I also brought along my pocket recorder. We were to meet at the school at 7:00 p.m. which would put us downtown shortly before 8:00. That would give us approximately a 12 hour condensed version of street life.

I checked in with Green Eyes a few days before our adventure. At that time he was sleeping on a hunk of foam under a tree on Beacon Avenue and had his shopping cart bulging with women's clothing which he was trying to sell. He said that we were welcome to tag along with him and that he would "introduce us to some of the girls." Little did I know how true that statement would prove to be!

Only a few hours before we were to leave, I received a phone call from Doug. He had hurt his knee in a football game the day before and could hardly walk. He would not be going with us. I was disappointed and wondered whether or not we should postpone the outing. But it had been such an ordeal to schedule it for that night that I thought it best to go out with just the three of us. A few minutes later the phone rang once more. It was Rob asking if he could bring along Nick, who had accompanied us when we went street witnessing with Victory Outreach. I was excited that the Lord had so quickly pushed our numbers back up to four!

Kyle was our fourth member and expectations were high as we piled into my car at Biola and headed downtown. Both he and Rob had crammed all weekend long for their exams the next day. We spoke excitedly and inquisitively of what we would see and experience together. I told them of Green Eyes' enthusiasm as our "host," and that we would be his "shadow" for the night. We spent time in prayer for God to protect us, teach us, and make us a blessing to whomever we would meet. We pulled up to the curb on the corner of 9th Street and Beacon Avenue around 8:15 p.m.

Green Eyes was waiting for us with a broad grin, standing beside his cart. We left anything of value crammed under the seats of the car. I had stashed a few dollars in the glove compartment in case of emergency. We were ready, or so we thought, to experience the streets! Since we had no agenda per se other than hanging out with Green Eyes we chatted with him on the sidewalk for a while. Kyle and Rob he already knew so he introduced himself to Nick, who truly was the "wide-eyed" freshman at this point. Green Eyes showed us his prized possessions in the basket, consisting primarily of clothing articles. I also noticed a large jug of water, a bunch of wooden beads, and a pair of old rubber boots among other odds and ends.

MEETING THE "NEIGHBORS"

He then invited us to go around the corner and meet some of his "friends." We made our way to his spot under the tree along the sidewalk on Beacon, where we were to spend the next several hours. A cluster of girls were about 15 yards down the sidewalk from our vantage point, all prostitutes. The first member of the group he introduced us to was China, a strikingly attractive, young Hispanic woman. Green Eyes had earlier informed me of her identification with the 18th Street gang. Two White girls named Donna and Sparky were a part of the group and Linda was the fourth member of the bunch.

Green Eyes had apparently alerted them in advance to our coming , explaining "He's the one I told you that's writing a book about me." They seemed to regard us with a curious mixture of amusement, indifference and relief. Relieved that we were not necessarily a threat to their "business," and amused at the sight of four naive, young men with note pads, not having the faintest idea of what was going on around them! But they were predominantly indifferent toward us, engrossed in their own little world of activities. A cement wall topped by a chain-link fence ran along the sidewalk behind us, separating us from several old and boarded up Victorian homes that faced the street. We were all just leaning up against that wall, under the scraggly branches of the tree by which Green Eyes had now parked his cart, next to his foam bed. The girls had huddled together on some broken concrete steps which formed a brief break in the wall.

It was still early in the evening and not much was going on, so we thought. I noticed a few cars (including my own which I had moved shortly after we arrived) and an old white van parked along the street. Green Eyes had provided us with a couple of "chairs" consisting of a plastic milk crate and a five-gallon paint bucket. Two of the guys had perched on them and the other simply sat down on the sidewalk. I could hear muffled conversation in both English and Spanish coming from the stairwell, so I mentioned that I was going over to talk to them for awhile. Green Eyes cautioned me against that, however, calmly stating that they were "shooting up" (heroin). This was the first of numerous realizations on our part, throughout the night, of the "street awareness" of our resident guide and instructor! Sensing that "class was in session" and all his students were present, "Professor" Green Eyes appropriately began his lecture for the evening. He spoke of how the streets are "to be feared" and how "they will eat you up" if you aren't careful. He admitted that "the streets are not great, but they are the best teacher."

It was now nearly 9:00 and we faithfully "took notes" while he spoke. But before we had an opportunity to comment on his discussion, the first of many "guest speakers" approached our open classroom. An articulate young Black man named Chauncey just walked up and began talking to us almost on cue! Green Eyes knew him and mentioned that we were students doing research. Chauncey seemed to pick up on that immediately, announcing that he had studied both business and psychology in college. He then launched into a monologue on a wide array of topics.

He emphasized that street people are "human, grown up people, not scum, not dogs." He spoke of how his father, whom he called "the rooster, because he would chase us," taught them rules. He then mentioned that "the street has rules too." He continued, "You have to live in fear out here. It's part of survival. It's best to be scared 'cuz it's the only way to survive." He rambled on about how "some people hate on the street" and that "you have to learn how to confuse [them]." He suddenly brandished a rusty old tire iron which he swung menacingly at us, exclaiming, "Don't you f___ with me!" He then burst out in laughter, as we all looked at each other in bewilderment.

He said that he was on "a mission" that night, and that he was not "drunk or high." That mission is "chasing girls," whom he called "whores," and he claimed to be "as big a whore as them!" Chauncey then mentioned that his livelihood on the street was selling penicillin pills for $2 a piece to the whores. He explained that he had "gotten broke" and ended up on the streets, where he had spent the past four years. He concluded as he sauntered away, "Degrees only prove you can learn. Experience in the world is the real teacher."

As we began to digest the subject matter of Chauncey's presentation, Green Eyes seized the opportunity to further enlighten us regarding creative financial enterprises on the street by showing us his "pipes" that are used to smoke cocaine. They are actually little tubes which he found in the dumpster and sells for $3 each. We were now beginning to understand why the area we were in (particularly around the corner on 9th) had been dubbed "who-stro" (whore stroll). He had somewhat of a sheepish look on his face as he admitted that he also sells condoms to the girls for $1. I knew the guys had a hard time with that and I felt sick about it myself.

"HE'S GOT A GUN!"

Green Eyes then excused himself and shuffled a few yards away to smoke some "rock" in one of his pipes. It was about 9:30 p.m. and we were still trying to process all that we had begun to see and hear, when the sound of an argument among the girls wafted our way. It didn't seem to faze Green

Eyes much, but it did cause a young Black woman who had been walking toward us on the sidewalk to suddenly do an about face and head the other way. I heard her say, "I'm gettin' the f___ outa here!" as she scurried off.

Suddenly, to put it in the vernacular (as everyone else we met that night seemed to do so freely), "all hell broke loose!" We heard the distinct sound of a "slap" and people running everywhere which brought us all to rigid attention (including Green Eyes) and focused our eyes on the fleeing girls. At this point everything seemed to happen in "fast-forward," but yet felt as if it would never end. It wasn't until the dust had settled minutes later that we were able to decipher just exactly what had "gone down."

I had not noticed (but Green Eyes had) two men approach the group as Chauncey was unfolding his story to us. One was a Puerto Rican young man named Jaime, who, according to Green Eyes, is Donna's boyfriend and a member of the 18th Street clique with China. The other was a Cuban drug dealer who generally works the area a few blocks further west on Olympic. It was the Cuban man who slapped China loudly across the face, causing everyone to scatter. The girls ran up the street, all but China who jumped into a parked car and sped away. Across the street a White homeless man named Marty, a friend of Green Eyes, had observed the incident as well. He was carrying a backpack and came charging toward the two men, yelling something about "that's no way to treat a woman!" They in turn had dashed down the street in the other direction to a red pickup truck parked on the curb.

At this point I clearly remember Rob, who was beside me along the wall, leaning over and whispering, "He's going to get a gun!," which seemed to us "about a foot long," as Kyle described it later. Life on the streets had quickly become far more dangerous than we had bargained for! It seemed as if we were watching a movie as we remained paralyzingly transfixed along the wall. We looked imploringly at Green Eyes for direction, but even he was soberly still and pressed up against the wall beside us.

Satisfied that the girls were long gone, the Cuban had run back up the middle of the street and stopped not more than 10 feet in front of us. He glanced our way for what was probably only a second, but seemed an eternity, and all eyes were riveted on that gun (which Green Eyes told us later was a .357-magnum). I remember thinking how we were literally "sitting ducks," witnesses of the whole incident and entirely at his mercy if he so desired to pull the trigger.

But Marty and his crusade on behalf of China had caught up with the Cuban by now, and he turned to face him. As the Cuban waved the gun in Marty's face, I leaned toward Rob and hissed, "He's going to get himself shot!" To complicate matters even further, Jaime had grabbed the backpack from Marty, which incensed him all the more. The Cuban, apparently feeling that he had sufficiently stared down all rivals, began walking back to his car. Jaime tagged along with him and Marty followed, yelling at him to, "Give me back my f__ backpack!" Jaime finally did throw it onto the sidewalk across the street and then he and the Cuban screeched away in the pickup. We were dumbfounded at how quickly those encounters had escalated to the point where anyone of us could easily have been shot!

We all cumulatively exhaled at this point, not really knowing what to say to each other. We had all felt the numbing effects of fear, and Nick in particular said that he was very afraid and suggested that "maybe we should all go home." But before we could even make a decision Marty approached us, having just retrieved his backpack. He was still visibly angry, exclaiming, "it's f__ up to hit a woman." I mentioned that I fully expected him to get shot and Green Eyes simply said that what he had done was "stupid." Marty defended his actions, particularly his persistence to reclaim his backpack, stating "that bag is all I own."

He and Green Eyes then concluded that the Cuban "must be in the same clique or he'd be a dead man by now." (They were referring to the power China supposedly wielded in the gang and thus the potential for retaliation she would have toward him for slapping her.) They both agreed we had not yet seen the end of that conflict, and that the Cuban would probably be back. That was not the kind of news we "researchers" had wanted to hear!

Marty then wandered off, although muttering to himself and obviously shook up. Just then the Black woman who had approached us earlier and immediately retreated down the street as the altercation had begun, came our way once more. Green Eyes knew her and introduced us to Roxie. She was the fifth prostitute which we had met in the last two hours, as it was approaching 10:00. She immediately exclaimed to him, "I didn't want any part of that s__!" which was why she had scurried away as the gun episode had begun. Green Eyes then gave her the details including China's blow to the face which seemed to start the whole thing. Roxie replied, "She (China) had it comin'. She always doin' dirt to people, premeditated s__ and stuff. Now her skeletons are comin' out of the closet!"

THE BEAT GOES ON

Activity on the street was picking up now. As Roxie walked away, after "putting China in her place," we watched a nicely dressed man pass by. He got into a car parked on the curb nearby, drove it across the street, and parked it once more, remaining inside. Puzzled we looked to Green Eyes, who matter-of-factly identified him as a cocaine supplier who has four men working for him 24 hours a day. He also informed us that the man pockets about $4,000 a day for his efforts!

Still somewhat rattled by the earlier confrontation on the street we were eager to gain Green Eyes' perspective. Although not articulated by anyone of us, I think we desperately wanted his affirmation that we were safe with him in our present location. I was also curious as to why he had not intervened on China's behalf, as Marty did, and as I had previously witnessed him do with Linda. He seemed to act as if he was trying to ignore the whole incident, and we asked him why. His comments shed light on the individualistic, "every man for himself" survival ethic of street life. He spoke impersonally, almost curtly to us, as if we should understand his actions without even needing an explanation. He responded, "I watch, but I don't see nothin'. I don't hear. I don't witness nothin'. I have no associations. I'm out here by myself. No one looks out for me." One of the guys asked if we had been "stupid" for just standing frozen along the wall when we realized the danger we were in. Should we have walked or even run away? He replied, "Why should I run? Can't outrun a bullet anyway!" He spoke of how running would have brought more attention to us and would have indicated "that we knew somethin'." What we did was all that we could have done.

It was evident that Nick in particular, and Kyle somewhat as well, were still quite afraid. I began to wonder about my responsibility to the group as a whole. I pictured myself trying to explain to the University that I had "lost a few students" in the process of my research! I hated to admit defeat and "run back home to the suburbs," but maybe this experience was a bit "too realistic?" Even Green Eyes admitted that "things might get worse." What a prophet the man turned out to be, when all of a sudden "things" did! After Marty had left us not more than half an hour ago he had apparently gone across the street to the white van. We had been unable to see from our vantage point, about 50 feet away, that another man was in it, whom Green Eyes later identified as Philip.

As we pondered our next move, Marty and Philip literally tumbled out of the van and onto the street in a flurry of profanity and flying fists. Philip quickly got the upper hand and began violently banging Marty's head on the sidewalk. It was extremely difficult to remain passive this time. It appeared that Philip was totally out of control and that Marty might not walk away as he did from his last skirmish. Just then Philip somehow "got a grip" on his sanity and released his grip on Marty's head, as Kyle and I had begun to walk that way (I don't have a clue what we would've done though when we got there had they still been going at it!) Philip yelled at Marty to "Stop f____ around or I'll really f__ up your life!" Then he climbed back in the van, slammed the door, and drove away with tires squealing.

197

Marty stumbled back toward us in a daze. He told us that he hadn't done anything to provoke Philip, but that Philip was "jealous" of him. Marty and Green Eyes talked for a short while, and it seemed that both were anxious for a "rock." Green Eyes had a few dollars on him and Marty had no money at all. So Marty asked if he could "sell a few pipes" for Green Eyes and come back with some cocaine. Green Eyes was obviously hesitant and untrusting, but nonetheless gave him two pipes to sell. Marty said he'd be back soon.

He left and we asked Green Eyes what he had meant when he said that Philip was "jealous" of him. We were also inquisitive of Philip's "role" in the neighborhood. Green Eyes answered that Marty is what is known on the streets as a "doctor," meaning that he is able to "shoot someone up" with heroin faster than they are able to do so themselves, giving them an even greater high. Philip's van had been functioning as the doctor's "office." Both he and Marty were beneficiaries of a certain amount of what Green Eyes called "kick down" for their services. The girls would "repay" them for heroin, but apparently Philip was envious of the fact that Marty was receiving more than his fair share of "affection" from the girls.

As Green Eyes continued to "school us" in the ways of the street, I noticed the return of a different white van that had driven by us a number of times during the past 2 hours. In response to my request, Green Eyes enlightened us to the fact that it was driven by an undercover cop who routinely drives past "just checkin' things out!" He said that "he's keepin' an eye out on the girls," noticing which ones have been recently released from jail, etc. Just then another car passed us, moving very slowly. Green Eyes recognized the driver as a guy who comes by every night "lookin' for White girls." He explained that he "dates for drugs," and was after "strawberries" (lower class prostitutes who give sex for drugs).

One of the guys thought he saw the red pickup truck drive by a block to the east of us, which snapped us all back to attention and reminded us of the fear we still felt but had tried to ignore. At this point we no longer wanted to return home (it was nearly 11:00), but did have a strong desire to relocate a few blocks away for the time being. Green Eyes was also frustrated that Marty had yet to return with his money, or his "medicine" (cocaine). He began fumbling through his clothes searching desperately for his hoarded funds. It appeared that he was $1 shy of what he had to have to buy his medicine, and apparently a bill had fallen out of his pocket. He actually got down on all fours, crawling around and hunting until he found it several minutes later in a crumpled wad. As we watched with interest we learned the value of money, even very little amounts of it, to people on the street. Green Eyes mentioned how important just $1 or even $.50 was, commenting, "If somebody took it you must take it back. You can't let them do that to you or you'll never survive on the street."

A TRIP TO THE "DRUG STORE"

With enough cash in hand now to buy a rock, Green Eyes suggested that we walk the three blocks with him so that he could get his medicine and we all could get a new lease on life! We heartily concurred and set out with him, laughing as we each pushed his shopping cart and seemingly "took turns being homeless" (not that it was a laughing matter, but it relieved some of the tension we had felt). Green Eyes thoroughly enjoyed the moment , and it must have been quite a sight to passersby viewing four young, White men pushing a basket and tagging along behind a Black homeless man on the who-stro. We headed up Beacon to 8th and went west to the intersection of Westlake. He instructed us to wait for him on that corner while he went down another block to Alvarado and got his medicine, shielding us from the illegal activity. (In the 2 1/2 years that I've known him he has always kept me at arm's length from this aspect of his life).

As we waited we watched what appeared to be a couple of gang members (BBC?) come out of an alley and cross the street. We then noticed with growing interest and some apprehension that we too were being watched by three Hispanic men standing on the other corner directly opposite from us. We figured something was odd when they remained at their post despite the pedestrian signal changing numerous times. Once again we were oblivious to the serious, even life threatening situation in which we were naively standing. We saw Green Eyes heading back our way. He cut diagonally across lanes of traffic and intercepted the men in the middle of the intersection. We overheard him say, "They're okay, they're with me," explaining that we were college students whom he was "teaching" about the streets. That seemed to satisfy them, but they still eyes us sternly as they walked by. We turned to watch them go, and it was then we noticed several others behind us who had been standing at a distance and keeping an eye on us as well.

Some of the guys had also noticed that a car had been circling the block several times and paying close attention to us. As we walked up to Westlake toward 9th, Green Eyes explained that they all had perceived us to be narcs because "you stuck out so bad." We were amazed as he told us that he had even noted people watching us from the apartments above. He then asked us if we had seen "the bulge" in the belly of one of the three men at their "post" across the street from us. None of us understood what he meant, so he calmly informed us that it was a gun! He also referred to those in the car as "hawkers," whose job was basically as a mobile guard unit, on the lookout for suspicious characters like us!

Green Eyes continued to get a kick out of our naiveté and innocence, his helpless and extremely vulnerable pupils! He especially seemed to relish how dependent we were on him and his role as our protector as well as our professor. We were astonished at our ignorance and lack of comprehension to the danger we had just been in once more. He further enlightened us to the fact that we had also been standing in a heavy drug-trafficking area, and the reason we drew so much attention was because they were "protecting their interests." In retrospect their "concern" about us seemed somewhat ironic in that we had not the foggiest notion about what was going on around us!

MIDNIGHT ON WHO-STRO

It was now 11:30 and we were in the heart of "who-stro." We stood on the corner of 9th and Westlake for half an hour and watched several different girls at "work." There was the sixth young woman we had seen so far that night, another Black girl, who paced back and forth along the sidewalk across the street. No one stopped to pick her up while we were watching, although many cars and a few men on foot eyed her lustfully as they passed slowly by.

Green Eyes expounded on the fact that most of the "johns" who "date" the girls are married men and have good jobs. He spoke of how they could "get women anywhere but like the control and mystery of something new." He continued, "Some of them don't even have sex with the girls, they just drive around and talk. There's a lot of lonely men out here."

A rather heavy White woman approached us as he was speaking, number seven in my unofficial tally, dressed in some very short shorts. Green Eyes asked her if she needed clothes. She politely replied, "No thanks!", eyed us alluringly, then walked down to the liquor store on the next corner. Moments later she reappeared, a car stopped to pick her up, and she was on her way. Next appeared a very sickly woman who was in dire need of medical attention. She asked if Green Eyes had any chiba (heroin), he did not (he has never used it), and they chatted for a short while. It was just after midnight, and she was the eighth different girl we had seen thus far.

BACK TO THE SCENE OF THE CRIME

Green Eyes felt it was now "safe" to return to our original location on Beacon, so we steered our cart in that direction. As we neared his "home on foam" he recognized Sparky being let out of a car driven by a girl named Lupe. Since the latter had been rebuffed in her affections by Linda, Green Eyes mentioned that now "she's eyeing Sparky." She filled the ninth spot on my list. There was no sign of China or Donna or Linda anywhere, nor our friends from the islands, much to our relief! Philip's van had returned, however, and was parked in his "reserved space" across the street. I stopped on the sidewalk enroute to jot down some quick observations, when two

Hispanic men pulled up to the curb in their car. Looking at me, they called Green Eyes over and he talked with them briefly through the car window. He came back smiling, informing me that they were selling chiba and thought that I may have been writing down their license number!

Meanwhile, Sparky was talking with another Hispanic man in a car parked only about 15 feet away from our vantage point. Green Eyes clarified that "he wants her to be with him, but she wants to be on the street." She then got out of the vehicle and walked over to Philip's van to replenish her supply of chiba. As she returned, Green Eyes called out, "Hey Sparky, where's my dollar?" She owed him that and more for some clothes he had "sold" her. She angrily replied, "Get it from your four friends!" She then climbed back into the car with her "old man" and drove away. Interestingly enough, that was the only time the whole night that anyone other than Green Eyes actually addressed us to our face at all.

"TRICKS" OF THE TRADE

It was after 1:00 a.m. and we were beginning to get tired, all except Green Eyes, who was still wired from his most recent smoke. Rob and Kyle were dozing off, seated respectively on the milk crate and paint bucket and leaning up against the wall. There was a rare lull on the street, and Nick took the opportunity to ask Green Eyes about his "coke habit." Green Eyes answered that he has been on it since '86 and became hooked after 6 months. He explained that he only uses it as medicine to dull the constant pain that he feels as the result of getting jumped and beaten.

As he spoke Lupe drove by once again, alone in the car this time, "looking for Sparky," Green Eyes commented. He then summarized "the neighborhood" and those who inhabit it in a very cogent manner:

> You either live in this area, you're lookin' for drugs, or girls, or you're a cop or a narc. No other reasons to come into this neighborhood. Ain't no tourists, that's for sure. It's a meltin' pot of misery. It's an alert when you enter the area, like a red flag, war. People here have to constantly be on the alert, know every car and person and recognize unfamiliar ones. You have to so that you don't get shot, 'cuz shooters are usually strangers.

We were gaining a better understanding of why we were constantly being eyed with suspicion and concern the whole night long. We were intruders, aliens as it were in this subculture where not only "the fittest" survive, but "the alertest" as well.

Having seen Lupe drive by a couple times I was puzzled about her involvement on the street. Green Eyes explained that she is "gay" and part of Gus' "harem" of girls, although she does not "turn tricks." She was "with" Linda for a number of years but is now in pursuit of Sparky. Like the others she is an addict and not only looking for love but drugs as well. He described how she literally tries to intercept Sparky when she returns from a "date" and still has the money and craving for a hit. Lupe then offers to drive her to the "drug man" and receives a portion of a rock for her shuttle service.

The time had crept along to 1:30, or so it felt to me at this point. Kyle was now lying on the sidewalk, Rob leaning up against the tree, and Nick had gone down on one elbow on his side. Our current context reminded me of the letter from Tanya that Green Eyes had let me read and I asked if she was still in jail. He replied disgustedly that within a few days of her release a couple weeks ago she was behind bars once again. He explained that she had returned to "working the streets" and had been picked up for soliciting an undercover officer. He commented on how "stupid" it was on her part, how "good she looked" when she got out of jail, and how "run down" her appearance had become in less than a week back on the street.

About ten minutes later, the tenth "lady of the night" we had seen that evening came our way. I should say rather that she "floated by," as she was "high as a kite" with cocaine pipe in hand. Forty-eight-year-old Gina, was wearing a short, low-cut dress and babbled on about being on the streets for the past 16 years. She had been in that neighborhood the last eight years, and was on her way to see Philip, still across the street in the van. She asked if we wanted a date, and we politely declined her offer.

As we watched her climb into Philip's van I asked Green Eyes what the girls do about venereal disease and AIDS. Many of the ones we had met appeared so "used," worn down and sickly. He responded that was due primarily to their drug addiction, particularly to chiba. Surprisingly he remarked that often "prostitutes are the cleanest, they have to be, 'cuz it's their job." We noticed another White girl now at "work" on the corner of 8th and Beacon, dressed in a pink outfit so "hot" it appeared to glow in the dark! Moments later it had fulfilled its purpose of attracting the attention of a date. She was number 11 on my "prostitute poll."

Lupe pulled up to the curb in her car once again, still frustrated in her search for Sparky. She sported an old baseball cap and had obvious masculine features. She spent the whole night long driving around in circles! We could hardly fathom Green Eyes' next remark. He nonchalantly mentioned that we had "picked the wrong night to see the 'he-she's' (transvestites)!" They apparently "work the who-stro" on Friday and Saturday nights, but do not stay on the streets. Green Eyes matter-of-factly noted that "some of them look better than the girls (I'm not sure what he meant by that comment!) and make more money too!"

A DONUT NEVER TASTED SO GOOD

Two o'clock in the morning had come and gone, and a couple of the guys had roused. I was feeling quite sleepy and we all were hungry and needing to stretch our legs. Green Eyes mentioned the Winchell's on the corner of Olympic and Burlington, and that sounded wonderful to each one of us! So I raided my "emergency" cash stash in the car and we were "on the road again," shopping cart and all!

Enroute Green Eyes pointed out another girl named Emily, the 12th we had seen thus far. Before we had a chance to say even a word to her she had gotten into the car of her next trick. We were all amazed at the amount of passing vehicles at this hour of the night. Less than a block further we crossed paths with Kitty, the 13th member of our group of girls. She was a young and attractive Korean woman who almost appeared out of place by comparison with the others. Green Eyes informed us that she was "high priced and only dates Koreans." He seemed to know everyone out here and most everything about them. I noted that we had met girls from every major ethnic group that evening.

We met Paula in the parking lot, our 14th lady of the night. She was White, probably in her 30's, but her features cried out that they had been hard years. Upon learning why in the world four young White men were with a

Black homeless man in a Winchell's Donut House at 2:30 a.m., she announced that she, too, had "many stories to tell." She regretted that she could not share them with us at that moment (she was in obvious need of a fix), but she knew Green Eyes' "address" on Beacon and said she would be by "to talk" before the morning light. She never showed.

We ordered donuts and large hot chocolates, both of which had never tasted so good. In the process I was both impressed with and challenged by Green Eyes' generosity. Positioned by the door as we were leaving, a Black young man, who had watched us enter, asked if we could spare "just one donut." Of the five of us it was Green Eyes who unhesitatingly gave him one, simply stating, "You never deny a person who's hungry." My mind flashed to Matthew 25, "I was hungry and you gave Me something to eat." I was ashamed that I had hesitated.

Sparky was back again when we returned to Beacon. She of all the girls seemed to be in high demand. Green Eyes affirmed that she was "very popular," but claimed that "she's just slummin' it tonight." Dressed only in jeans as she was that evening, he estimated that she would make only around $150. But when she "dressed up," he exclaimed, "cars line up to use her services" and she brings in $300-400 a night plus "all the drugs she wants." He added though that she easily does $100 of cocaine and heroine a day.

Shortly after 3:00 two guys pulled up to the curb in front of us in a sharp, sleek black car, rolled down the window and bluntly inquired, "Where's the women?" The street was surprisingly lean on that "commodity" at the moment, and so they drove off. Green Eyes dismissed them as "pimpin'." Rob then asked if China and Donna and Sparky had pimps. Green Eyes replied, "The dope man is pimpin' 'em all and he's guaranteed to get his money."

Nick was now asleep on a blanket provided for him by Green Eyes when a young Black man approached us asking for cigarettes. We told him that we didn't smoke, and he asked us what we could possibly be doing out here. We explained our purpose and he eloquently but painfully replied, "You'll never know the deepest agony of the street unless you're addicted to drugs." Having said that he just disappeared into the night. Green Eyes confirmed that young man was an addict, which was the reason he was on the streets. He then summarized that encounter by reiterating how drugs are simply "a way of life for people out here." Minutes later Sparky burst out of her old man's car muttering profanities and headed toward Philip's van. She then began desperately crawling around on her hands and knees in the dirt between the van and the sidewalk. Green Eyes deciphered that "she must be lookin' for her outfit" (heroin syringe and needle), and sure enough we watched her return to the car with one in hand.

Two more Black passersby came our way about 3:30, and noticing our unique and weary little group politely inquired, "How's it goin'?" "Alright, thanks!" we groggily responded, although it seemed like an odd exchange at that hour of the morning! Green Eyes identified that pair as "jackals," due to their common tendency to "jack people up" (rob them). He told us that they probably thought we were narcs, which would explain their politeness anyway. I tucked away "jackals" in my growing glossary of street jargon, right between "hawkers" and "strawberries!"

At this point Kyle announced, "That's it, I'm gonna lie down!" and did so at 3:45. I noticed that as he was retiring Sparky was just getting warmed up again! She and her old man, rejuvenated by the heroin, were becoming extremely "friendly" in the car a mere ten feet away. I also observed another vehicle drive up to the curb across the street and park there. It was driven by a Hispanic man, and Green Eyes predicted that "he's gonna take a hit." Moments later we saw him light his pipe and enjoy his "piece of the rock." He picked this area "because it's a dark street," Green Eyes clarified for us (none of the street lights on Beacon were functioning). Ten minutes later he drove away.

It was 4:00 a.m. and Rob and I were watching and writing and pacing to keep warm and awake in the midst of pestering Green Eyes with questions. Meanwhile he had begun stringing some bead necklaces which he informed me were presents for myself, my wife and my daughter. I recognized them now as from a car seat mat, which I had seen earlier in his basket. At first I was amazed at how wide awake he still was, but then quickly realized that it was the lingering effects of his last dosage of medicine.

LAUNCHING OUT ON OUR OWN

Fighting a losing battle with sleep, and wanting to explore a bit more of the surrounding streets, Rob and I decided to go for a walk around 4:15. It also gave us a chance to reflect a bit on the array of experiences we had faced. We walked a big square up 9th to Bonnie Brae, down to 8th, followed it to Union, then back up 9th and around the corner to Beacon. The whole excursion was very tame and lasted all of 15 minutes. However we commented to each other how much more vulnerable we felt without Green Eyes. We realized the extent to which we had depended on him for our well-being that entire night. Although traffic on the street had subsided a bit, we did hit the intersection of 8th and Union just in time to witness the prostitute in pink, whom we had seen earlier from a distance, arrange a transaction with a trick in a van and drive away.

As we walked we both admitted to feeling a bit overwhelmed by the depth of addiction to both sex and drugs of those we had met that night. In our own strength it seemed almost hopeless to intervene, and we agreed that nothing short of the power of God could effectively break its stronghold on their lives. We were both sobered by the realization that God longs to act powerfully on their behalf through encounters they have with such as us! We returned to find out that Green Eyes had awakened Nick to watch over Kyle shortly after Rob and I had set out on our stroll. Green Eyes had then gone off to a nearby dumpster and come back with an entire bag full of odds 'n ends, including men's shoe polish, women's shoes, and a child's doll house. He was even munching happily on a large carrot he had dug out of the dumpster!

Nick asked Green Eyes if he had any plans to find a job and get off the streets. Green Eyes replied that he liked the fresh air and frequent interaction with all kinds of people that was such a part of street life. He alluded to his years in prison which not only confined him alone to a cell but also took away his freedom to be a part of society. Now he was truly "free" and happy, eating what he wants and sleeping when he wants, with no one to tell him what to do. This said, I noted, as he was finishing off his carrot from the dumpster and soon to go to sleep on a piece of cardboard on the sidewalk!

"NOW I LAY ME DOWN TO SLEEP"

Green Eyes did lie down at about 4:30, so the rest of us decided to do the same. It was noticeably quieter on the street now, the first real break all night long. Rob and Nick shared the foam, while I reclined luxuriously on another piece of cardboard. Kyle was still asleep under a blanket, and I could hear Green Eyes breathing heavily only moments after retiring. His head was propped up against the tree, and his only covering was his short-sleeved shirt.

I on the other hand was cold and uncomfortable despite wearing a jacket! Kyle told me later that he too had been cold even though under a blanket. My cardboard "mattress" did little to cushion me from the hard ground, and in particular, from the protruding roots of the tree. The view from my bedside along the curb was a curious mix of branches above and the right rear wheel of my car not more than two feet from my head! I struggled to get comfortable, surprised at how much the cool breeze managed to creep its way under my jacket, even at ground level. I ended up on my back, with my knees bent and legs leaning against the car.

I don't think I slept more than 20 minutes at a stretch, dozing in and out for the next two hours. Noises seemed amplified from the sidewalk and the street, particularly approaching daybreak. Buses and garbage trucks, cars and voices of passersby caused me to often lift my head and look their direction. I remember glancing at my watch at 5:30 as a shabbily dressed White prostitute stopped to eye us inquisitively and then continue on her

211

way. She took the 15th spot on my list, and I could hardly believe she was still soliciting dates at that hour of the morning.

I watched Rob get up at 6:00, perch on the milk crate and write some notes of our experiences that night. He told me later that he was shocked to see three more women turn tricks in a space of about 20 minutes during that time frame. Finally, around 6:30, the rest of us "dragged ourselves out of bed," which is not all that difficult to do when you're sleeping on cardboard on the sidewalk! "Making one's bed" is also a fairly easy task. Just "pick up your bed and walk!" I remember how sore my hip bone felt, and most of us looked as if we had been run over by a truck! All but Green Eyes that is, who laughed at the way we looked and felt and announced that he had "slept great!" He gave me the bead necklaces he had made and finished before he went to sleep, and we thanked him for what had been a most incredible evening. At that point we were simply grateful to have survived it!

It seemed fitting that as we were about to get into the car, Green Eyes introduced us to the 16th and final girl I counted that night. She was a very pretty Hispanic woman with long black hair, arguably the most attractive of the girls we had met. She said that she was looking for China, who we realized had still not returned to the area. It did serve as a reminder of that entire amazing episode however, the details of which Green Eyes was providing her as we drove away.

DID WE REALLY DO THIS?

Our conversation in the car during the forty-minute ride back to Biola was punctuated by nervous laughter as we recounted the harrowing events of the previous twelve hours. Emotions rode the roller coaster from gratitude and relief for emerging weary yet physically unscathed to amazement bordering on shock for all that we had seen. Of particular concern was how to deal with it all psychologically and spiritually. Furthermore, there was the small matter of having to quickly regroup mentally and become a college student once again in a setting of great contrast from where we had just spent the night! Kyle had his biology exam at 8:00, and Rob had a class at 8:30. Nick was free until 10:30, and the other two kidded him playfully about whether or not he would make it to chapel at 9:30. All three however were eager to share their adventures with their peers.

The overriding experience by far of the entire evening was the gun episode. Their incredulity at how fast it had happened and how helpless and afraid they had felt came tumbling out in a rush. We discussed again how easily we could have been shot and whether we should have run or simply just walked away, as Rob reaffirmed. Nick still could not believe that we hadn't left and returned home immediately. We all acknowledged our thankfulness to the Lord for his protection despite our vulnerability and naiveté.

We laughed at Nick's recounting of Green Eyes waking him and designating him to stand guard over his stuff and a sleeping Kyle while he went "dumpster diving" and Rob and I were out "sight seeing!" He was scared out of his wits to be alone on the streets, at 4:00 a.m., and we all realized it to be another example of God's keeping and our own oversight once again.

Kyle especially was deeply stirred by the lifestyles of those we had observed. He questioned whether or not many of them could ever be untangled from the web of sex and drugs. We recalled the testimonials we had heard the previous weekend from those at Victory Outreach and reflected on our mandate to regard those in need with compassion, as we had been exhorted to do just days earlier by Bernard. We reviewed the truths of Matthew 9:13, Mark 6:34 and Luke 10:37 in light of our experiences and Nick in particular was challenged by their message.

We arrived on campus at 7:15, and Kyle headed straight for the shower with 45 minutes and counting until class. I was home by 7:30 and in bed by 8:00 until shortly after the noon hour. I was at my desk writing and reviewing our collective experiences when the phone rang. It was my professor, anxious to hear of our adventures. As I replayed them for her, in particular the situation with the gun, I was humbled and amazed as she excitedly revealed how the Spirit of God had nudged her to pray specifically for us around 9:30 that night. Her obedience to intercede on our behalf may actually have saved our lives! Furthermore, I learned later that God had also burdened Sandra to pray for us every hour, all night long, until 5:30 a.m.

I too had needed to take inventory of my emotions after that evening. Despite knowing Green Eyes quite well, I was still surprised at how interwoven his life was with the girls in that area involved in prostitution. I was also dismayed at how many we had witnessed, and how heavily drug dependent they were. They all deserved the opportunity of a better life, yet what a pity to see them all throwing it away. The powerful grip of drugs and its devastating consequences was indelibly imprinted upon my mind.

214

I was very proud of the guys and the way they handled the entire evening. Asking questions, taking notes, withholding judgment and seeking to gain insight into the troubled world of the streets by experiencing it personally. My only real regret was that the tightness of their schedules did not allow us to immediately sit down with a cup of coffee and really debrief the events of the night as a whole. In fact, since Nick was not part of the ongoing research of the class that semester, I rarely saw him over the succeeding months, let alone helped to process his reactions.

Several days later, in our next class period, one of the students asked if we could summarize the experience for them. I gave Rob and Kyle the opportunity to do so, eager to hear their renditions myself. Rob gave a general summary of what occurred that night, highlighting the saga of the gun. Another student asked why we did not run, and Rob replied that "it would've shown that we were more than just passive observers and involved in some way" (with what was going on). He explained how Green Eyes had just looked down at the ground and told us that he didn't see or hear anything. Rob then touched on our walk around the block and our discussion of the daunting task of being used of God to help change lives on the street. He was really challenged by that responsibility, concluding "about all that we saw was sin."

Someone else asked if we slept at all, and I looked over at Kyle with a grin and replied, "Some of us more than others!" Rob said he had laid down for an hour or so but then had gotten up to chronicle our experiences. He commented on the fact that cars were stopping and girls were turning tricks even at 6:00 in the morning. He explained that prostitution was a "24-hour

215

business," despite the presence of undercover cops which Green Eyes recognized and pointed out to us as they drove by. He included the "good talks we had with Green Eyes" in his summation, and ended with our naiveté in accompanying him on his drug expedition and how oblivious we were once again to the danger of a man with a gun right in front of us.

Rob concluded that the whole evening "showed me how much I don't know and that I just need to sit down and listen (to people)." He then reaffirmed how glad he was that we were with Green Eyes, how much we had needed him as a "translator," and that without him to translate for us the streets really are a "jungle."

Kyle followed Rob and shared on much more of a personal nature, catching me somewhat off guard in the process and rekindling my disappointment in not having the opportunity to help the guys work through the intensity of what we had witnessed. Kyle related to the class that he had literally felt sick to his stomach upon returning to Biola, as if he had "witnessed a crime that must be reported." He spoke of being "confused" and of getting into the shower and wanting to "wash off all the evil" that we had seen. He claimed to be "physically drained" by the activity and especially "shook up" by the gun experience. Kyle related quite prophetically how deeply grieved he was by the sinful activities and wrong choices of those we had observed on the streets. He recalled that when he was in high school and knew of his peers doing sex or drugs he would "take a stand and speak out" against it, affirming his own convictions in the process. But that night he felt "like a helpless bystander" and simply "sat and watched and wrote."

THE REST OF THE STORY

Three days later I dropped in again on Beacon to visit Green Eyes. How much less intimidating it felt in the daylight than at night! The street was relatively quiet and Green Eyes was actually sweeping the sidewalk with a gnarly old broom he had found. He was wearing a t-shirt that afternoon which said, "Golfers do it 18 times a day!" It did seem sadly relevant to all whom we had met and observed a few nights earlier.

He had accumulated two more shopping carts and even a chair since we had left him that morning and was pleased to show them to me. He proudly mentioned that several people had asked him about who we were and why we were with him on the street that night, providing him with the opportunity to explain his role as our "teacher." I noticed that Philip and his van were not parked along the curb, and Green Eyes mentioned that he had not seen him for the past couple days. I learned as well that Marty had been arrested that same night at a "chiba house," and thus Green Eyes had not gotten his money back. He also shared that China and Donna had returned the next day, and that China had "diss'ed" (disrespected) the Cuban man, which began the entire scene with the gun. Apparently, no retaliation was ordered against him by the gang because Jaime vouched for the fact that it was she who was out of line and therefore deserved to be slapped for what she had done.

Sparky was asleep on his hunk of foam under the tree. Green Eyes awakened her so that we could chat for a few minutes, but she was in no mood to talk. She sat up and asked him for a cigarette and then lay right back down, barely able to carry on a conversation. The thought struck me that I was now witnessing the "real" Sparky, and on a larger scale, the life of the prostitute/drug addict in general. No makeup, matted and greasy hair, old jeans and a sweatshirt, and badly in need of a fix. There were hardly any girls on the street at that moment, but I knew that come nightfall, Sparky and all the rest would be dressed and ready for yet another night on the endless parade that is who-stro.

IMPRESSIONS AND OBSERVATIONS

A summary of the significant observations and impressions of our night on the street is as follows:

1. The incredible diversity, creativity and individuality of men and women on the streets.

2. The willingness of street people who have so little to freely share with others in need.

3. The importance of understanding and respecting the networks and unwritten rules or laws of the street.

4. The often violent, around-the-clock survival ethic of street life and activity.

5. The massive and tragic effects of drugs and prostitution on those who live on the streets.

6. The receptivity and openness of street people to allow caring, non-judgmental individuals access to their world.

7. The desperate need for a Christ-like, incarnational witness to those on the street.

8. The array of emotions one experiences in an initial encounter with that world. These include fear, vulnerability, shock, anger and disgust.

9. The realization that reaching out to street people requires commitment, compassion and consistency over the long haul.

Table 4

<u>A Glossary of Street Terms</u>

Chiba - heroin
Chiba house - home where heroin is used
Coke - cocaine
Clique - gang affiliation
Diss'ed - disrespected
Doctor - one who injects heroin addicts
Fix/Hit - dose of drugs
Hawker - one who guards an area
He-she - transvestite
Jackal - robber
John - a prostitute's date
Kick-down - repayment
Medicine - drugs
Narc - narcotics officer
Outfit - heroin syringe and needle
Pimp - one who procures prostitutes
Pipe - tube used to smoke cocaine
Pusher - one who deals drugs
Rock - hardened form of cocaine
Shooting up - injecting heroin
Slummin' it - dressing casually
Strawberry - a girl who trades sex for drugs
Trick - a prostitute's date
Who-stro - whore stroll

CHAPTER 8

A SEARCH FOR MEANING:

ON FEELINGS, FINDINGS, AND FULFILLMENT

Indispensable to the research with the students were the opportunities
to debrief, reflect on and draw meaning from our experiences together. This
occurred after every activity even though it is recapped here as a specific
entity in its own right. The purpose is to convey the crucial learning process
in a condensed format providing a panoramic view of the semester in its
totality. Each event or encounter is once again recapped with our significant
impressions.

PRAYER TOUR

The initial prayer tour embodied in microcosm a large part of the
student's responses to what occurred on an ongoing basis during the Fall
months. Feelings of guilt, anxiety, fear, and insecurity were all expressed as
well as that numbing sense of being overwhelmed and helpless in the midst
of such blatant need. Comments were made about the incredible paradox of
luxury and disparity between those in the Biltmore Hotel and those on the
streets outside its doors. Tammy shared her struggle to justify the lifestyle of
her own upper-middle class suburban heritage in light of the homeless men
and women we had just met. She questioned her own stewardship and then

sincerely exclaimed, "the money people spend for one night at the Biltmore, what could that do for so many on skid row?"

Brenda picked up on the same tension as she related her amazement over the lavish, extravagant hotel, singling out its "marble corridors, plush carpeting and glamorous people." She honestly admitted however to being more "comfortable" in that rich, clean environment, despite its "ostentatiousness," than she was in being with the poor out on the streets. She knew that she needed the love of Jesus to change her heart. Another student echoed similar genuine sentiment, asking "How do we deal with it all? How do we love them? When do we break down and cry?" Tammy concurred and acknowledged the much easier tendency to simply "turn off" our emotions so as not to have to deal with all that we had seen and heard. She confessed, "I can't feel all that is here or my heart will break!" Already we were on the road to learning compassion!

Others contributed their perspectives as we pondered our impending semester-long involvement. One claimed that the issues of poverty are "more real to me now" and that we "can't just pass off the poor." Susan testified to the fact that her "eyes have been opened" in particular to the "blatant" reality of drugs on the streets and she puzzled over what could be done to intervene. Sandra suggested, "Despite its crime and problems, as we get to know more of the city we understand it more." Jeff built on this sociological vein by noting the overlap of the refugee, business and homeless communities we had passed through that evening and the importance of being aware of that diversity. As we sought to bring together our random thoughts the realization of our propensity to "do" something and to "solve

221

the problems" was very evident! But we agreed that God's priority was for us to "be" something, namely, a loving people on a quest to build relationships so that Jesus may be seen in us. One of the students succinctly concluded, "We go to love!"

Significant Impressions:

- The stark, widening contrast between the rich and the poor in our cities raises difficult questions about stewardship, lifestyle and values.

- The first glimpse of thousands of men and women on Los Angeles' skid row is an overwhelming experience for most people. Too often, however, we simply "turn off" our emotions instead of embarking upon the pain-staking process of dealing with what we have seen.

- Personal encounters with the poor "put faces on" the reams of harsh, cold statistics that otherwise leave us helpless and hopeless in our efforts to "make a difference."

- God is not necessarily calling us to "do" great things "for" the poor as much as to "be" a compassionate presence "among" the poor.

INTERVIEW WITH GREEN EYES

Reaction to the session with Green Eyes in our apartment was not nearly as diverse nor emotionally charged. This was due in part to the fact that both the context and the agenda were more familiar to and controlled by the students. I had also spoken of him substantially so there was a basic prior awareness of his situation. In class the following day several of the students voiced their response to his presentation. Doug admitted to being rather skeptical initially of what Green Eyes had to say and Brenda agreed, admitting that she struggled with "being a learner from a guy who had attempted murder and had made so many wrong choices in life." But as he shared his perspective and challenged us all to set aside our prejudices and accept him for what he was, the group as a whole acknowledged that they truly did learn a great deal. We spent some time talking about and clarifying Green Eyes' taxonomy of the poor, that being the street, skid row and drug cultures (Table 3).

A number of the students commented that he didn't fit the "typical stereotype" of what they thought homeless people would be like. Specifically he actually enjoyed being on the street, considering it "home" and its fellow occupants "family." They puzzled over his choice to remain there and particularly to return to the sidewalk after having spent so many months in a hotel. There was further critique of elements of his "philosophy" and the seeming contradictions of claiming to be "happy" and yet confessing to being bound by cocaine. This included his warning about "homeless con artists," while to some extent he fits into the same category. Yet despite these valid indictments there was a growing awareness in the hearts of many that God was at work. Brenda personally noted, "He's showing me His standards for loving the poor."

Significant Impressions:

   - It is often a humbling process for the believer to willingly submit as a "learner" under one who has been immersed in an array of "wrong choices" so as to become more familiar with that individual's context and companions.

- Street people long to be accepted for who they are, regardless of their lifestyle. This is generally a first step toward establishing a relationship and ultimately reaching them with the gospel.

- Similar to the way that gangs serve as a "substitute family" for numerous young people, the streets become "home" to many of its occupants and some find it very difficult to leave their "family" behind.

VICTORY OUTREACH

Only the night on who-stro surpassed the group's experiences with Victory Outreach for dramatic, front-line encounters and sheer, eye-opening exposure to human need. In actuality it was our most satisfying contact with gang members and certainly "whetted our appetite" for more. Kyle was impressed with V.O.'s "go get 'em mentality" and their vision to "save the city." Rob expressed his surprise over the receptivity we were granted by the gang members themselves, commenting, "The gang culture being so open to the gospel was such a revelation to me. I have always thought that 'gang-bangers' would scoff or take you out soon as a blink." But instead he explained, "They are very respectful of those who come to them with the Word." I was greatly encouraged by his concluding discovery, "I have a new assurance that the gospel can be preached throughout all the land, even through me."

Another who was deeply challenged by our participation with V.O. was Nick. After the first, more "timid" of the two evenings, he shared his fears while we were driving back to Biola. At the close of the service earlier that night, the speaker asked us all to join hands. He then encouraged us to pray for those next to us who so indicated their need of prayer. Nick was seated beside me and wanted me to pray for him. I did so, not fully knowing his need. I asked the Lord to free him from anxiety and to supply real boldness in its place as we were soon to go out on the streets. He then admitted that he had sought prayer and the fullness of the Spirit because he had felt so inadequate and unprepared to minister in contrast to many of the other students and especially the V.O. staff members. He further confessed to having doubts about his gifting and struggling with doing evangelism. He wondered if he was simply "over his head" in that environment and should not bother coming back again with the group the next Friday.

Nick, in his first semester, had little if any experience in sharing his faith, let alone articulating it to gang members. All of us in the vehicle began to really encourage and build him up. We acknowledged that evangelism is a gift and we all admired and were challenged by the zeal of Paco, Tomas and Alberto and their ability to identify with and contextualize the gospel to gang members. It was obvious that God had effectively enabled them to do so and had, in some cases, miraculously freed them from similar lifestyles. But despite our not having "been there," we recalled the biblical injunction to "do the work of an evangelist" (II Timothy 4:5). We agreed that much like any other skill or task in life our fears are increasingly overcome as we obediently learn the art of relevantly sharing our faith. We also concurred that we needed aggressive opportunities like these with V.O. as an impetus to "just do it!"

Bolstered by our overwhelming show of support on his behalf, Nick asked how you actually go about making personal contact with a gang member. He exclaimed excitedly, "That's what I really want to do!" I smiled and shared of my attempts with Funee Man, acknowledging that I felt God had ultimately allowed me to find favor with him and thus access to his world. We experienced that process unfold before us the very next week, expedited by the prayers and guidance of V.O. During the return trip home such descriptive adjectives as "intense," "incredible" and "amazing" were all voiced by various ones in recapping the night's events.

Kyle and Rob and I found Nick's enthusiasm to be particularly enjoyable. He was "really pumped," to borrow his phrase, as our confrontation with Bullit, Yogi and friends had been exactly what he had hoped for, and more. We laughed loud and long as he recapped how scared he had been at the sight of every passing car, thinking he might be the next victim of a drive-by shooting! This from the one who had thirsted so for just such excitement. Nick then asked, with youthful innocence, as to what had "happened" during the service that night. He had followed the crowd to the front and, along with the pastor, had laid hands on a man only to have him fall flat on his back moments later! Kyle especially took great delight in dispelling Nick's naiveté in this regard. Personally embracing the charismatic tradition, Kyle claimed to "know about those things" and eagerly fielded his questions.

One of those inquiries had to do with shedding light on being "slain in the Spirit," which Nick sincerely reiterated "the pastor had called it!" He wondered if it was "real or just emotion" and we shared varying opinions on the matter, concluding that some displays truly are genuine while others may be fabricated. I explained that even though its authenticity is frequently decried or downplayed by evangelicals, it often takes on real meaning for such a one as that individual in V.O.'s rehabilitation program who has hit rock bottom. We may not understand, but God seems at times to literally touch lives in very dramatic and powerful ways and numerous testimonies bear this out. Regardless of its verification in this instance it had certainly etched itself indelibly in Nick's mind.

One other of the many insightful discoveries on the part of the students was that of a graduate and his wife. He had been deeply moved by the contacts on the street, while she had been stirred by the worship service and interaction with several on the rehab program. They commented on the relevancy of the message and how genuine and expressive the people were, particularly in their worship (I had observed the two of them to be much more stilted and reserved in that regard). She in particular was struck by the emotional dimension of the ministry. A student of psychology, she wondered if they used any formal psychological counseling with those on the program. It was obvious that their entire philosophical approach was not what she was accustomed to, nor had been exposed to in her schooling thus far. This led to a discussion of traditional Anglo, conservative methodology used to minister in the average middle-class setting. We reflected on its distinctive cerebral, programmatic style, in such contrast to those we had just heard testify of how God had "touched them" or "did a miracle" in freeing them from drugs and gangs. We agreed that our appreciation for the vast diversity within the body of Christ had been richly expanded in our rewarding involvement with Victory Outreach!

Significant Impressions:

- There is a greater degree of receptivity to and respect for the gospel on the part of gang members than we often give them credit for. In reality, what is too often lacking is our willingness to go and share the message with them.

- God has uniquely gifted many of His children as evangelists and has strategically positioned some of them within intense urban subcultures. Yet we each have the opportunity of partnering with them in propagating the gospel. Much like any other skill or task in life, our fears to that end are increasingly overcome as we obediently learn the art of relevantly sharing our faith.

- Numerous testimonies bear out the fact that God often chooses to work in dramatic, miraculous ways to deliver men and women who are helplessly in bondage to various vices as they cry out in faith to Him.

UNION RESCUE MISSION

Evangelistic Service

Another extremely positive opportunity for the group was the orientation session with Bernard followed by our participation in the evening service at Union Rescue Mission. The students were deeply impressed with both he and Ruth. In fact, of the latter, Tammy adoringly acclaimed her to be "like Jesus!" Brenda reached a personal milestone in that she had felt no fear while in the heart of skid row and had caught my eye during the meeting and whispered, "This is really good!"

The guys couldn't resist teasing Brenda, our resident "maestro," about her latent piano playing expertise and she joked along with us, recalling her horror at having been asked to perform in such an impromptu manner. We laughed even louder (with the exception of Brenda that is) when Tammy could no longer stifle her guilty conscience and admitted to being no slouch on the piano herself! She claimed to have been "too embarrassed" to volunteer however, and Brenda could have belted her for it!

This playful interaction soon led to a discussion of the songs that had comprised the service, specifically, all traditional hymns. Brenda shared how much she missed them and had enjoyed singing them. Tammy concurred, referring to how she had grown up with them and was "tired of singing choruses all the time." I mentioned that Doug and I, seated beside each other on the platform, had whispered among ourselves during the service that about the only place you sing hymns anymore is in rescue missions! It does not bode well for a contextualized ministry approach when that environment is the last bastion of hymnology! It was also noted with interest that "Amazing Grace" seems to be the rescue mission equivalent to the Billy Graham Crusade's "Just As I Am"! We collectively mused, "Are all the 'wretches' of the world necessarily confined to skid row?"

Everyone seemed to have a pertinent evaluation about various aspects of the service. Brenda felt it was, for the most part, unrelated to the street people and Shelley pronounced it "depressing and uninteresting." Doug suggested that the best part was Bernard's welcome, "mini-message" during

229

the offering, and the altar call. He exclaimed, "Those were the most effective, relevant and loving parts of the whole program!" He even wished that we could go back another night and do a service "the right way this time!" We laughed initially as we recalled Bernard's efforts to awaken the audience, but then admitted how incredibly tragic it was that half of them had fallen asleep in the first place. Tammy recorded how sad it is that in general many volunteers from the various churches doing the services "have no experience or point of contact with the homeless until they stand up to preach a sermon to them."

Further dialogue ensued regarding how the service seemed to benefit the church and their need for "outreach" more than it did those to whom they were supposedly "reaching." We remembered how uncomfortable they had been and I noticed that while we were all mingling after the service they had remained together as a group. We could not recall seeing even one of them in a single conversation with a street person. Shelley insightfully noted that the entire format of a program for several hundred men is simply not conducive to getting to know them personally. Furthermore, she suggested, "These men have an emotional side that is difficult to reach in such an environment." Her overall synopsis was that, "If I was down and out I do not think that a service like that would motivate or inspire me to get out from the position I was in." She concluded, "Contextualize it and make it sound new!"

Brenda pointed out how little of God's power is evident in the average rescue mission service these days. Many sermons, much preaching, but few lives being changed. All in such stark contrast to the "heyday" of rescue ministry dating back to the previous century when a movement of the Holy Spirit had gripped men's hearts in revival through anointed messengers. We pondered whether missions had dwelt far too long on a ministry model which had reached its apex decades ago. With the drug abuse and mental health problems unique to our generation, we discussed the premise that the most valuable contribution of rescue missions' today may well be their rehabilitation components. This in contrast to the traditional "soup, soap and salvation" mentality where men seem only to come and go, in and out of a revolving door between the street and a bed for the night.

Our "profound critique" notwithstanding, I was very pleased to later read Brenda's pertinent reminder of God's outlook on it all. She aptly concluded:

> Throughout the service, as I sat at the piano, I studied the faces of the men I could see. Almost 350 men were there. Were they hearing anything? What did they think about these efforts to evangelize them? Was any of it really getting through? What held these men in bondage?...I began to understand a little of what Jesus must have felt when He was "moved with compassion" for the multitude that was "like sheep without a shepherd" (Matt. 9:36). Behind the empty stares were people of great value to God.

Significant impressions:

- Regardless of how in-step or out-of-sync our outreach programs may be, it is by-and-large the people serving faithfully in them that impact lives.

- It would seem that de-emphasizing the programmatic in favor of the relational and rehabilitational approach to ministry among street people is the need of our day.

231

- It is an intriguing dynamic in ministry that on occasion our "evangelistic" efforts are more suited to our own needs than to those we are seeking to reach.

Youth Ministry

Sandra and Shelley in particular made significant discoveries during our participation with Union's youth ministry. Since the timing of our visit was only a few days prior to Halloween, the young people spoke excitedly about their upcoming "haul" of assorted goodies. While seated in the van, our laps full of wiggling, enthusiastic children, Sandra and I were amazed to realize that the extent of their trick-or treating was to go from room to room down the hallway of the floor in the hotel in which they lived! Driving back to Biola later that afternoon we recapped our realization for the rest of the group, who responded with similar surprise. The kids mentioned that their mothers (most all were fatherless) would not allow them on other floors because it was too dangerous and we were struck by the reality of daily life in the hotels. Several commented on how they could hardly imagine what it must be like to grow up in such a place, cooped in and feeling almost like a prisoner in one's own home.

Shelley also added her perspective on the hotels. She and Doug had been in the other vehicle and had gone inside one of the units, along with a staff member, to track down some of the children who had not been waiting for them when they pulled up to the curb. She described the building as "dirty, noisy and freaky" and was grateful for the secure company of two other males. She reported her disbelief over the fact that there was only one functioning elevator for that entire multi-story facility and claimed that the "scariest part of it" was the ride itself. It moved slowly, smelled badly and the lights indicating which floor it was passing also did not work. Having gotten just a glimpse of that world we all had a much deeper appreciation for the outlet U.R.M.'s activities provided for the young people, to say nothing of their spiritual value.

The group had also become more aware of the desperate need for affection on the part of the children. Leslie had encouraged the volunteers to sit beside and hold the younger kids in particular and Sandra had spent most of the afternoon doing just that. We discussed the power of and craving for the human touch and the tragic consequences of an upbringing devoid of love and affirmation. Shelley had spent the prior summer serving with an urban youth ministry and shared how the staff had been warned by leadership about being overly affectionate due to the volatile nature and numerous accusations of abuse. Its intent was not an either/or proposition but was rather to avoid extremes and to specifically caution male staff members with female young people. We acknowledged the vital necessity of tangibly expressing true, Christ-like love and tenderness to the children and admitted our sadness over how easily it can be distorted in society today.

One final observation of the students was that while all the kids were Black and Hispanic all the staff and volunteers were White! We recalled that the Victory Outreach staff, on the other hand, were all non-Anglo. Leslie had mentioned that her Hispanic co-worker was gone that day, nonetheless we spoke of how typical this often is of many para-church inner-city ministries whose upper level leadership is White. This led to interaction about the varying underlying factors such as issues of control, contextualization, staff recruitment, and the challenge of raising support in the Black and Hispanic communities. Evident to all was the pressing need to raise up ethnic leadership among young people such as those we had just met.

I thought of little eight-year-old Keith, a bright Black boy who had approached me during the craft session of the club. I was in the back of the room jotting down notes and had pen and paper in hand. He curiously inquired about what I was doing and I explained that I was writing a big paper for school about many different kinds of people downtown. He asked if he could be in it and proceeded to proudly record his full name for me on the notepad. I replied that I would be honored to include him.

Significant impressions:

- The "dirty, noisy and freaky" skid row hotels should be viewed in their own right as veritable mission fields of hurting, neglected, disadvantaged people.

- There are few substitutes for the power and affirmation of the loving human touch. But there are also numerous examples of men, women and children having grown up without it and whose lives bear the scars of its tragic neglect.

- Indigenous, ethnic leadership continues to be a dire need in urban ministry settings.

Crossroads Rehabilitation Program

In keeping with the theme of ethnic leadership, one of the highlights for the group of our visit to Crossroads was the opportunity of getting acquainted with Paul. The fact that he and his family lived on-site was a real challenge to the students, so much so that it sparked a conversation on the way home in the car about the tenuous balance in ministry between work and family time. We recalled his struggles with the constant demands on their time and his wife's remark about how they frequently just need "to get away." Shelley speculated that this constant proximity to people's need was "unhealthy" and that if they did not have "some place to retreat and be alone" it could ultimately "take a toll on them." Doug on the other hand, was impressed by their constant availability and the opportunities it afforded to "model Christian behavior and principles." Despite the "stress" of such a lifestyle, as Paul had characterized it, he emphasized that they are "committed to do so" in order to provide "the best possible help." We noted that all of the staff are quite young and surmised that this phase of intense, "on-call" involvement was in all likelihood a limited one.

The students were also impressed with the program's job training component as well as the commitment of the staff to connect the young men to the local church for ongoing fellowship and accountability. Shelley also noted that the home was not located on "some far away island," but was rather somewhat of a "safe house" in the urban environment, thus ensuring a smoother transition back into "the real world."

I was very much encouraged by our further dialogue as we drove back to the dorms. A few days earlier I had spoken in a Theology of Mission class on material pertaining to a theology of the city. Half of the group was taking that course as well and several shared that the discussion had been motivating and meaningful. We reviewed some of the pertinent Scriptures, acknowledging the stirring challenge of Jeremiah 29:7 to "seek the welfare of the city." Doug had been particularly impressed with Linthicum (1991a) and Shelley had even gone out and bought the book, in addition to McClung (1991) and Dawson (1989). She eagerly expressed her desire to minister in an urban community upon graduation. Doug echoed his own increasing openness to the city, to the extent of considering pastoring an inner-city church. I was pleased at the way the students were processing concepts of urban outreach theoretically as well as experientially.

Significant impressions:

At the heart of urban ministry philosophy is the pertinent issue of living among those to whom one is ministering. The potential does exist for the constant wear and tear to "take a toll" on individuals and families alike. Certainly time to "be alone" and "to get away" are a frequent necessity. However, those demands and sacrifices "come with the territory" if one is "committed to model Christian behavior and principles."

CENTRAL CITY COMMUNITY CHURCH

One of the truly impacting highlights of the semester for the entire group was our exposure to Central City Community Church. Once again the students were primarily impressed with an individual, Scott himself. Kyle noted his very relational demeanor and "vision to empower people." He was also impressed with how well the street people responded to him and suggested that may be due in part to the fact that he "respected them for who they were." We were all touched by his loving and very real down-to-earth manner. Julie recalled a phrase from Lupton (1989:75) that had stuck with her and which she had earlier read to the entire class, that being, "The fundamental building blocks of the kingdom are relationships."

Doug picked up on this theme and shared how intrigued he was with Scott's commitment to community, accountability, and discipleship. He noted that he "accepts anybody" and that "his church is filled with what middle-class people call 'hobos' and 'bums!'" Doug was also challenged by the testimonies and Scott's free and interactive teaching style. He inquired of Scott about the dialogical, question-asking dynamic of his "sermon" and related enthusiastically, "It's because he believes in the priesthood of all believers." Doug was particularly enamored by its application among the street people as he exclaimed, "a homeless person is a priest!" He spoke further of how this "reflected their specialness to God," instilled confidence in them, "and made them feel that they were worth something."

Tammy noticed that during the prayer time people had asked God to give them strength in their environment and not to necessarily get them off the streets. She mentioned that this had been a real challenge to her own situation. I later read with interest and pleasure her assessment of Scott's fledgling flock of believers:

> I expected to find a group of people who were upset with their present condition, and possibly even angry at God. After all, they were dealing with a lot of pain and uncertainty…What I found instead was…they were all praising the Lord and praying for one another…My faith was definitely stretched as I saw so many people trusting God completely to

take care of their needs-even their very basic physical needs. They were certainly not without problems...And yet, there was a true joy in that little room that caught me completely by surprise.

Julie admitted that the visit had been a bit unnerving to her initially. We had purposely chosen to disperse ourselves throughout the "congregation," and she therefore had to field questions about where she was from and if she had ever come before. Julie explained that she had felt rather vulnerable and then realized that it was probably not unlike the feelings of those who come in off the street.

Sandra also shared an interesting perspective which opened up further dialogue. Noting that the church had begun in the park and was now meeting in a building, she expressed concern that they may lose their evangelistic connection with the street. She affirmed the constant priority "to go back out and reach their own." We all agreed and acknowledged that this aggressive, "harvest mentality" is what impressed us so with Victory Outreach and certainly is the hallmark of that ministry and its zealous new converts. We noted the irony in the fact that the potential is just as great for a homeless church to lose its vision and become ingrown as it is for an insulated middle-class, suburban congregation to do the same. However, in Scott's defense, I mentioned he had told me that they are in the process of beginning their first adult Sunday School class and the initial topic to be addressed is evangelism. It was his intent for the church to not lose sight of its roots and its mission field.

The remainder of our drive back to school was spent in a very timely and thought-provoking conversation about incarnational ministry. I had sensed that theme "brewing" after our contacts with Cambria and more recently the Crossroads' staff members. It surfaced that day in great relevancy after the group met Scott and his family and learned that they lived only two blocks from the church. The students had just finished reading Bakke (1987) in the class and recalled the priority of loving the city and the simple truth that it is very difficult to live and work in it if you don't even like it. Kyle reminded us of our journey to understand the meaning of "suffering together with" and Doug asked if the concept is limited necessarily to targeting the economically disadvantaged. We pondered the fact that irregardless of the locale it is simply biblical and was practiced and modeled for us by the Lord Himself, specifically, the principle of identification. But we also recalled that Christ "became poor" on our behalf (II Cor. 8:9) and that the every essence of His calling was "to preach the gospel to the poor" (Luke 4:18).

One of the girls, feeling a bit overwhelmed by it all, sincerely asked how you actually go about doing it! She wondered if you just "pick an ethnic group and move in" or what? I shared some of our experiences of living in low-income neighborhoods and we spoke of such necessities as targeting a specific community, a team approach, and participation with a local body of believers. Further questions surfaced as to whether or not one had to be involved in "full-time ministry" in the community in order to live there. We talked about the nature of tent-making roles and the impact one can still have in modeling the gospel and a Christian home and family while building relationships with one's neighbors.

This led to the inevitable discussion of raising children in the inner city and we recalled the exhortation of Jeremiah 29. Another asked what you should do if "your kids hate it" and are really struggling. "Do you still stay?", she inquired. We talked about not sacrificing your family on the altar of ministry and I mentioned several I knew of who, for the sake of their children, were forced to pull out of an incarnational ministry, at least for a season. But on the other hand we agreed that it can be a very healthy learning process and ultimately is a decision of each individual family to act upon what they feel God is calling them to do.

Significant Impressions:

- "Community, accountability and discipleship" are vital, yet often neglected, ingredients in an effective ministry with the homeless.

- Applying the biblical concept of "the priesthood of all believers" in the context of men and women off the street who come to Christ implies that "a homeless person is a priest!" This gives tremendous "dignity and self-worth" to the individual, instills confidence and "reflects their specialness to God."

- Our faith is stretched as we come face to face with men and women experiencing "a lot of pain and uncertainty" and yet are "praising the Lord" and "trusting God completely to take care of even their very basic physical needs."

- The potential exists for a church among the homeless (or a rescue mission) to become "ingrown" and lethargic in its "harvest mentality", despite its proximity to skid row, as it does for an "insulated" middle-class, suburban congregation far removed from the intensity of urban need.

- The Lord Jesus is our ultimate model in an incarnational identification with mankind. In seeking to follow His example though, we must keep in mind a team approach, involvement with a local body of believers, and sensitivity to the needs of one's children.

FIRST EVANGELICAL FREE CHURCH

Much of the reflection over our involvement with First Evangelical Free Church was on the part of the graduate students and seemed to center on our thwarted efforts as much as anything else. But in the end it turned out to be a very good learning experience for us all. In our initial planning meeting with church leadership we had strongly appealed for their involvement with us among the homeless in the community but quickly realized that their agenda was more in tune with local immigrants. This accounted for their strong and pertinent emphasis on tutoring and ESL. But the proximity of a street people's encampment in their own backyard (albeit a somewhat resistant group) seemed to be a unique and ready-made mission field in which to flesh out the gospel message in a compassionate manner.

But as we talked it over with them we sensed a greater concern for continuity and ultimate follow-up which, unfortunately, often translates into doing nothing at all. In contrast to Victory Outreach's aggressive "take it to the streets" mentality and Scott's specific focus on the homeless poor ,we had gotten a glimpse of some of the criteria whereby a traditional church evaluates and prioritizes its outreach energies. Brenda had initially entertained high hopes of seeing and participating in ministry among the poor through a local church. Although that did not come about, she did however provide a succinct summary of some of the issues that surfaced during our interaction with them:

The "church people" were cautious and hesitant of our involvement. We, the "zealous student group" were willing, but unsure of the level of our commitment...At first, it seemed that they were slow to enter into ministry with these people. Yet, as I pondered the issue from their perspective, I realized that they were trying to be accommodating to us. Yet ultimately they would have to carry on anything we started. Anything we tried would require commitment on their parts...These church leaders knew the weight of responsibility when beginning a new ministry endeavor.

Jeff had been given the opportunity of teaching an adult Sunday School class on the subject of City Life and Ministry, which would potentially have run concurrently to our project that semester. When he first mentioned it to me and I realized the significant relationships he had already developed with numerous church members, it appeared to be a weekly gathering with great potential. He and I talked with enthusiasm about possibly recruiting lay members from the class to participate with us in attempting to make contact with the homeless community behind the facility. We thought of how this would allow for congregational ownership and continuity of the ministry had we been able to make inroads. But as it turned out our efforts in both the class and the community more closely resembled a dead end!

We had even discussed a curriculum containing elements of urban theology and sociology and envisioned the group meeting in an abbreviated session so as to allow time to meet and mingle experientially with the homeless. Although strong in vision our dreams were weak in realism. Despite the fact that the members were a highly committed group neither the burden for the homeless nor the time and motivation to establish a rapport with them was present and the class was ultimately discontinued after only a few short weeks.

It is generally easier and more effective to plant a church among the homeless than it is to channel the energies of the existing congregation in that direction. Ultimately, a group or a key individual must possess a deep, God-given burden for those on the street in order to pour one's energies into ministry with them.

THANKSGIVING DINNER UNDER THE BRIDGE

We reflected on our Thanksgiving "potluck" with the guys under the bridge during the next class period several days later. I recapped our valuable discovery for all the students in the course, namely Big Jed's preference of our fellowship over the food which we had brought. We laughed about how they weren't even hungry but agreed that overall it was a fitting reminder that the giving of ourselves is the essence of our message.

While Sandra, the professor, and I had gone over to visit with Tony beside his bush, Brenda and Kyle had sat and chatted with Jed. Kyle shared with the class that despite Jed's initial bravado and supposed contentment with his life he ultimately admitted that he wished he had a wife and kids to go home to. Brenda relayed her surprise over the perception that the guys under the bridge have of themselves. She noted Jed's reference to others on the streets as "bums" and "tramps," while they regard themselves as living under what more closely resembles a "shelter" (she recalled that he had referred to it as their "house" when we arrived).

We had also listened with interest as Jed had touched on a number of ways that the homeless manage to accrue money. As we rehearsed them to the class we sensed their value in the form of a taxonomy. The list began with panhandling which included "haggling" (Tony, et al. - asking people for money), "working a sign" (Lenny's approach) and playing on people's emotions (Dirty Jake and Lefty's forte - dirty, smelly and handicapped). Then there was "walking paper," what Lefty had done when he handed out fliers. Next was canning and "dumpster diving," which Red and Billie had mastered. This was followed by government checks (welfare, disability, and S.S.I.), which they all had made use of on occasion. Finally, Jed admitted to having resorted to theft for many years to make ends meet (although he swore that was behind him now and placed himself squarely in the panhandler category!)

Table 5

A Taxonomy of Financial Accrual by the Homeless

Category	Representatives	Description
Panhandling	Big Jed	Extending ones hand, hat, etc.
-Haggling	Beached Whale	Asking, badgering people for money
-Working a sign	Lenny	Holding a cardboard sign
-Emotional appeal	Lefty, Dirty Jake	i.e. Dirty, smelly, handicapped
Walking Paper	Lefty	Distributing fliers
Canning	Red Dog, Billie,	Scrounging in dumpsters
Government Checks	Green Eyes, Red Dog, Billie, et al.	Welfare, disability, S.S.I.
Theft	Big Jed	Robbery
Sales	Green Eyes	Clothing, assorted merchandise

Significant Impressions:

- The giving of ourselves is the essence of our message as Christians.

- Many of those who "live" under the bridges or in homemade shanties, yet are technically "homeless," perceive themselves as "sheltered" and a step up from the "bums" and "tramps" who literally make their "home" on the street.

As the semester progressed my intent was to try and monitor the learning process of the students. This quest was at the heart of all our reflection and debriefing. A mid-point evaluation also shed light on their development as did their eventual oral and written summary of our ethnographic explorations to their peers and professor. The goal was to unearth feelings and findings on their initial journey along the rocky road toward ultimate urban ministry fulfillment. A summary of these discoveries is presented at the end of the chapter.

FEELINGS

One of the real challenges for me during my months with the students was watching them struggle with an array of unresolved feelings resulting from our ministry encounters together. My tendency was often to want to tie up the loose ends of their fractured emotions. But I knew that was simply not possible and even attempting to do so would be counter-productive to the very nature of the research.

Perhaps what was even more difficult was to arrive at the "end" of the project only to find that most, if not all, were still struggling. Granted, progress had been made and invaluable lessons learned, but all would attest to the fact that we were somehow different people than when we commenced this experiment just a few months before. I can only surmise that we had begun to experience for ourselves that tried and tested New Testament triad of seeing need, feeling compassion and taking action. It is that all-consuming second stage of "suffering together," with its myriad of feelings, which most found to be the essence of that struggle. Excerpts of those feelings of many of the students follow.

Expectations were understandably mixed at the start of the project, running the spectrum of eagerness and enthusiasm to being completely clueless and even afraid! Tammy recapped her early emotions toward our adventures together:

> My initial feelings were excitement and anticipation as to what we'd be experiencing, but a lot of fear also. I had just seen so much about the city - all negative - from the media. Being female and White, I felt very threatened by the environment of the inner city. It intimated me.

Rob also admitted to a similar perspective in the beginning:

> The concrete jungle was my name for it. A geographical area that was filed under "unknown" in my brain...The product of the unknown: confusion. This was my view of the city. The city environment... would bring fear to my heart because it never made sense in the world I knew. A mass of people all going in different directions, so impersonal, so cold, so fast, big, strange.

Reality quickly set in as the group began processing their responses to even the initial glimpse of skid row. Julie recalled her reaction, "I saw Blacks, Whites, Hispanics, Asians, some obviously were mentally unstable, some looked like they hadn't had a bath in days...people all over. All of a sudden my confidence began to fade." Tammy recorded a comparable response, including a sense of helplessness and vulnerability. She noted, "There were so many homeless people, just milling around...I had a very strong feeling of not belonging. I felt like everyone was staring at us...like we totally stuck out...It was a very frightening and vulnerable feeling...like I was no longer in 'my city' but in some strange land."

As the one responsible for leading them into such an "emotional state of disarray," I could only "comfort" them with the heartless consolation that it would probably get worse before it got any better! Julie remembered her perplexity and inadequacy, "The weight of the inner-city problems overwhelmed me. There are so many people here who need help...so many who are hopeless...so many who need Jesus. But what can I do and would they even listen to me? How can anyone even begin to make an impact among all these people?"

Tammy concurred:

As the semester progressed my excitement changed to a real sense of disillusionment over what I was seeing and experiencing every week. At times I felt overwhelmed and helpless because the need just seems so great...I saw a lot of brokenness and despair and it was hard at times to know how to respond.

This painful admission that "it was hard" was echoed not only by Tammy but by Kyle as well. He reflected, "It was very taxing emotionally to see the evil that encompasses the City of Los Angeles...I did not realize that it would be so emotionally draining...I had a hard time...because of the hurt I felt. The pain of the city was sometimes too hard to bear." For some, these feelings of confusion and anxiety teetered on the edge of despair! Ryan confessed, "I felt overwhelmed to the point of heavy depression by the problems I was seeing and hearing." Susan revealed a parallel propensity, "I feel discouraged and depressed after leaving the city. I want to feel challenged, not discouraged."

As we came to the end of the semester and took "emotional inventory," many of the students found lingering feelings of frustration over such things as compassion (or a perceived lack thereof), lifestyle and future involvement in the city. Susan pondered, "I am frustrated with my desire to help the city's needs but not knowing if I really have the loving attitude to work in the city."

Julie shared:

I have not resolved the frustration of living a middle-class, comfortable life with the ability to share the gospel with these people. I feel that I have no basis to share with them because my life is so easy in comparison and I just drive down to spend a few hours and then drive back into the "Biola bubble." I'm not sure how to handle these feelings of guilt and confusion. Sometimes they get so overwhelming that I just have to shut them off.

Tammy summarized:

I feel a lot of frustration, because I'm not sure what my next step should be. How can I remain involved? I don't want to forget all that I've experienced and yet I cannot let it fill my thoughts completely or I would be overwhelmed. Where do I go from here?

FINDINGS

In the midst of such bombarding emotions it was a source of great encouragement to me to watch their insights unfold and to interact with them on their eventual findings and conclusions. Patterns could be identified as some students made similar discoveries from our joint investigations. Others chose rather to highlight a certain need, ministry emphasis or specific individuals.

Several admitted to having their eyes opened to the coping mechanisms of the urban poor. Doug summarized:

I cannot emphasize enough how much my inner-city experience has changed my thinking. I am amazed at the resourcefulness of Green Eyes...I am amazed at how the "bridge people" continue to survive in the midst of city pollution and adverse conditions. I am amazed by

249

Red Dog who is able to...put up with all of the crime, prostitution and drug pushing that goes on in the housing project he lives in. The urban poor are survivors despite their circumstances.

He further noted "the remarkable environmental awareness the urban poor possess." He concluded respectfully, "They seem to have an acute sense of when things are dangerous and when they are harmless." Julie added her perspective:

> I have learned that people in the inner-city are real...I have developed a large respect for these people and their lifestyle. Although many people view it as a lifestyle of failure, in many ways they are successful just to survive on the street. They have learned things about life that I will probably never learn and they have a keen sense of how frail our humanity is.

Tammy shared insightfully of her own growing awareness in this regard:

> The city is more than a place. I have come to discover that the city is an organism, a "creature" that never stops moving and never sleeps. For some, it is filled with great prosperity and wealth. For many others however, it is a place of great poverty and need. Along with that there is often a great deal of pain, both physical and emotional. In order to survive they must find a way to deal with the barrage of things that confront them day and night. There are a lot of options available to the poor and homeless that help them to cope with their situations...They don't always choose options based on right and wrong. It's more a matter of survival.

Many of the students made mention of the tragic fact that one of the "wrong options" so frequently resorted to is drugs. Tammy referred to people's "emotional scars" and Julie commented, "When people can't turn off their emotions, they resort often to substance abuse." Tammy in particular was struck by its blatant usage, rampant extent, and firm control over people which "keeps them on the street" and makes them "willing to give up everything to have the drug." She shared her perplexity about the "relatively minimal intervention by the police force to stop the sale of drugs on the street." Referring to law officers she continued, "It seems that they have turned their backs on the inner-city. Maybe they feel it is a lost cause, that it is beyond hope. I don't really know. All I know is that the catalyst for a lot of the problems in inner-city Los Angeles is drugs, and a lot of people are turning a blind eye on the whole situation."

Kyle and Shelley dug a bit deeper to explore the spiritual root cause underlying people's vulnerability to drugs and other negative influences. Much of what shaped Kyle's perspective was the night on the street. He likened himself to "the believer who wishes to see the kingdom of God reign in the city," yet, what he found in its place, was "poverty, violence, and abuse." He soberly concluded that "sin is running rampant in the city." He explained, "The night on the street opened my eyes to the world of the city. It gave me a different perspective...The things which I saw showed me the incredible and overwhelming needs of the city...homelessness, prostitution, gang activity...and sinful habits such as drug addictions."

Shelley benefited not only from her exposure to human need but also from extensive reading in Linthicum (1991a), Dawson (1989), and McClung (1991). She shared how she too had "felt the heaviness of the city," but noted with excitement, "After reading these three books I started to view the city differently." The following are excerpts from her succinct and salient discoveries:

> The city is often looked at as an evil place; a place where sin runs rampant and God is forsaken...Through the journey that God has taken me this semester...and...by looking at the Scriptures I now understand His attitude and intentions for His creation...He does not want us to forsake the city...He also wants us to work for the betterment of the

city...God never intended it to be evil. The evil came in with the fall of man...I can now see that the city is not evil in itself and that it was meant for good. God created it and purposed for His people to live in it. Therefore the evil in the city must be present not because the entity in itself is evil, but because there is something else deeper going on...the city is a battleground between God and Satan...Satan uses this sin to disrupt the work that the people of God are trying to accomplish...I see it as an opportunity to serve Him and reach many hurting people.

Doug found himself struggling as well in this urban arena of conflicting values and lifestyles. He was bewildered by the fact that many of those he had met (he cited Green Eyes, Red Dog and Funee Man) "know of God but continue to live in sin." Although this tendency is certainly not limited to the urban poor, he noted, "Somehow individuals have allowed themselves to divorce their knowledge of God from their every day actions." Kyle recorded his thoughts on this "blurred morality grid," claiming, "Their standards for right and wrong have not been established by anything other than their own experiences of what the streets have taught them. It is not based upon the truth of God's kingdom. The importance of bringing a righteous standard cannot be stressed enough."

Many of the group members reached similar conclusions regarding the desperate need for this "righteous standard" to be raised high in the streets of our cities. Julie, reacting to the systemic mistreatment Red and Billie have had to endure, strongly claimed, "The solution is not agencies, but individuals." Susan, who had spent equal time with them, summarized, "The government is not helping much with homelessness and poverty. It seems the church should be attempting to do something about the problem of the street...we need a loving and helping group of people."

Deeply impressed with Scott's ministry at Central City, Doug was in full agreement with the necessity for "a loving and helping group of people" to minister among the urban poor. Kyle and Brenda, among others, echoed identical conclusions. Doug surmised, "The members which compose the 'culture of poverty' need an incarnational presence a church offers." He then highlighted the dynamics of an incarnational ministry to include "a degree of permanence" with those one is seeking to reach, a "sense of community," a "support group that keeps people accountable," and the opportunity to "teach as well as model Christian principles and standards." Kyle agreed with this premise and noted with corresponding zeal, "In order for effective ministry to take place among the homeless and gang members, Christians must live and minister among them." He too mentioned Scott as "a great example of this" and went even further to acclaim how Scott "didn't just minister to them but with them." Kyle concluded with a sobering realization however, claiming, "The lack of people who are willing to live among the poor and give their life away is depressing. In order for an army of God to be raised up to fight in the city, troops need to be recruited. It seems that they are all being deported to the suburbs."

Brenda also planted her flag with this lifestyle of identification as she deduced, "The primary goal of ministry to the poor is to join them in the process of being freed from their bondage." She sounded the cry for an empowering ministry mentality as well, affirming it to be an integral part of our servanthood. She submitted, "The poor seem to take pride in that which they feel a sense of responsibility and ownership...This plays into exhibiting servanthood to the poor- allowing them to take responsibility...in areas that require vulnerability and the relinquishment of power on the part of the helpers."

Brenda in turn had been challenged by the L.A. Mission's rehabilitation program and its holistic impact on the lives of numerous recovering street women. She acknowledged, "in the long run, churches are more effective than rescue missions or parachurch agencies in truly changing lives." But she appealed for a wider definition of the traditional body of Christ, as she explained, "I came to realize that the 'church' must be seen in a broader sense than just the local congregation." She then offered this interpretation, "It is any group committed to His Word and to evangelizing and discipling the poor and the lost."

She concluded, "Ministries need to provide sound biblical counseling to meet the deep emotional wounds of people. Committed friendship is an important part...and intensive discipleship by a person committed to the growth of that individual should be a priority for the church." Julie was also in line with Brenda's thoughts here as she concurred that "personal relationships and one-on-one contact...makes a difference." Her in-depth conversations with Billie led her to infer that "people need to be accepted, respected, heard from, and allowed to talk." She reasoned that applying these attributes "will start to chip away at the hardness in the city." She further noted, "We need to develop programs and plant churches...that take these things into account."

Sandra, Susan, Rob and Kyle were all in harmony with coming to the city as Rob put it, "with an open mind" and a "big ear to listen." Kyle summarized, "Another principle which I see as key to ministry in the city is treating people with honor and respect. The people in the city respond so well to a respectful question and an understanding heart...we need to listen...and let them tell us about their hardships and successes."

A final discovery of those same two young men focused on the crucial concept of networking. Kyle once again acts as spokesperson:

> The most important factor to seeing the city changed or not changed centers around networking...it must take place for more people to be reached. The communication between the church and the parachurch groups needs to become broader...There seemed to be little networking...They function independently.

FULFILLMENT

But even more satisfying to me than the student's findings was the incredible privilege of sharing with them in significant moments of personal fulfillment resulting from their embryonic experiences in urban ministry and research. By "fulfillment" is meant not the ultimate sense of completion or coming to the end of the journey, but rather the small glimpses, insights and realizations along the way that are such an integral part of our Christian pilgrimage. Such delightful affirmations as Brenda's enthusiastic declaration, "I have to admit, I'm hooked!" (on the prospects of future relational ministry among the poor). Or Rob's sincere announcement, " I have learned more about the city in this semester than I have ever in my entire life (all years combined)!" Another that comes to mind was the pleasure in hearing Julie announce, in our last class together, how she wished she could "move into the building" where Red and Billie live, so as to put into practice her newly confirmed discoveries of accepting, respecting and listening to people.

Several of the students admitted to their overall inadequacy upon reaching the end of the project. Rob confessed, "It showed me how much I don't know." Brenda acknowledged, "I learned how much I have to learn." Julie concurred, "It's important to approach and respond to people as a learner." Many members of the group professed to have made real headway in overcoming their initial fears of the city and its people. Rob testified, "I used to hate cities, I was afraid of them." Susan noted similar trepidation about "things I might see or run into." But she later shared, "The more I went to the city to talk with people it became easier each time. I was not afraid anymore." Julie agreed, "The first time I went...I was scared to death. But after that first visit I was much more confident...I am no longer scared of the city and its people...I know it's possible to conquer that fear...I have learned how to build respect with people and not to be intimated." Brenda revealed her development in this regard as well:

> At first I was intimidated by the city and the devastating lives there. I dreaded going because I didn't have the emotional energy to deal with it. Now I look forward to going and I see the people differently. I guess, over time, I began identifying more with the people. The bridge between us narrowed.

Both Tammy and Brenda commented on how they had gained a deeper awareness of what it means to be less critical. Tammy noted, "I found that I need to put myself in the place of people before I judge their actions." Brenda added, "Everything I learned this semester helps me not to make generalizations and be so judgmental."

Julie attested to having been challenged anew in the matter of true priorities in life:

I have learned that people in the inner city...wake up each morning and realize the success of just making it through another day. I take that for granted - I, who knows that not only did I make it through, but Jesus, who holds all together, has given me another day of life. This is missing in my complicated life. I have found a lot of healing just by being with them and learning that all the "important" things in my life are not so important after all. The important things are people, life, and the one thing that is missing from many of their lives, Jesus.

Susan reported growth in several areas such as deepening her convictions, widening her horizons and challenging her ongoing ministry involvement:

Now that I look back on the whole process, I feel that I have a better grasp on what I believe concerning the homeless and the poor. I am glad that I took the time to hear these unbelievable experiences first hand...This project has also put many questions in my mind about my responsibility to the poor. As a result of these individuals I have a new perspective on urban life.

Brenda too professed to being stretched along these lines, claiming, "This project made me uncomfortable, challenged my preconceived notions and shifted my existing paradigms of theology." She also made meaningful progress in the crucial matter of discovering her spiritual gift. She explained, "I became more aware of my gifts. My conviction that my primary gift in ministry is that of showing mercy to those who are suffering has been reinforced." Overall, our experiences together," reinforced my conviction for holistic ministry," she concluded.

Some of the details of her exposure to and activities in the various ministry settings shed light on the crucial process of clarifying her calling and ministry focus:

I learned that I am much more effective in one-on-one or small group discipleship where I can become emotionally involved in the lives of people...I need further exposure and growth in the area of evangelism

257

and outreach. These have always been difficult for me, and this project has challenged me to further expose and stretch myself in these areas. I was least comfortable visiting homeless men and resistant to street evangelism ministries...I want to...share my faith while building relationships.

Another who was deeply challenged in this matter of motivation in ministry was Tammy. She genuinely shared her understanding of and desire for a true servant's heart:

The biggest thing that I have learned is that the people in the city don't need me. They could live their lives perfectly fine if they never came in contact with me...That was like a slap in the face when I finally realized it, because I thought, "Then why in the world would I want to be here?"... My motivation for going to the city cannot be to "help" those "poor" people. I must go as a servant, not expecting any gratitude because I probably will never see any displayed in the people I'm trying to serve. If I'm going to the city for the wrong reasons, I might as well not go...I realized that I need to think long and hard about my motivation for working in the city and be sure that God is truly calling me there.

Brenda and Shelley were particularly moved by portions of Scripture which took on new meaning for them during the Fall months. Brenda noted, "God's call in the Bible to the poor, the widows, orphans and refugees...struck me to the core and I knew immediately...if that was where God's heart was, that I needed to align my heart to the same."

Shelley, reflecting on the truths of Ephesians 6:12, shared her insights:

This verse has been not only familiar to me for years, but also memorized. Yet, only this semester have I really understood the reality of it...I must pray against these forces and their power...Now when I enter a city, I am that much closer to seeing it in the same manner that God does. I now understand more of what I am up against and am on my way to battling the spiritual realm in a way that is more productive and less fearful.

Finally, our semester-long quest toward a compassionate lifestyle bore fruit in the lives of many. Tammy and Brenda are here representative of the group as a whole. Tammy suggested, "Something I do think could have an impact is...the genuine love and caring that Jesus had for all those He ministered to. It is not pity, but true compassion. If we can learn God's true love for the city, then we could be taking the first step to bringing some kind of improvement to the situation."

Brenda shared her perspective:

In spite of the frustrations, I wouldn't trade this project for anything! I'm learning so much and God is using this project more than anything else right now to chisel me and challenge my attitudes and assumptions about the poor...As I observe situations through the eyes of the poor, I am beginning to understand what true compassion means...God revealed to me that...I cannot muster up compassion on my own, but only through His strength...I'm learning that working for justice for the oppressed and poor is an exhausting road to take, but it's the way of Jesus and the way I choose!

Tammy then concluded with a genuine summary of her own personal pilgrimage in "God's School":

I learned about true compassion. I learned to see the people as individuals, humans just like me, and not just "those people"... I learned that God loves the city. Most of all, I learned that God is teaching me to love the city and its people...My heart breaks for the city. Often I find myself overwhelmed with the vastness of the problem. I wonder what one young person can contribute to the overwhelming need...Sometimes that really scares me, and I try to resist it...But, I have to remind myself that God has been taking care of the city for a long time. All He asks is that I be available. He'll take care of the rest.

Table 6

A Review of the Journey

Feelings	Findings	Fulfillment
Enthusiasm, excitement, eagerness, expectation	Brokenness, despair, pain, poverty, sin, emotional scars	Overcoming fears, intimidation, and disgust of the city
Anti-city bias, negative media perspective=cold, strange, impersonal, fast-paced, unknown	Violence, abuse, addiction, gangs, prostitution, homelessness	Gaining confidence - God can use me to reach the city!
Threatened, intimidated, insecure, confused, hurt	Coping skills of urban people, resourceful, environmental awareness, survival	Improved relational ministry skills
		Less judgmental, more accepting
Fear, anxiety, helplessness, vulnerability, frustration	City as battleground-God vs. Satan, opportunity to serve and minister	Gratitude for what one has, blessed
Overwhelmed, inadequate, discouraged, disillusioned, emotionally drained	Blurred morality grid on the street (situational ethics)	Reassessed priorities
		First-hand awareness of the urban poor
Guilt	Ministry philosophy=incarnational, holistic, righteous standards, servanthood, identification	Expanded paradigms, new insights, deepened convictions
Challenged, sobered	Viable churches and ministries=accountability, community, teaching, counseling, discipling, empowering, modeling	Deeper awareness of God's calling, gifting, and ministry motivations
	Acceptance, respect, honor, understanding are crucial	Embracing biblical theology of the city and the poor
	Priority of networking	Entering into compassion

CHAPTER 9

OF LESSONS LEARNED AND TO BE LEARNED

This study has used the analogy of a "journey" in urban experiential learning. The various "stops" enroute have been the array of ministry experiences and encounters with the students among disenfranchised men and women. Those episodes have been portrayed and debriefed on the previous pages. This chapter brings us to the "end" of the journey and evaluates its overall strengths and weaknesses in training students for urban ministry. Some final thoughts and significant discoveries conclude the study.

LIMITATIONS AND WEAKNESSES

1. Restricted Time Period

A 15-week semester is a restricted time period in which to train students in urban ministry. As a result their experiential learning was intense yet very abbreviated. Other than a general orientation in the initial class periods there was no opportunity for extensive pre-field instruction. This is to be expected though when one is training college students and has no contact with them prior to the course. This limited time frame also prohibited longevity in the training process. Each member of the group submitted a written evaluation of their overall experience at the end of the project. But monitoring the application of what students "learned" beyond the confines of the semester is prohibitive. Graduation absorbs many and other classes consume the time and energy of those remaining on campus.

A 4-month experiential immersion is not a sufficient period of time to fully equip students for urban ministry. However the "end" in view was the process of discovery itself, which is beneficial whether the exposure is a weekend "urban plunge" or a short-term missions excursion. The semester "window," with all its limitations, is the primary time frame in which to train college students and is still twice as long as the average summer missions program. Significant contributions to our urban training agenda can still be made within those parameters.

2. Diverse Student Schedules

The diversity of students' schedules handicapped us to some degree. It was almost impossible to get the whole group together on a consistent basis for observations and ministry participation due to conflicts with other classes. This is made more of a challenge when the students are a mixture of majors as well as both grads and undergrads. For the most part we were able to work around competing class schedules and decide on a common time which was conducive to all.

But inevitably some of the students missed out on learning experiences because of unavoidable alternative activities. Only a few were able to gain the full intent of the "holistic" exposure I had originally planned for them. Yet, the various aspects of the project in which different ones took part shaped the direction of their research. Noteworthy examples are Kyle and Rob and the unforgettable night on the street and Julie and Susan with their focus on Red Dog and Billie.

3. Commuting Ministry Mentality

The incarnational model is a significant vehicle for ministry training. One of the students regretted that he was "too closely connected with suburbia" during the semester and would have preferred to be "submerged in the culture" of the disenfranchised. A contextualized urban field education model is also highly effective and provides consistent in-depth exposure to the city. But we did not have the opportunity for either of these avenues. The alternative was to commute.

Those "kamikaze raids" into skid row were troubling to many of the students. It forced them to wrestle with the contrast between their life in relative case in the suburbs and those they were meeting who lived in cardboard boxes or under a bridge. Furthermore, those one and a half hour drives on congested freeways significantly limited the time we could spend in research and involvement with the various ministries and individuals. Commuting did provide an excellent opportunity, however, for group interaction and reflection on our activities together. It is the rare Christian college or seminary that is located in the urban environment and transporting students from campuses to city centers is a very real part of the experiential training process.

4. Insufficient Debriefing of Experiences

This study purposely marshalled an array of intense experiences in the city for the students. But we were immersed in the project before I realized how overwhelming so many of our encounters were for them. I had not fully comprehended the fears harbored by many of the girls in particular or how disillusioned several were becoming over their perceived helplessness and vulnerability in the midst of such blatant urban need. Comments by one about being "sick to his stomach" and another who was feeling "depressed" served as somewhat of a wake-up call for me. I had become accustomed to the tragedy of the world we were exploring and I needed to see and feel it all over again, through the eyes of the students. But it never seemed to be "convenient" for the group to sit down and debrief upon our return from an event. It was nearly 1 a.m. when we got back to the dorms after our Victory Outreach excursions. Day-time activities were often squeezed by an upcoming class or exam. One of our visits to First E. Free fell on the afternoon of the presidential election! I sought to maximize every free moment I had with the students. This included one-on-one and small group mentoring opportunities as well as brief sessions before, after, and during the break time of our class period together. Those times of reflection were invaluable, as were our conversations on the road. But in retrospect they were still inadequate.

5. Unfamiliarity with the City and its Networks

Because I was new to Los Angeles, I was unaware of the significant urban outreaches and individuals in the city center. I was familiar with rescue mission ministry and had prior contact with Victory Outreach in another city, but I was not well informed of the local urban churches in the downtown area. This was an initial liability and tended to portray a hectic nature to the project in the early stages while setting up the activities. Yet in some ways it was valuable as the students sensed that I was in a similar process of discovery along with them. One contact led to another, although it was several weeks into the semester by the time this occurred. It would potentially be more effective to duplicate the project now after having done a trial run and established the networks.

6. More Exposure to Organizations than Individuals

It was more difficult than I had anticipated to match up students with individuals from the various subcultures under study. This was particularly true for the girls interested in establishing rapport with a homeless woman or a prostitute. Compounding the problem was that I was in the process of building relationships with many of the likely doorkeepers into those communities myself (i.e. Funee Man, Red and Billie, etc.). Although Red did provide entree for us into the unstructured world of the "bridge" and "bush" people, the project was well underway before that introduction took place. Most of the female students were only able to get face-to-face interaction with women on the street through the L.A. Mission. Furthermore, were it not for our participation with Victory Outreach, the group's exposure to gangs would have been very limited.

I underestimated the amount of time it takes not only to make contact with individuals on the street, but to establish trust and credibility whereby one can bring students into their world. I had hoped for a balance between interfacing with organizations and individuals and this did occur to some extent. Green Eyes was an invaluable sounding board for the students in raising thought-provoking issues and opening their eyes to life on the streets. I would have liked to see the students experience even more spontaneous, one-to-one interactions apart from the protective umbrella of a church or rescue mission. I now realize that was an unrealistic desire for our particular situation.

265

7. Imbalanced Interface with the Various Subcultures

I also envisioned a relatively equal amount of interaction for the students with those in the homeless, gang and prostitute communities. As it turned out, the project primarily offered contact with the homeless. Green Eyes had much to do with that because it was our pre-established friendship that led to meeting Red and Billie and ultimately the guys under the bridge. It was also Green Eyes who put me in touch with Funee Man and the girls on the street with whom, unfortunately, the students had minimal interaction.

But as was typical of the study overall, we were learning things along the way. I did not know that the homeless would be much more approachable and receptive to students than those in the other two lifestyles. This was not always the case, as Funee welcomed me into his confidence. Furthermore, we were rebuffed in our attempts at befriending those under the overpass behind First E. Free. But for the most part we found the homeless to be more conducive to the project's ethnographic research component, specifically, participant observation, interviewing and gathering case studies.

We soon learned that it was very difficult for a group of naive, though well-meaning, young people to quickly gain favor with members of the very closed and untrusting circle of gangs and prostitution. The illegality of their activities makes it a challenge for even the most experienced and street-wise individual to penetrate their world, to say nothing of students with limited time and background. This does not mean to imply that students cannot be trained experientially in those arenas as well as with the homeless. I certainly believe that they can and should be equipped to minister among gangs and

266

prostitutes, which are arguably some of the most needy and neglected subcultures. It was my intent and attempt to do so in this project, but I found that I lacked the crucial relational foundation within those two communities for it to take place.

8. Macro Vs. Micro Perspective

A final limitation of the study is that its approach was purposely a broad and diverse examination of urban subcultures and ministries as opposed to a more specific and indepth analysis of one particular community or ministry model. In their evaluations, several students recorded their struggles over wanting to focus on just one aspect of all that we experienced over the length of the semester. They felt bombarded by the array of troubled lives and the various outreach approaches to respond to them. But that was an integral part of the project itself. Most of the students eventually filtered through the maze and directed their research on a single component of what we had seen. In the end, they agreed that they needed the overall exposure and were grateful for it.

STRENGTHS AND SUCCESSES

The project succeeded in meeting its primary objectives, as were specified in the opening chapter. Those are now recapped along with additional highlights of the study.

1. Personal Experience of Urban Need

Experiential learning, in the context of disadvantaged subcultures, brings students face-to-face with very needy individuals. It offers them a first-hand glimpse of gang members, prostitutes and street people, those comprising the "underside" of the city. It transcends the statistics of those "seedy subcultures", puts names on faces, allows for the beginning of relationships and even the forming of friendships. It is the first step in the process of learning compassion, namely, to see need. Poverty, violence, vagrancy, graffiti, hustling, and addiction were no longer confined to the pages of a textbook or daily newspaper nor limited to the numbing, mesmerizing television evening news. It now became real to them, something to be felt, struggled with and acted upon.

2. Exposure to Multi-Cultural Role Models

A highlight for many of those in the group was making the acquaintance of numerous urban leaders from a variety of cultures and lifestyles. Several of these men and women had great impact on the students as they heard their testimonies and saw them in action in their various ministry capacities. These individuals are a rich array of Black, Hispanic and White men and women whose lives have been transformed by Christ and devoted to ministry among the poor. The students themselves are on the threshold of significant ministry decisions in the coming years. Rubbing shoulders with such quality "kingdom people," watching their lives and absorbing their priorities is an invaluable contribution to that end.

3. Greater Awareness of Agencies Serving the Poor

The project set out to expose the students to various ministry approaches among the poor. It enabled them to personally reflect on and evaluate church and para-church distinctions as well as to discover for themselves the ultimate inadequacy of governmental programs. For some it was the first time they had ever set foot in a rescue mission. Many had never experienced the dynamic of a truly contextualized inner-city church or community of believers. Most had never seen anything like the zealous "go-get-em mentality" of Victory Outreach.

During their investigations they saw the tragic rescue mission tendency of "warehousing" or "processing" the poor and came to realize anew the value of people vs. programs. Scott's congregation reiterated to them the church's unique capacity to nurture and disciple the urban convert. But they also glimpsed its ever-present inclination to become ingrown to the neglect of evangelism (which is obviously the forte of V.O.). The group discovered that the strengths of one ministry approach can help to counteract the weaknesses of another and arrived at the simple yet profound conclusion that they need each other! They need to "network."

Teamwork, communication, partnerships, networking...each an essential ingredient to effectively further the gospel among the poor. Regretfully, they are items of great tension and polarization among well-intentioned ministries which are too often blinded in the pursuit of their own agendas. These young people are potential urban missionaries in their own right. The earlier they can embrace a partnering ministry mentality the better off they, and the agencies with which they serve, will be.

4. Deeper Appreciation of Group Dynamics

An offshoot of our collective explorations in research and ministry was the opportunity for the group to experience team work. Serving together at the rescue mission, reaching out to the homeless camp behind the church, building relationships under the bridge and sharing their faith on the streets were all a part of functioning as a team.

269

Prayer times helped to deepen their commitment to each other as well as to the project at hand and the comraderie we shared enhanced the notion of team-oriented ministry in their eyes. They caught glimpses of each other's strengths and limitations and saw how emphasizing the former while minimizing the latter can contribute to the overall success of the team.

But a broader group dynamic took place as these experiences spilled over into the classroom. The class as a whole benefited vicariously as the team recapped their adventures week by week. These included the dramatic experiences with Victory Outreach and the intimidating encounters of our night on the street. This led to an even deeper unity as an entire group and served as an ongoing base of prayer and encouragement throughout the semester.

5. Increased Flexibility and Effectiveness with Limited Numbers

Although the group totaled ten students, teams roughly half that size tended to comprise most of our adventures. This allowed for better interaction with each student and enabled smaller clusters to focus their research on specific areas of interest. It was also more conducive to building relationships with men and women on the street and under the bridges and was much less obtrusive into their world. Many "hard core" inner-city neighborhoods simply do not warrant bringing in big groups of young people for training or any other purpose. This was true of our night on who-stro and the efforts to reach the homeless camp behind the church. Group sizes can often be increased once trust is established and relationships are built but in most cases it is still much more functional and productive to work with smaller numbers.

6. Debunking of Stereotypes

Several students testified that the project helped dispel many of their preconceptions of the city and its people. One member of the group concluded:

> My upper-middle class world tells me that I am better than they are and that I have something to offer them and they have nothing to give to me. That is so wrong. They have more things to give to me than I could ever give...as a Christian, I have Jesus and He is the best thing we can offer anyone. Yet they teach me more of what it is to be a Christian so even in that aspect they can offer me something.

Another shared very honestly of his bias prior to the start of the project. He admitted that it had been easy for him to "downgrade the value of urban humanity," formerly acknowledging them to be "incapable of doing anything, so they deserve the place where they are." But he soon learned that "they are able (and willing) to discuss (not to be 'preached at') issues of extreme importance such as the eternal destiny of their souls. This has caused me to elevate my thinking of the urban poor."

Several students registered their surprise about how "amiable" and "gentle" Green Eyes was for one who was living in a cardboard box. They were unprepared for his "openness" and challenged by how he spoke so "intelligently" about life on the streets. They were equally caught off guard by some of those they met within the gang and prostitute communities. One of the grads recalls her impressions upon first meeting Funee Man:

> Funee Man reached in [to the car] and shook our hands as John introduced us. He seemed friendly and respectful to us and to John. I couldn't help but think how different he was than my stereotyped image of a gang leader. I would have expected him to be rough, profane and carrying a weapon...It seemed strange that someone so seemingly friendly to us was involved in such hard-core criminal acts. I knew, at this point, that the people of the city are complex and it

would take a lot of time to even begin to come to an understanding of their world.

The students discovered that the city and its people were not nearly as "big and bad" as they had been led to previously believe. Their fears and distorted perspectives had kept them away and prevented them from meeting and getting to know other such personable, receptive and intelligent men and women. Their experiences brought a sense of balance and realism to their understanding of the city and has ignited many of them for future urban ministry involvement.

7. Clearer Perspective of God's Calling and Gifting

An exciting long-term effect of the project is the insight several students gained regarding their gifting and burdens in ministry. A graduate at the end of the course is enthused about getting involved in a low-income urban community. Another who finished last Spring, set aside her teaching aspirations in light of pursuing urban missions. Two of the students discovered that they "really thrive in one-on-one relationships". One of them, assured of her gift of mercy, aspires to urban holistic ministry in the years ahead. Yet another is contemplating pastoring in the inner-city.

I know of no better way for students to gain a deeper awareness of whether or not God is calling them to the city than by strategically immersing them in its array of subcultures and carefully monitoring their reactions. Supplement this with an understanding of a biblical theology of the city and the additional inspiration of significant urban leaders, and the young people are well on their way to processing and personalizing God's unique place for them in the ripening urban harvest fields of our world.

8. Lessons Learned in the School of Compassion

Early in the semester we addressed the scriptural admonition to "go and learn" compassion (Matt. 9:13;Luke 10:37), noting as well the biblical steps to that end of "seeing, feeling, and acting" as outlined in Mark 6:34. This issue was one of the chief struggles of many of the students, but several learned their lessons well under the tutelage of the Master Teacher.

As I reflected on their journey into a "suffering together with" ministry mentality, I was intrigued by the similar patterns and distinct stages in their development. I have wondered whether it is possible to visualize or map out that vital yet painful path of following Jesus into a compassionate lifestyle. Could we guide people in this learning endeavor, and if so, what would it look like? Our experiences together in this study shed a great deal of light on that process.

I noticed four "stages" in this "compassion continuum". The first is a pre-exposure mentality toward the city and its people in which all the students found themselves, in varying degrees, prior to the start of the research. Although not exclusively confined to these categories, the initial attitudes seemed to fall into a positive, neutral, or negative posture toward the urban environment. Positively this included enthusiasm, teachability and naiveté. The neutral classification was that of indifference, and the negative involved attitudes of over-confidence, prejudice, fear and guilt.

The second stage was actually the first step in Mark 6 of "seeing" need and encompassed our array of exposure and experiences in the city. Stage three, the most intriguing, intricate and indispensable of the biblical triad flows out of those diverse encounters. This crucial "feeling" component is

273

the heart of the entire process and the point at which many recoil and retreat from embracing the cross of compassion.

This stage lends itself to varying levels or degrees as well. Level one responses to urban need include those of feeling vulnerable, intimidated, overwhelmed, anxious, hurt and angry. A transition period generally follows in which feelings of frustration, disillusionment and discouragement set in resulting in a state of helplessness and perceived inadequacy. This plateau then becomes the decisive crossroads at which one can either turn back or plunge ahead. Choosing to go forward puts in motion the cycle of accepting our inabilities and confessing our shortcomings while committing ourselves anew to a compassionate lifestyle which is then forged into conviction. The final climactic stage is the "active" expression of "suffering together with" the urban poor. This lifestyle of servanthood is reflected in brokenness and unconditional love. It is incarnational in its very essence and embodies the dynamics of empowerment and identification with those in need.

Table 5

A Compassion Continuum

Matthew 9:13 - "Go and learn what this means, 'I desire compassion...'"
Matthew 9:36 - "Seeing the multitudes, He felt compassion for them..."

Pre-exposure

+ Enthusiasm
+ Teachability
+ Naiveté
o Indifference
- Overconfidence
- Prejudice
- Fear
- Guilt

Stage 1

"Seeing"

EXPOSURE
TO
URBAN
NEED

Stage 2

"Feeling"

LEVEL I
Vulnerable
Intimidated
Overwhelmed
Anxious
Hurt
Angry

TRANSITION
Discouraged
Frustrated
Disillusioned
Helpless
Inadequate

LEVEL II*
Acceptance
Confession
Commitment
Conviction

Stage 3

"Acting"

COMPASSION:
"TO SUFFER
WITH"
Incarnation
Identification
Empowerment
Servanthood
Brokenness

Stage 4

Key: + Positive, o Neutral, - Negative
*Denotes a cyclical pattern

275

SUMMARY THOUGHTS AND SIGNIFICANT DISCOVERIES

1. Ministry Among the Urban Masses Flows from a Biblical Theology of the City and the Poor.

A Biblical theology of the city and the poor is the bedrock upon which all our efforts are based, the stimulus to our every activity. Scripture clearly challenges Christians to "seek the welfare of the city" (Jer. 29:7) and to "practice kindness and compassion" among "the widow, the orphan, the stranger and the poor" (Zech. 7:9, 10). Without the inspiration of God's love and concern for the Ninevahs' and Jerusalems' of our world (Jonah 4:11; Luke 19:41) we would quickly tire and easily lose hope.

2. The Process Rather than the Product is the Emphasis of Experiential Learning.

Too often in our Western world we are product-driven, accentuating the end in view while underestimating the crucial steps along the way. Each experience is itself the training process, not simply the project or course as a whole. The same can be said for the Christian life. God is interested in the moment by moment formation of our character, which is all a part of the overall plan of conforming us to His image. As educators we must not lose sight of the parts for the whole. The end product will be a viable one if we are mindful to seize and maximize every opportunity that comprises the painstaking learning process.

3. Self-discovery Should Be a Vital Component of our Urban Ministry Training.

Those being trained need to experience and grapple with the harsh reality of urban need. While they are doing so we must resist the urge of intervening too quickly and undermining their painstaking personal growth and ministry development. As a mentor, it is difficult to watch one's trainee struggle, overwhelmed with fear, hurt and disillusionment. Our tendency is to immediately jump in and resolve their problems or shield them from the pain. It is crucial that we allow them to wrestle through those initial experiences as they move toward "seeing the city with the eyes of God" (McClung 1991).

4. Debriefing the Trainee's Urban Ministry Experiences Cannot Be Underestimated or Overlooked.

This study appeals for a far greater emphasis on learning experiences outside of the classroom. But debriefing those encounters is equally valid, in fact, it is vital. Without it students remain unnecessarily overwhelmed and may even shy away from further involvement. Reflection helps them sort through and make sense of what they have been exposed to. It draws meaning from each situation and connects those fresh discoveries with their previous body of knowledge. It is the passageway from past experience to new horizons of learning.

5. A Heart for Urban Ministry is Easier Caught than Taught.

Those who would be effective servants of the city and its diverse subcultures need to be shown, not simply told, how to do so. This fact speaks loudly for the place of modeling and mentoring in urban ministry. It is a call for teachers and trainers to also see themselves as coaches. Inherent to that profession is one who is chiefly a practitioner, able to personally demonstrate the nature of his craft. To teach is not just to tell. It is to show, to model, to merge knowing with doing, theory with practice. The old Chinese proverb still applies, "I listen and I forget; I see and I remember; I do and I understand" (Sollanky 1984: 161).

6. Classroom and Community Should Complement, Not Compete with Each Other.

Espousing experiential learning does not necessarily entail denigrating formal classroom instruction. The two are allies rather than adversaries. Experiential training begins in the classroom with the presentation and discussion of pertinent urban issues and supplementary reading material. Debriefing and reflection as well as corporate prayer for the city and its people take place there throughout the learning experience. Critique and evaluation are also relevant to the classroom setting as the project draws to a close. Each needs the other and functions most effectively as a unit.

7. Establish and Cultivate Key Contacts in the City.

Experiential learning projects or practicums must tie in with local church and para-church ministries. Partnerships should be established whereby students can gain valuable experience while contributing to the outreach efforts of the organizations. Equipping men and women for urban ministry hinges upon the viability and credibility of these contacts in the field. This includes significant "gatekeepers" in the various subcultures to be explored. The project leader must also network and build relationships in those communities of need. This is extremely time-consuming and particularly challenging for those in the academic arena. Acknowledging ones limitations and allowing for the assistance of others must be a priority if we are to fully equip students for urban ministry.

8. Seek a Balance Between Wide Exposure to Diverse Urban Need and Selected Ministry Sites with Spontaneous, One-on-One Interaction Among the Poor.

The curriculum of an urban training program is understandably broad and varied and needs to be contoured to the specific locale. Aim for a harmonious exposure to existent ministries along with opportunities for the students to spontaneously experience urban need in an unstructured environment. For those whose dichotomous outlook on life demands considerable structure, these times of impromptu interaction are often met with hesitancy and discomfort. But because so much of urban ministry is notoriously unscheduled, relational expertise and adaptability are qualities of great value and are wisely cultivated. Strive for a blend between wide introduction to the various subcultures with focused, face-to-face interaction with individuals from a specific community. These personal encounters provide a realistic, eye-witness account of life on the streets in contrast to the shielded climate of a mission setting. It also models an incarnational approach, a willingness to "meet them on their own turf" rather than insisting that they come to us.

9. The Crucible of Urban Ministry Training is by its Very Nature Experiential.

While the foundation of the missionary enterprise is theological and theoretical, its expression is profoundly practical. A similar ideology should characterize our training endeavors as well. How do we expect our future "apostles to the city" (Greenway 1978) to ultimately tackle extremely complex and highly intimidating urban subcultures without actually teaching them how to build a relationship with a gang member, befriend a prostitute and mingle with the homeless on the streets? These intensely needy communities cry out for our utmost attention and are deserving of our finest missionary candidates.

10. Urban Experiential Training Can Be Implemented by any Educational Institution.

Immersing students in experiential learning situations is not dependent upon money or restricted by departmental budget deficits. Unlike many start-up programs within the educational institution, it does not necessitate hiring new faculty. An existing faculty member, a teaching assistant, an experienced student with a burden for the urban poor, exposure to inner-city ministry and the necessary time and contacts can initiate an experiential learning project. Another option would be a local urban ministry staff member who could mentor the students on a short-term basis. Mature male and female team leadership would be the ideal to effectively guide the students in their learning experiences. While not a full-scale "urban" semester, it surpasses a merely cognitive analysis of the city, classroom simulations, or the sporadic "tourist-run" into disenfranchised communities. An experiential learning component can be added to any existing course and carries with it the opportunity for students to experience the integration of faith and learning.

CONCLUSION

This journey in experiential learning confirms the tremendous receptivity of disenfranchised urban subcultures. It also revealed the eagerness and ability of university students to embrace the city in all its diversity and complexity. The current deficiency lies not in the messenger nor the receptor, but in the source, the formal training institution. The major task for Christian educators this decade and into the next century is to equip men and women to penetrate urban society. But we are still inexcusably hesitant, unsure of our approach and out of touch with an increasingly urban world.

Michael Pabarcus (1992:8) shares these pertinent and challenging comments:

> The contemporary world and the cities that dominate them call the Christian college and the theological seminary to relevance. Educators must heed their call by giving serious thought to those biblical emphases, educational theories and contemporary necessities that should shape our current educational effort...Generally speaking, Christian colleges and seminaries are culturally oriented to the white, middle class, rural or suburban setting...As a consequence, effectiveness in divergent settings is diminished.

In a subsequent article, Thomas Austin (1992:34) furthers the argument and offers this timely advice:

> We need to reevaluate our institutions...and consider the appropriate changes...we need to accept the city, to become a part of it. We need to allow the city to infiltrate our walls and to become part of us. We need to begin to listen to the cries of the city with "urban ears" and to see its needs with "urban eyes".

Harv Oostdyk (1983:191) drives home the point with greater force as he boldly predicts, "If every biblical scholar, student and preacher spent one month living among the poor, no church would ever be the same. Neither would any poor neighborhood". Might I add, neither would any training institution?

As educators we need similar exposure. In the words of Harvie Conn (1992:5), "It's not simply that the city needs us; we need the city." We need to draw near its hurting people, to feel their pain. We the instructors must become the instructed in "suffering together with" the urban masses. We cannot hope to instill a burden and a love for the city in our students unless we ourselves are embracing the way of compassion. Excuses pale in light of the significance of the task and the urgency of the hour.

BIBLIOGRAPHY

Amberson, T. R.
    1980   Reaching Out to People. Nashville, TN: Broadman.

Appleby, Jerry L.
    1986   Missions Have Come Home to America. Kansas City, MO: Beacon Hill.

Argyris, C. and Donald A. Schon
    1974   Theory in Practice: Increasing Professional Effectiveness. San Francisco: Jossey-Bass.

Aschenbrenner, Joyce
    1975   Lifelines: Black Families in Chicago. New York: Holt, Rinehart & Winston.

Austin, Thomas
    1992   Integrating City and Seminary. Urban Mission 10(2):28-38.

Bahr, H. M. and G. R. Garrett
    1976   Women Alone. Lexington, MA: Lexington.

Bakke, Ray
    1987   The Urban Christian. Downers Grove, IL: InterVarsity Press.

Bassuk, Ellen L.
    1984   The Homelessness Problem. Scientific American 251(1):40-45.

Baxter, Ellen and Kim Hopper
    1982   The New Mendicancy: Homeless in New York City. American Journal of Orthopsychiatry 52:393-409.

Beals, Art
    1985   Beyond Hunger. Portland, OR: Multnomah Press.

Bernard, H. Russell
    1988   Research Methods in Cultural Anthropology. Newbury Park, CA: Sage.

Berte, Neal R. and Edward H. O'Neil
    1977   Old and New Models of Service. *In* Redefining Service, Research, and Teaching.Warren Bryan Martin, ed., pp. 17-21. New Directions for Higher Education V(2). San Francisco: Jossey-Bass.

Bing, Leon
    1991   Do or Die. New York: Harper Collins.

Bingham, R. D., R. E. Green, and S. B. White
    1987   The Homeless in Contemporary Society. Newbury Park, CA: Sage.

Bird, Brian
    1990   Reclaiming the Urban War Zones. Christianity Today (January 15):16-20.

Blackwood, V., B. Reichardt, and S. Schreiner
    1992   SCUPE Urban Theological Education Programs Directory. Chicago: Seminary Consortium for Urban Pastoral Education.

Boot, R. and P. Boxer
    1980   Reflective Learning. *In* Advances in Management Education. J. Beck and C. Cox, eds. London: John Wiley.

Brake, Robert K.
    1991   A Ministry to the Homeless in Urban America. Urban Mission 8(5):48-55.

Brown, Gerald F.
    1980   Three Types of Experiential Learning: A Nontrivial Distinction. *In* Developing Experiential Learning Programs for Professional Education. Eugene T. Byrne and Douglas E. Wolfe, eds., pp. 47-55. New Directions for Experiential Learning 8. San Francisco: Jossey-Bass.

Bruning, Carol L.
    1993   Practical Help for the Homeless. World Vision (April/May):7-10.

Burt, Martha R. and Barbara E. Cohen
    1989   America's Homeless: Numbers, Characteristics, and Programs that Serve Them. Washington, D. C.: The Urban Institute.

California Council on Criminal Justice
1989 State Task Force on Gangs and Drugs. Sacramento, CA: Author.

California Legislature, Joint Committee on Organized Crime and Gang
 Violence
1989 Gang Violence: Recommendations for Legislative Solutions.
    Sacramento, CA: Author.

Canales, Isaac
1989 Chicano - Growing Up in the Barrio. Youth Worker, Winter.
    32-36.

Carney, Glandion
1984 Creative Urban Youth Ministry. Elgin, EL: David C. Cook.

Chickering, Arthur W.
1977 Developmental Change as a Major Outcome. *In* Experiential
    Learning: Rationale, Characteristics, and Assessment. Morris T.
    Keeton, ed., pp. 62-107. San Francisco: Jossey-Bass.

Chow, Wilson
1982 An Integrated Approach to Theological Education. *In*
    Evangelical Theological Education Today: An International
    Perspective. Paul Bowers, ed., pp. 49-60. Nairobi: Evangel.

Christensen, Michael J.
1988 City Streets, City People: A Call for Compassion. Nashville, TN:
    Abingdon.

Chung-choon, Kim
1984 The Contextualization of Theological Education. *In* Missions
    and Theological Education in World Perspective. Harvie M.
    Conn and Samuel F. Rowen, eds., pp. 41-54. Farmington, MI:
    Associates of Urbanus.

City Confronts
1983 City Confronts "Bombshell" in Crowded Hotels. Los Angeles
    Times, July 10, Metro Section, p. 1.

Claerbaut, David
1983 Urban Ministry. Grand Rapids, MI: Zondervan.

Clark, Roger L.
    1989   Toward 2000: Transformed Colleges and Curricula. Polis 1
              (Summer):42.

Clinton, J. Robert and Richard W. Clinton
    1991   The Mentor Handbook. Altadena, CA: Barnabus Publishers.

Coleman, James S.
    1977   Differences Between Experiential and Classroom Learning. *In*
              Experiential Learning: Rationale, Characteristics, and
              Assessment. Morris T. Keeton, ed., pp. 49-61. San Francisco:
              Jossey-Bass.

Commission on California State Government Organization and Economy
    1989   Meeting the Needs of California's Homeless: It Takes More
              Than a Roof. Sacramento, CA: Author.

Congressional Research Service, Library of Congress
    1991   Homeless: What Should be Done to Meet the Needs of the
              Homeless in the United States? Washington, D.C.: U.S.
              Government Printing Office.

Conn, Harvie M.
    1984   Eternal Word and Changing Worlds. Grand Rapids, MI:
              Zondervan.

    1987   A Clarified Vision for Urban Mission. Grand Rapids, MI:
              Zondervan.

    1992   Theological Education for the City. Urban Mission 10(2):3-5.

Conn, Harvie M. and Samuel F. Rowan
    1984   Missions and Theological Education in World Perspective.
              Farmington, MI: Associates of Urbanus.

Costas, Orlando E.
    1984   Christ Outside the Gate. Maryknoll, New York: Orbis.

Cross, K. P.
    1981   Adults as Learners: Increasing Participation and Facilitating
              Learning. San Francisco: Jossey-Bass.

Danwing, Enrique
    1988   God and Large Cities. Urban Mission 6(2):27-32.

Davis, Mike
    1988   War in the Streets. New Statesman & Society 23(11):27-30.

Dawson, John
    1989   Taking Our Cities For God. Lake Mary, FL: Creation House.

D'Ercole, A. and E. Struening
    1990   Victimization Among Homeless Women: Implications for
               Service Delivery. Journal of Comm. Psychology 18:141-152.

Dewey, John
    1938   Experience and Education. New York: Macmillan.

De Wolfe, Evelyn
    1982   Hotels Vanishing as Living Space for 10,000 People. Los Angeles
               Times, Real Estate Section, April 25.

Doherty, Austin, Marcia M. Mentkowski, and Kelley Conrad
    1978   Toward a Theory of Undergraduate Experiential Learning. *In*
               Learning by Experience - What, Why, How. Morris T. Keeton
               and Pamela J. Tate, eds., pp. 23-35. New Directions for
               Experiential Learning 1. San Francisco: Jossey-Bass.

Donovan, John
    1988   An Introduction to Street Gangs in California. Sacramento, CA:
               John Garamendi.

DuBose, Francis M.
    1978   How Churches Grow in an Urban World. Nashville, TN:
               Broadman.

    1984   Urban Poverty as a World Challenge. *In* An Urban World:
               Churches Face the Future. Larry L. Rose and C. Kirk Hadaway,
               eds., pp. 51-74. Nashville, TN: Broadman.

Duley, John S.
    1977   Service as Learning, Lifestyle, and Faculty Function. *In* Redefining Service, Research, and Teaching. Warren Bryan Martin, ed., pp. 23-26. New Directions for Higher Education V(2). San Francisco: Jossey-Bass.

Duley, John S. and Jane Szutu Permaul
    1984   Participation in and Benefits from Experiential Education. Educational Record (65)3:18-21.

Elifson, Claire Sterk and Kirk W.
    1992   Someone to Count On: Homeless, Male Drug Users and their Friendship Relations. Urban Anthropology 21(3):235-251.

Ellison, Craig
    1974   The Urban Mission. Grand Rapids, MI: Eerdmans.

Ellison, Craig and Edward S. Maynard
    1992   Healing for the City. Grand Rapids, MI: Zondervan.

Elmer, Duane H.
    1984   Education and Service: A Model for Praxis Education. *In* Missions and Theological Education in World Perspective. Harvie M. Conn and Samuel F. Rowan, eds., pp. 226-244. Farmington, MI: Associates of Urbanus.

Erickson, Jon and Charles Wilhelm
    1986   Housing the Homeless. New Brunswick, NJ: Center for Urban Policy Research.

Evans, Anthony T.
    1983   Stretching Your Reach. Grand Rapids, MI: Radio Bible Class.

Ezekiel, Raphael S.
    1984   Voices From the Corner. Philadelphia: Temple University Press.

Flack, Michael J.
    1981   Experiential Learning in Transnational Contexts. *In* Cross-Cultural Learning. Charles B. Neff, ed., pp. 11-20. New Directions for Experiential Learning II. San Francisco: Jossey-Bass.

Flenniken, Trudy
    1993   "I Wanted Them to Disappear." Decision 34(6):36.

Ford, Andrea
    1993   County's Homeless Population Up 13%. Los Angeles Times,
                Metro Section, June 30.

Freire, Paulo
    1970   Pedagogy of the Oppressed. New York: Seabury.

Frias, Gus
    1982   Barrio Warriors: Homeboys of Peace. Los Angeles: Diaz.

Frick, S.
    1977   Toward a Definition of Experience. Liberal Education 63:495-499.

Fung, Raymond
    1981   Evangelizing the Sinned Against. Your Kingdom Come:
                Mission Perspectives. World Council of Churches.

Gardner, Sandra
    1983   Street Gangs. New York: F. Watts

Gmelch, George and Walter P. Zenner
    1988   Urban Life. Propect Heights, IL: Waveland.

Grant, George
    1986   The Dispossessed: Homelessness in America. Ft. Worth, TX:
                Dominion.

    1988   Bringing in the Sheaves. Brentwood, TN: Wolgemuth & Hyatt.

Greenway, Roger S.
    1976   Guidelines for Urban Church Planting. Grand Rapids, MI:
                Baker.

    1978   Apostles to the City. Grand Rapids, MI: Baker.

    1989   A World of Giant Cities. City Watch 4(4):1-2,4.

    1992   Discipling the City. 2nd ed. Grand Rapids, MI: Baker.

Greenway, Roger S. and Timothy M. Monsma
    1989   Cities: Mission's New Frontier. Grand Rapids, MI: Baker.

Grigg, Viv
 1984 Companion to the Poor. Australia: Albatross.

 1992 Cry of the Urban Poor. Monrovia, CA: MARC.

Grigsby, C., et al.
 1990 Disaffiliation to Entrenchment: A Model for Understanding
     Homelessness. Journal of Social Issues 46(4):141-156.

Harper, D. A.
 1975 The Homeless Man: An Ethnography of Work, Trains, and
     Booze. Unpublished Doctoral Dissertation, Brandeis University.

Harrington, Michael
 1963 The Other America. New York: Macmillan.

 1984 The New American Poverty. New York: Holt, Rinehart &
     Winston.

Hastings, Deborah
 1983 Owner of Skid Row Hotel May Face City Prosecution. Los
     Angeles Times, Metro Section, July 25.

Hollowell, Martha
 1990 Evangelizing the Homeless. Urban Mission 7(3):36-42.

Hombs, M. E. and Mitch Snyder
 1983 Homelessness in America: A Forced March to Nowhere.
     Washington, D. C.: Community for Creative Non-violence.

Homeless, Joe
 1992 My Life on the Street. Far Hills, NJ: New Horizons.

Honey, P. and A. Mumford
 1983 Using Your Learning Styles. Berkshire, England: Ardingly
     House.

Hope, Glenda and Penny Sarvis
 1992 Teaching Ministry in the City. In Envisioning the New City.
     Eleanor Scott Meyers, ed., pp. 327-338. Louisville, KY:
     Westminster/John Knox.

Hope, M. and J. Young
    1986   The Faces of Homelessness. Lexington, MA: Lexington.

Hopper, K. and J. Hamberg
    1986   The Making of America's Homeless: From Skid Row to New
               Poor, 1945-1984. *In* Critical Perspectives on Housing. R. Bratt, C.
               Hartman, and A. Meyerson, eds., pp. 12-40. Philadelphia:
               Temple University Press.

Horowitz, Ruth
    1982   Adult Delinquency Gangs in a Chicano Community. Urban Life:
               A Journal of Ethnographic Research 11(1):3-26.

Houle, Cyril O.
    1977   Deep Traditions of Experiential Learning. *In* Experiential
               Learning: Rationale, Characteristics, and Assessment. Morris T.
               Keeton, ed., pp. 19-33. San Francisco: Jossey-Bass.

Huff, C. Ronald
    1990   Gangs in America. Newbury Park, CA: Sage.

Hurst, J.
    1986   Houses of Horror: "Slum Busters" Cracking Down on
               Dangerous, Dilapidated Apartments. Los Angeles Times, Metro
               Section, June 8.

Hutchings, Pat and Allen Wutzdorff
    1988   Knowing and Doing: Learning Through Experience. *In* New
               Directions for Teaching and Learning 35 (Fall). Robert E. Young,
               ed. San Francisco: Jossey-Bass.

Jackson, Robert K.
    1985   Understanding Street Gangs. Sacramento, CA: Custom.

James, Samuel M.
    1984   Training for Urban Evangelization. *In* An Urban World:
               Churches Face the Future. Larry L. Rose and C. Kirk Hadaway,
               eds., pp. 189-206. Nashville, TN: Broadman.

Johnson, A. K. and L. W. Kreuger
    1989   Toward a Better Understanding of Homeless Women. Social
               Work 34:537-540.

Joiner, Bill
    1980   Dilemmas in Experiential Learning Programs: Toward a Holistic
                Approach. *In* Developing Experiential Learning Programs for
                Professional Education. Eugene T. Byrne and Douglas E. Wolfe,
                eds., pp. 79-95. New Directions for Experiential Learning 8. San
                Francisco: Jossey-Bass.

Keeton, Morris T.
    1977   Experiential Learning: Rationale, Characteristics, and
                Assessment. San Francisco: Jossey-Bass.

Keeton, Morris T. and Pamela J. Tate
    1978   Learning by Experience - What, Why, How. *In* New Directions
                for Experiential Learning 1. San Francisco: Jossey-Bass.

Keiser, R. Lincoln
    1979   The Vice Lords: Warriors of the Streets. New York: Holt,
                Rinehart & Winston.

Knowles, Malcolm
    1980   Modern Practice of Adult Education, From Pedagogy to
                Andagogy. Chicago: Follet.

Koegel, Paul and Audrey M. Burnam
    1988   Alcoholism Among Homeless Adults in the Inner City of Los
                Angeles. Archives of General Psychiatry 45(11):1011-1018.

Koegel, Paul, Audrey M. Burnam, and R. K. Farr
    1988   The Prevalence of Specific Psychiatric Disorders Among
                Homeless Individuals in the Inner City of Los Angeles.
                Archives of General Psychiatry 45(12):1085-1092.

    1990   Subsistence Adaptation Among Homeless Adults in the Inner
                City of Los Angeles. Journal of Social Issues 45(4):83-107.

Kolb, David A.
    1976   Learning Style Inventory: Technical Manual. Boston: McBer.

    1984   Experiential Learning: Experience as the Source of Learning and
                Development. Englewood Cliffs, NJ: Prentice-Hall.

Krupat, Edward
    1989   People in Cities. New York: Cambridge University Press.

Ladner, Joyce A.
  1971   Tomorrow's Tomorrow: The Black Woman. New York:
            Doubleday.

La Gory, M., K. Fitzpatrick, and F. Ritchey
  1990   Homeless Persons: Differences Between Those Living on the
            Street and in Shelters. Sociology and Social Research 74 (3):162-
            167.

Landes, A., C. Foster, and B. Caldwell
  1991   Homeless in America: How Could it Happen Here? Wylie, TX:
            Information Plus.

Landry, Paul
  1983   Poor in America. World Vision. November, pp. 8, 9.

Lewin, Kurt
  1951   Field theory in Social Sciences. New York: Harper & Row.

Liebow, Elliot
  1967   Tally's Corner. Boston: Little, Brown.

Lingenfelter, Judith
  1992   Getting to Know Your New City. In Discipling the City: A
            Comprehensive Approach to Urban Mission. Roger S.
            Greenway, ed., pp. 183-194, 2nd ed. Grand Rapids, MI: Baker.

Lingenfelter, Sherwood G. and Marvin K. Mayers
  1986   Ministering Cross-Culturally. Grand Rapids, MI: Baker.

Linthicum, Robert C.
  1991a   City of God, City of Satan. Grand Rapids, MI: Zondervan.

  1991b   Empowering the Poor. Monrovia, CA: MARC.

Lochhead, Carolyn
  1988   Compassion and Disgust: Dealing with the Homeless. Insight
            (May 16):8-18.

Locke, L. W., W. W. Spirduso, and S. J. Silverman
  1987   Proposals That Work. Newbury Park, CA: Sage.

Logan, Richard D.
    1983   Bridging the Traditional and Non-Traditional: A Model for
             Higher Education. Liberal Education 69(3):233-243.

Long, T. J., J. J. Convey, and A. R. Chwalek.
    1985   Completing Dissertations in the Behavioral Sciences and
             Education. San Francisco: Jossey-Bass.

Lupton, Robert D.
    1989   Theirs is the Kingdom: Celebrating the Gospel in Urban
             America. New York: Harper & Row.

MacLeod, Jay
    1987   Ain't No Makin' It. Boulder, CO: Westview.

Marienau, Catherine and Arthur W. Chickering
    1982   Adult Development and Learning. *In* Building on Experiences
             in Adult Development. Betty Menson, ed., pp. 7-30. New
             Directions in Experiential Learning 16. San Francisco: Jossey-
             Bass.

Marshall, C. and Gretchen B. Rossman
    1989   Designing Qualitative Research. Newbury Park, CA: Sage.

McClung, Floyd
    1991   Seeing the City with the Eyes of God. New York: Fleming H.
             Revell.

McGavran, Donald A.
    1980   Understanding Church Growth. Grand Rapids, MI: Eerdmans.

McLean, Gordon
    1991   Cities of Lonesome Fear. Chicago: Moody Press.

McNeill, D. P., D. A. Morrison, and Henri J. M. Nouwen
    1982   Compassion. New York: Doubleday.

Moore, Joan W.
    1978   Homeboys: Gangs, Drugs & Prison in the Barrios of Los Angeles.
             Philadelphia: Temple University Press.

Moore, Joan W. and James Diego Vigil
    1989   Chicano Gangs: Group Norms and Individual Factors Related to
            Adult Criminality. Aztlan 18(2):27-44.

Morales, Armando
    1982   The Mexican-American Gang Member: Evaluation and
            Treatment. *In* Mental Health and Hispanic Americans. Rosina
            M. Becerra, Marvin Karno, and Javier I. Escobar, eds., pp. 139-155.
            New York: Grune & Stratton.

Murrell, Patricia H. and Charles S. Claxton
    1987   Theory and Ideas for Training. Counselor Education and
            Supervision 27(1):4-14.

Neff, Charles B.
    1981   Introduction: Cross-Cultural Encounters. *In* Cross-Cultural
            Learning. Charles B. Neff, ed., pp. 1-10. New Directions for
            Experiential Learning 11. San Francisco: Jossey-Bass.

Nelson, Marcia Z.
    1986   Street People. *In* Housing the Homeless. Jon Erickson and
            Charles Wilhelm, eds., pp. 17-25. New Brunswick, NJ: Center
            for Urban Policy Research.

New American Standard Bible
    1973   New American Standard Bible. La Habra, CA: Lockman.

Oostdyk, Harv
    1983   Step One: The Gospel and the Ghetto. Basking Ridge, NJ: Son
            Life.

Ortiz, Manuel
    1992   Being Disciples: Incarnational Christians in the City. *In*
            Discipling the City: A Comprehensive Approach to Urban
            Mission. Roger S. Greenway, ed., pp. 85-98, 2nd ed. Grand
            Rapids: Baker.

Pabarcus, Michael
    1992   A Call to Relevance. Urban Mission 10(2):6-15.

Palen, J. John
    1987   The Urban World. New York: McGraw-Hill.

Pannell, William
  1992   Evangelism from the Bottom Up. Grand Rapids, MI:
          Zondervan.

Perkins, John
  1982   With Justice For All. Ventura, CA: Regal.

Phillips, Keith
  1975   They Dare to Love the Ghetto. Glendale, CA: Regal.

  1985   No Quick Fix. Ventura, CA: Regal.

Piaget, Jean
  1971   Psychology and Epistemology. Middlesex, England: Penguin.

Pinson, William M., Jr.
  1982   Our Mandate for Reaching Urban America. *In* The Urban
          Challenge: Reaching America's Cities with the Gospel. Larry L.
          Rose and C. Kirk Hadaway, eds., pp. 34-39. Nashville, TN:
          Broadman.

Quinn, Mary Ellen and Louise Sellars
  1974   Role of the Student. *In* Implementing Field Experience
          Education. John Duley, ed., pp. 31-38. New Directions for
          Higher Education II(2). San Francisco: Jossey-Bass.

Rahimian, Afsaneh
  1990   Migration and Mobility of the Urban Homeless. Unpublished
          Doctoral Dissertation. Los Angeles: University of Southern
          California.

Ramsey, William R.
  1974   Role of the Agency Supervisor. *In* Implementing Field
          Experience Education. John Duley, ed., pp. 45-54. New
          Directions for Higher Education II(2). San Francisco: Jossey-Bass.

Raths, James
  1987   Enhancing Understanding Through Debriefing. Educational
          Leadership 45(2):24-27.

Redburn, F. S. and Terry F. Buss
  1986   The Invisible Homeless. New York: Human Sciences.

Roehlkepartain, Eugene C.
1989   Youth Ministry in City Churches. Loveland, CO: Group.

Rooy, Sidney
1992   Theological Education for Urban Mission. *In* Discipling the City: A Comprehensive Approach to Urban Mission. Roger S. Greenway, ed., pp. 223-245, 2nd ed. Grand Rapids, MI: Baker.

Ropers, Richard H.
1986   The Rise of the New Urban Homeless. Public Affairs Report 26(5, 6):1-14.

1988   The Invisible Homeless: A New Urban Ecology. NY: Human Sciences Press.

Rose, Larry L. and C. Kirk Hadaway
1982   The Urban Challenge. Nashville, TN: Broadman.

1984   An Urban World: Churches Face the Future. Nashville, TN: Broadman.

Rosenthal, Rob
1991   Straighter From the Source: Alternative Methods of Researching Homelessness. Urban Anthropology 20(2):109-126.

Rossi, Peter H.
1989   Down and Out in America. Chicago: University of Chicago Press.

Rowe, Stacy and Jennifer Wolch
1990   Social Networks in Time and Space: Homeless Women in Skid Row, Los Angeles. Annals of the Association of American Geographers 80(2):184-204.

Ryan, Mary
1988   The Teachable Moment: The Washington Center Internship Program. *In* Knowing and Doing: Learning Through Experience. Pat Hutchings and Allen Wutzdorff, eds., pp. 39-47. New Directions for Teaching and Learning 35(Fall). San Francisco: Jossey-Bass.

Santoli, Al
  1991   "What Can Be Done About Teen Gangs?" Parade Magazine
           24(March).

Scanlan, A. Clark
  1984   Planning a Holistic Strategy for Urban Witness. *In* An Urban
           World: Churches Face the Future. Larry L. Rose and C. Kirk
           Hadaway, eds., pp. 167-187. Nashville, TN: Broadman.

Schon, Donald A.
  1983   The Reflective Practitioner. New York: Harper Collins.

  1987   Educating the Reflective Practitioner. San Francisco: Jossey-
           Bass.

Scott, Waldron
  1980   Bring Forth Justice: A Contemporary Perspective on Mission.
           Grand Rapids, MI: Eerdmans.

  1988   Man at His Best and Worst: A Biblical View of Urban Life.
           World Christian (January/February):27-29.

Seeman, Howard
  1988   Why the Resistance to Experiential Learning? Education Digest
           LIV (4):28-30.

Shannon, T. R., N. Kleniewski, and W. M. Cross
  1991   Urban Problems in Sociological Perspective. Prospect Heights,
           IL: Waveland.

Sider, Ronald J.
  1980   Cry Justice. Downers Grove, IL: InterVarsity Press.

  1984   Rich Christians in an Age of Hunger. Downers Grove, IL:
           InterVarsity Press.

Sikkema, M. and A. M. Niyekawa-Howard
  1977   Cross-Cultural Learning and Self-Growth. New York:
           International Association of Schools of Social Work.

Skolnick, Jerome H.
1990   Gang Organization and Migration: Drugs, Gangs, and Law
        Enforcement. Sacramento, CA: State of California Department
        of Justice.

Slavinsky, A. T. and A. Cousins
1982   Homeless Women. Nursing Outlook 30(June):358-362.

Snyder, Howard A.
1976   The Problem of Wineskins. Downers Grove, IL: InterVarsity
        Press.

Solansky, Anil
1984   A Critical Evaluation of Theological Education in Residential
        Training. *In* Missions and Theological Education in World
        Perspective. Harvie M. Conn and Samuel F. Rowan, eds., pp.
        156-168. Farmington, MI: Associates of Urbanus.

Spates, James L. and John J. Macionis
1987   The Sociology of Cities. Belmont, CA: Wadsworth.

Spotts, Dwight and David Veerman
1987   Reaching Out to Troubled Youth. Wheaton, IL: Victor.

Spradley, James P.
1970   You Owe Yourself a Drunk. Boston: Little, Brown.

1980   Participant Observation. New York: Holt, Rinehart & Winston.

Stack, Carol B.
1974   All Our Kin. New York: Harper & Row.

Stanley, Paul D. and J. Robert Clinton
1992   Connecting: The Mentoring Relationships You Need to Succeed
        in Life. Colorado Springs, CO: NavPress.

Steffen, Tom A.
1993   Passing the Baton: Church Planting that Empowers. La Habra,
        CA: Center for Organizational & Ministry Development.

Stefl, Mary E.
1987   The New Homeless: A National Perspective. *In* The Homeless in Contemporary Society. Richard D. Bingham, Roy E. Green, and Sammis B. White, eds., pp. 46-63. Newbury Park, CA: Sage.

Steward, Harry B.
1989   A Neighborhood Ministry for the Unreached People of the Urban Communities. Unpublished Doctoral Dissertation, Eastern Baptist Theological Seminary.

Stoil, Julie
1983   Women on the Street. Working Woman 8(April):84.

Stoner, Madeleine R.
1983   The Plight of Homeless Women. Social Service Review, December:565-581.

Sugarman, Leonie
1985   Kolb's Model of Experiential Learning: Touchstone for Trainers, Students, Counselors, and Clients. Journal of Counseling and Development 64(4):264-268.

Svinicki, Marilla D. and Nancy M. Dixon
1987   The Kolb Model Modified for Classroom Activities. College Teaching 35(4): 141-146.

Tessler, R. and D. Dennis
1989   A Synthesis of NIMH - Funded Research Concerning Persons Who Are Homeless and Mentally Ill. Washington, D.C.: National Institute of Mental Health.

Tillapaugh, Frank R.
1982   The Church Unleashed. Ventura, CA: Regal.

Tillman, Martin J.
1981   The Lisle Fellowship: A Case Study. *In* Cross-Cultural Learning. Charles B. Neff, ed., pp. 45-58. New Directions for Experiential Learning II. San Francisco: Jossey-Bass.

Today's English Version Bible
1976   Today's English Version Bible. American Bible Society.

Tonna, Benjamin
    1982   Gospel for the Cities. Maryknoll, New York: Orbis.

Underwood, Jackson
    1990   An Ethnography of a Homeless Camp. Unpublished Doctoral
                  Dissertation. Los Angeles: University of California.

United Nations General Assembly
    1985   International Year of Shelter for the Homeless: Report of the
                  Secretary-General. New York: Author.

United States Conference of Mayors
    1990   A Status Report on Hunger and Homelessness in America's
                  Cities. Washington, D. C.: Author.

United States Department of Health and Human Services
    1984   A Report to the Secretary on the Homeless and Emergency
                  Shelters. Washington, D. C.: Office of Policy Development and
                  Research.

    1989   A Report on Homeless Assistance Policy and Practice in the
                  Nation's Five Largest Cities. Washington, D.C.: Office of Policy
                  Development and Research.

United States General Accounting Office
    1985   Homelessness: A Complex Problem and the Federal Response.
                  Washington, D. C.: Author.

United States House Committee on Banking, Finance, and Urban Affairs
    1983   Homelessness in America. Washington, D.C.: U.S.
                  Government Printing Office.

Valentine, Bettylou
    1978   Hustling and Other Hard Work. New York: Macmillan.

Van Houten, Mark E.
    1988   God's Inner-City Address. Grand Rapids, MI: Zondervan.

Vigil, James Diego
    1988   Barrio Gangs: Street Life and Identity in Southern California.
                  Austin, TX: University of Texas Press.

Walter, Gordon A. and Stephen E. Marks
    1981   Experiential Learning and Change. New York: John Wiley.

Ward, Ted
    1984   Servants, Leaders and Tyrants. *In* Missions and Theological
               Education in World Perspective. Harvie M. Conn and Samuel F.
               Rowen, eds., pp. 19-40. Farmington, MI: Associates of Urbanus.

Waters, R.
    1984   Trickle-down Tragedy: Homelessness in California.
               Sacramento, CA: California Homeless Coalition.

Whyte, William F.
    1955   Street Corner Society. Chicago: University of Chicago Press.

Wiersma, William
    1991   Research Methods in Education. Needham Heights, MA:
               Simon & Shuster.

Williams, Melvin D.
    1981   On the Street Where I Lived. New York: Holt, Rinehart &
               Winston.

Wolch, J. R., M. Dear, and A. Akita
    1988   Explaining Homelessness. Journal of the American Planning
               Association 54(4): 443-453.

Worden, Steven K.
    1987   Bums, Barrios, and Baptists: An Interactionist Inquiry into the
               Pieties of Place. Ph.D. dissertation, University of Texas at Austin.